Contract Law in England and Wales

Contract Law in England and Wales

James C. Fisher

This book was originally published as a monograph in the International Encyclopaedia of Laws/Contracts.

Founding Editor: Roger Blanpain
General Editor: Frank Hendrickx
Volume Editor: Jacques Herbots

Wolters Kluwer

Published by:
Kluwer Law International B.V.
PO Box 316
2400 AH Alphen aan den Rijn
The Netherlands
E-mail: international-sales@wolterskluwer.com
Website: lrus.wolterskluwer.com

Sold and distributed in North, Central and South America by:
Wolters Kluwer Legal & Regulatory U.S.
7201 McKinney Circle
Frederick, MD 21704
United States of America
Email: customer.service@wolterskluwer.com

Sold and distributed in all other countries by:
Air Business Subscriptions
Rockwood House
Haywards Heath
West Sussex
RH16 3DH
United Kingdom
Email: international-customerservice@wolterskluwer.com

ISBN 978-90-411-9465-7

e-Book: ISBN 978-90-411-9486-2
web-PDF: ISBN 978-90-411-9507-4

The Author

James C. Fisher is a Project Associate Professor at the University of Tokyo Faculty of Law & Graduate Schools for Law and Politics, and a visiting lecturer at Meiji University, Japan. He was born in South Wales and studied law at the University of Oxford (St Catherine's College), United Kingdom, and Leiden University, the Netherlands. James' teaching and research focus chiefly on the law of obligations and property in England and Japan. His work is published in leading scholarly journals, and he is a member of numerous scholarly and legal societies.

The Author

Table of Contents

The Author 3

List of Abbreviations 11

Preface 13

General Introduction 15

§1. The General Background of the Country 15

§2. The Common Law Family 16

§3. Primacy of Legislation 16

§4. The Position of the Judiciary 17

§5. Distinction Between Public Law and Private Law 18

§6. Distinction Between Civil Law and Commercial Law 18

Introduction to the Law of Contract 21

§1. Definition of Contract 21

§2. Historical Background of the Law of Contract 21

§3. Classification of Contracts 22

§4. Contract and Torts 23

§5. Contract and Quasi-contract 24

§6. Contract and the Law of Property 25

§7. Contract and Trusts 26

§8. Good Faith and Fair Dealing 27

Table of Contents

§9. STYLE OF DRAFTING 27

§10. SOURCES OF THE LAW OF CONTRACT 28

Part I. General Principles of the Law of Contract 31

Chapter 1. Formation 31

§1. AGREEMENT AND QUID PRO QUO (RECIPROCITY) 31

I. Offer and Acceptance 31
A. Offers and Invitations 32
B. Termination of an Offer 34
C. Withdrawing an Offer 34
D. Communication of Withdrawal 35
E. Communicating Acceptance 36
F. Objectivity 39
II. Intention to Create Legal Relations 41
III. Consideration 42
A. The Doctrine of Consideration 42
1. The Consideration Debate 45
B. Gratuitous Promises 46
C. Absence of 'Natural Obligations' 46
IV. Modifications of the Contract 47
A. A Special Case: The Variation of Debts 49
B. Promissory Estoppel 51

§2. FORMAL AND EVIDENTIAL REQUIREMENTS 55

I. Formal Requirements 55
A. Effect of Non-compliance 57
II. Evidential Requirements 58
A. The Parol Evidence Rule 58
B. Lack of a Role for Notaries 59
III. Burden of Proof 59

§3. LIABILITY AND NEGOTIATIONS 60

I. Pre-contractual Liability 60
A. Liability for Non-disclosure 60
B. Liability for False Statements (Independent of Contract) 61
II. Breakdown of Negotiations 62

Chapter 2. Conditions of Substantive Validity 64

§1. Capacity of the Parties 64

I. Capacity of Minors 64
II. Mental Incapacitation 65
III. Corporate Legal Capacity 66

§2. Defects of Consent 66

I. Mistake 66
A. Unilateral Mistake of Contractual Nature 66
B. Unilateral Mistake as to Contractual Terms 67
C. Unilateral Mistake of Identity 67
II. Misrepresentation 69
A. Exclusion of Liability for Misrepresentation 72
III. Improper Pressure 73
A. Duress 74
B. Undue Influence 77
IV. Gross Disparity 79

§3. Other Conditions of Validity 80

I. Existing and Licit Cause 80
II. Determined or Determinable, Possible and Licit Object 80
III. Initial Impossibility 81
IV. Illegality and Public Policy 84
V. Other Unenforceable Contracts 87

§4. The Consequences of a Defect of Consent or a Lack of Substantive Validity 88

I. Avoidance of the Contract 88
II. Retroactive Effect of Avoidance or Nullity 88
III. Damages 90

Chapter 3. The Contents of a Contract 91

§1. The Different Clauses 91

I. Ascertaining the Express Terms 91
A. Incorporation of Other Terms 92
B. Signature 93
II. Implied Terms 94
III. Standard Terms and Exemption Clauses 96
IV. Penalty Clauses 98
A. What Kind of Clauses can be Reviewed under the Penalty Rule? 99

B. What makes a Clause 'Penal'? 100
V. Arbitration Clauses 102

§2. Interpretation 104

Chapter 4. Privity of Contract 108

§1. The Rule of Privity of Contract 108

I. Third Parties and the Contract 108
A. The Case for Reform 109
II. Contracts for the Benefit of a Third Party 111

§2. Transfer of Contractual Rights 114

§3. The Special Case of a 'Sub-contract' 116

§4. Actio Pauliana 117

Chapter 5. The Termination of the Contract 119

§1. Performance and Breach 119

§2. Impossibility, Frustration and Hardship 119

I. Accounting for Discharge for Impossibility 122

§3. Discharge by Agreement 122

Chapter 6. Remedies 123

§1. General Provisions 123

§2. Specific Performance and Injunctions 123

§3. Termination 124

I. Termination under the Express Terms of the Contract 125
II. Termination for Breach at Common Law 126

§4. Exceptio Non Adimpleti Contractus 128

§5. Faulty Behaviour of the Debtor 129

§6. Limitation of Actions 129

§7. DAMAGES AND EXEMPTION CLAUSES 130

§8. RESTITUTION 134

Part II. Specific Contracts 135

Chapter 1. Agency 136

Chapter 2. Bailment 140

Chapter 3. Gaming and Wagering 141

Chapter 4. Sale of Goods 142

Chapter 5. Building Contracts, Hire of Work & Skills 143

Chapter 6. Lease, Commercial and Agricultural Leases 144

Chapter 7. Compromise Settlement 145

Chapter 8. Suretyship 146

Chapter 9. Pledge 147

Chapter 10. Loans 148

Chapter 11. Contracts with the Government and Other Public Administrations 149

Chapter 12. Contract of Partnership 150

Chapter 13. Quasi-contracts 151

§1. NEGOTIORUM GESTIO 151

§2. ENRICHMENT WITHOUT CAUSE 151

§3. MONEY PAID BUT NOT DUE 152

Selected Bibliography 153

Table of Cases 155

Table of Legislation 171

Index 173

List of Abbreviations

AC	Appeal Cases
All ER	All England Law Reports
Ch	Chancery Division
CLJ	Cambridge Law Journal
EWCA Civ	England & Wales Court of Appeal (Civil Division)
EWHC	England & Wales High Court
KB	King's Bench Division
LQR	Law Quarterly Review
QB	Queen's Bench Division
UKPC	United Kingdom Privy Council
UKSC	United Kingdom Supreme Court
WLR	Weekly Law Reports

Preface

This work presents and reflects upon the law of contract in England and Wales and aims to state the law as it stands in July 2017. The English law of contract is complex and in a state of constant evolution. In dealing with areas of legal uncertainty or debate, I provide what I consider the best-supported account of the law in question.

I am grateful to the University of Tokyo for the opportunity to pursue this project, and to my intimidatingly gifted students, for consistently challenging my knowledge and ideas about the law. The work is dedicated to my grandparents.

James C. Fisher
Tokyo 2017

General Introduction

§1. The General Background of the Country

1. England and Wales are two of the four countries that make up the United Kingdom of Great Britain and Northern Ireland. Together they make up one of the discrete legal jurisdictions that operate within this state.[1]

2. The UK is one of the world's largest economies, a permanent member of the UN Security Council, and a prominent member of numerous multinational organisations, including NATO, the Council of Europe, and the European Union (EU).[2]

3. It is a Parliamentary liberal democracy with a bicameral legislature and a constitutional monarch. The main legislative chamber is the House of Commons, composed of 650 Members of Parliament elected from single-member constituencies by a first-past-the-post system. Control of the House of Commons typically oscillates between the Conservative (centre-right) and Labour (centre-left) Parties.[3] Most members of the House of Lords are life peers appointed by the Queen (on the advice of the Prime Minister or the House of Lords Appointments Commission).[4] The House of Lords also includes ex officio members, such as certain Bishops of the Church of England. It also contains a small number of hereditary members, who were retained as a notionally transitional measure following the reform of the House of Lords in 1999.[5]

4. The head of Government is the Prime Minister, appointed by the Queen, who by convention appoints the leader of the largest political party in the House of Commons.

1. There is also a growing body of discretely Welsh law, following the devolution of certain legislative functions to the National Assembly for Wales, a regional legislature constituted and empowered by Act of Parliament (Government of Wales Acts 1998 and 2006). However, England and Wales remain a single jurisdiction except for issues that are devolved, and devolution has not produced any changes of relevance to the general law of contract.
2. On 30 Mar. 2017, the Prime Minister issued notice to the European Council of the UK's intention to withdraw from the EU, following a referendum decision to that effect. The EU Treaties will therefore cease to bind the UK not later than two years from that date, subject to the terms of any agreement concluded before that date between the UK and the European Union: Treaty on the EU, Art. 50(2) and (3).
3. Coalition governments are rare but not unknown, such as the 2010–2015 coalition between the Conservatives and the Liberal Democrats.
4. The Prime Minister invites nominations from the leaders of other political parties so as to maintain political balance in the Lords.
5. House of Lords Act 1999. The state of the House of Lords is widely felt to be unsatisfactory, but no significant reform has occurred since the removal of the bulk of the hereditary peers.

The Prime Minister in turn appoints other Ministers, each of whom must be a member of one of the Houses of Parliament.

§2. The Common Law Family

5. England is the progenitor of the common law, which was exported worldwide thanks to British colonial expansion during the eighteenth and nineteenth centuries, and came to replace or reshape a large amount of indigenous law across much of the globe.

6. Even following the decline of the British Empire, for many years English law enjoyed unofficial recognition as overseer of the common law's development. The decisions of English courts carried a privileged degree of authority in the courts of many former colonies, whose citizens often had a right of final appeal to the Privy Council, sitting in London.

7. However, the institutional umbilical cord that once tethered the common law to the courts of England and Wales is now almost entirely severed. The Privy Council is no longer the court of final appeal for any of the major Commonwealth jurisdictions.[6] While English law remains conscious of its enduring relationship with the wider common law world, that relationship has become conspicuously more balanced. It is common for English courts to engage intimately with the decisions of appellate and supreme courts from other common law jurisdictions in developing the law of England and Wales.

§3. Primacy of Legislation

8. In constitutional terms, English law respects the primacy of legislation in that there is no source of law higher than an Act of Parliament. There is no codified Constitution limiting the powers of the legislature, and conventional constitutional theory regards Parliament as unlimited in its legislative powers.[7] The usual legislative

6. Canada and India abolished it in 1949, Australia in 1986 and New Zealand in 2003. Rights of appeal to the Privy Council – technically to the Queen acting *on the advice* of the Privy Council – are retained by minor jurisdictions such as The Bahamas, Jamaica, and the Republic of Trinidad and Tobago.
7. The UK is a party to numerous international legal instruments that purport to impact this legislative supremacy, such as the European Convention on Human Rights. However, the UK is a 'dualist' legal system in which international law and domestic law are discrete, unless and until an Act of Parliament incorporates international legal obligations into domestic law, a principle recently reaffirmed in *R (on the application of Miller and others) v. Secretary of State for Exiting the European Union* [2017] UKSC 5, [55]. The traditional picture has also been complicated by the UK's membership of the EU, one effect of which is that EU law can prevail over inconsistent UK primary legislation in domestic legal disputes. Nonetheless apparent interferences with UK legislative supremacy can be attributed to the enduring operation of an Act of Parliament, such as the European Communities Act 1972: *see Miller* at [60] and [65].

process requires a Bill to be approved by both Houses of Parliament, and then to receive symbolic Royal Assent from the Queen.[8]

9. All other sources of law, such as secondary legislation and case law, are subordinate to Acts of Parliament.[9] Parliament can validly overturn even the most fundamental doctrines of the common law,[10] and indeed it is not unusual for Parliament to legislate specifically to reverse the law as developed by the courts in certain areas.[11] Courts, however, are frequently slow directly to abandon established doctrines of the common law, even when these are felt to be inconvenient or anachronistic, resulting instead in a complex web of exceptions and counter-exceptions. Legislation can therefore play an important role in overcoming this complexity.

10. However, despite its constitutional primacy, legislation has only secondary practical importance in many areas of English law. Although specific statutes operate to reverse, refine or supplement the law developed by the courts, most of English private law is contained primarily in case law rather than in statute. There are no comprehensive Codes (of a kind familiar to Civilian lawyers) to define axiomatic legal principles and deduce from them specific legal rules. While some legislative enactments purport to systemise the law in a particular area,[12] even these in fact presuppose and rely upon an existing body of judge-made jurisprudence.

§4. The Position of the Judiciary

11. English judges have an important and conspicuous responsibility for the development of the common law.[13] This is particularly so of senior judges, sitting in

8. However, the consent of the House of Lords is no longer indispensable, as a result of the Parliament Acts 1911 and 1949.
9. The devolved legislatures in Scotland, Wales and Northern Ireland also have lawmaking powers, although these are not sovereign legislatures since the scope of their legislative competence is defined by Acts of the UK Parliament.
10. Cf *R (Jackson) v. Attorney General* [2005] UKHL 56, [2006] 1 AC 262, [102] per Lord Steyn, suggesting (*obiter*) there are some fundamental doctrines that 'even a sovereign Parliament... cannot abolish.' Lord Hope and Baroness Hale made similar claims, which are legally unsupported and incompatible with the UK's fundamental constitutional principle: the sovereignty and supremacy of Parliament.
11. For example, the Compensation Act 2006 was enacted specifically to reverse the effect of the House of Lords' decision in *Barker v. Corus (UK) Plc* [2006] UKHL 20, [2006] 2 AC 572 (a tort law decision concerning liability for the claimant's asbestos-related disease). Examples relevant to contract law include the Law Reform (Frustrated Contracts) Act 1943.
12. For example, the Companies Act 2006, Law of Property Act 1925, and Land Registration Act 2002.
13. It was once the orthodoxy that judges did not make or change the common law, but only discovered and applied its principles – notionally timeless and unchanging – to novel situations. This is no longer taken seriously as a practical reality, and it is generally accepted that judicial decisions do not merely reflect the law, but constitute sources of law in their own right: *see* for example *Kleinwort Benson Ltd v. Lincoln City Council* [1999] 2 AC 349, 377, per Lord Goff, disparaging the merely 'declaratory theory of judicial decisions'.

the Court of Appeal and the Supreme Court, whose decisions are binding on inferior courts (and in the Court of Appeal's case, on itself).

12. As a result of the strong doctrine of precedent that applies in English law, individual judges have an identifiable influence within the legal system. Decisions are usually rendered in individual judges' own names, dissenting judgments are common, and judges are required to explain their reasoning thoroughly. Many judges have made tangible personal contributions to the development of the common law that endure long after retirement. Leading judges can in this way cause considerable and lasting legal change in accordance with their own values and legal opinions.

13. Although some fee-paid positions exist and can be combined with continuing legal practice, for the most part judges are full-time salaried Crown employees. Judges must be legally qualified,[14] and most are former barristers and solicitors with long and successful careers in legal practice, although it is becoming more common for legal scholars to take up judicial office, provided they also hold the requisite professional qualifications.

14. Judges are politically independent, and are appointed by an independent Judicial Appointments Commission, which fills judicial vacancies through an open process of advertisement and application. Judges serve until they reach the statutory retirement age applicable to holders of judicial office.

§5. Distinction Between Public Law and Private Law

15. English law contains no authoritative statement of the parameters of public and private law, and the very division itself has come under increasing pressure from courts and commentators, who have been particularly critical of the distinct remedies available against public and private litigants.

16. As regards the law of contract, English law recognises no doctrinally distinct category of public, or administrative, contracts. A contract between a private person and a public body is governed by the ordinary rules of contract doctrine, and is in this sense not legally distinct from a contract between private persons.

17. However, the activities of public bodies are subject to legal constraints that do not apply to private persons, by virtue of administrative law, which permits judicial review of public authorities. Administrative law imposes standards of conduct on public bodies, for instance by prohibiting actions that are unreasonable, arbitrary or beyond the powers of the public body in question. These restrictions can also apply to public bodies when negotiating, concluding and performing contracts. Crucially, however, these restrictions are not products of the law of contract but of general administrative law.

§6. Distinction Between Civil Law and Commercial Law

18. English law does not regard civil and commercial contracts as being governed by discrete bodies of law; a single body of contract law doctrine governs all contracts.

14. Tribunals, Courts and Enforcement Act 2007.

However, the law of contract does contain certain rules applicable only to contracts in which one party is a consumer and another acting in the course of business. For instance, many statutory provisions relevant to contracts apply only – or at least differently – to contracts between commercial parties.[15]

19. In addition to these distinctly applicable legal rules, doctrinal rules relevant to consumer and commercial contracts alike are sometimes applied differently in practice.[16]

15. For example, the Consumer Rights Act 2015.

16. For instance, where it is unclear whether one party has provided valuable consideration, courts are more likely to find consideration in a commercial context. Likewise it has been suggested that courts will presume an intention to create legal relations in a commercial context.

Introduction to the Law of Contract

§1. Definition of Contract

20. There is no authoritative definition of a contract in English law, although one can be constructed from an examination of the relevant jurisprudence. A workable definition might be that a 'contract' is a personal obligation that one party is deemed to have undertaken in favour of another party, to whom the law will award a remedy if the first party fails or refuses to perform in accordance with her undertaking.[17]

§2. Historical Background of the Law of Contract

21. The modern law of contract involves the interaction of rules and doctrines created by the courts of common law and equity, supplemented by those contained in statute.

22. The common law derives ultimately from the activities of the early royal Justices who, from the reign of Henry II, travelled the realm, adjudicating in accordance with a body of law 'common' to the whole of England. This gradually came to replace the feudal manorial justice that had followed the Norman conquest of England in 1066.[18] The common law courts operated based on a system of judicial formulae known as writs. These provided for a specified remedy where the claimant could show her case satisfied the requirements of an appropriate writ. One of these actions – the action of *covenant* – provided damages for the non-performance of an obligation undertaken by deed. The action of *debt* enforced undertakings to pay a sum of money. However, the early common law did not contain a general action to enforce informal promises to perform actions other than a payment of money, which were actionable by the writ of debt.

17. It is common to define contracts in English law by reference to an agreement between the parties, or an exchange of undertakings. However, while English law requires informal contracts to be a reciprocal exchange of value, an obligation entered into in the form of a deed is enforceable even if gratuitous. It is also sometimes possible to create 'unilateral' contracts, which are valid even though only one party owes any executory obligations to the other.

18. Alongside the development of the common law in England, Wales was becoming subject to the increasing control of the English Crown from the late thirteenth century. The incremental annexation culminated in the Laws in Wales Acts of 1536 and 1542 (27 Henry VIII c. 26 & 34 & 35 Henry VIII c. 26.), which formally made Wales a part of the Kingdom of England, ending its status as a separate legal jurisdiction. It is customary to speak of 'English law' in referring to the law applicable in the combined jurisdiction of England and Wales.

23. The shortcomings of the common law, and especially its evidential and procedural limitations, meant that many claimants could not obtain justice. Early in the history of the common law, such claimants would attempt to appeal directly to the King, who maintained a personal prerogative to do justice between his subjects, independent of the common law. The task of handling these petitions eventually became the responsibility of the King's Chancellor, leading ultimately to the development of the Court of Chancery, which would adjudicate in accordance with the dictates of conscience, or *equity*. The doctrines and practices of the Court of Chancery gradually coalesced into a system of rules based on precedent and applied by the judicial officers of a court system that paralleled the courts of common law.

24. At least partially in response to the emerging rival jurisdiction of equity, the common law courts had begun the creative adaption of existing writs in order to fashion a general action for the enforcement of executory obligations not contained in a deed, which became known as the action for *assumpsit*.[19]

25. The enduring division between the courts of law and equity obstructed the efficient administration of justice, since each maintained distinct rules of procedure and made distinct remedies available to claimants. The two sets of courts were combined by the Judicature Acts of the nineteenth century. These created the 'Supreme Court of Judicature',[20] comprising principally of the High Court and the Court of Appeal, empowered to apply both equity and the common law in the same courts. While the courts were combined, the jurisdictions of law and equity remained (and still remain) distinct, and both will often be relevant to the disposal of a given case. Where rules of equity and law diverge, the rules of equity always prevail.[21]

§3. Classification of Contracts

26. English law rejects the *ex ante* classification of contracts that is common in Civil law jurisdictions, and which derives ultimately from the Roman array of nominate contracts. While it is possible to identify categories of contract by reference to certain characteristics – for example it is possible to distinguish informal contracts from contracts by deed, or bilateral contracts from unilateral ones – this is not to suggest that the categories thus created are subject to special or distinct legal rules.

27. The rules of formation, vitiation, substantive validity, breach and remedies exist as general principles applicable across the law of contract. Specific rules can operate with respect to certain kinds of contract only, and can be introduced either by the common law or by statute. But this itself presupposes the general principle that all contracts are subject to the same doctrinal rules unless some specific derogation is to be found.

19. Contracts in the form of a deed – enforceable even if gratuitous – are often represented as an exception to the doctrine of consideration. However, in historical terms, it is more correct to regard informal contracts supported by consideration as exceptional, in that the law enforces them despite the lack of a deed.
20. Now known as the 'Senior Courts' to avoid confusion with the UK Supreme Court, which has since replaced the House of Lords as the court of last instance in the UK.
21. Supreme Court of Judicature Act 1873, s. 25(11), now Senior Courts Act 1981, s.49(1).

§4. Contract and Torts

28. The law of contract and the law of tort are often both materially relevant to the same events, such as when tortious liability arises between parties in a contractual relationship. While a contractual relationship will necessarily impose liabilities that would not exist were it not for the contract, it is also possible through contract to exclude other forms of liability that might arise between the parties in question, especially liability in tort.

29. A contract can contain duties that would anyway have existed between the parties by virtue of the law of tort. This is a particularly prominent issue concerning contractual duties to take care, which frequently overlap with the duties recognised by the tort of negligence.[22] Where liability is thus concurrent in both contract and tort, the traditional rule required the claimant to bring her action in contract only,[23] but the law subsequently came to permit the claimant a free choice between advancing her claim in contract or in tort.[24]

30. The change was prompted to avoid the situation wherein a person who provided services for free would be more vulnerable than someone who provided the same services for profit, because actions brought in contract are subject to a stricter limitation period than actions in tort.[25] However, while in some senses contractual liability is preferable to liability in tort, the reverse can also be true. For instance, a defendant in contract is liable for pure economic losses caused by his breach of duty, while defendants in tort actions are generally not. Moreover, the remoteness rule that limits liability in damages is less strict in tort than in contract, on the basis that contracting parties have the opportunity to decide specifically what the extent of the defendant's liability will be, and that their contract price should be taken as reflecting an agreement of some kind on this point.[26] An entirely free election between claims in contract and tort might therefore put claimants in an unjustifiably strong position

---

22. *See* for example tortious liability for negligent misstatements independent of a contractual relationship: *Hedley Byrne & Co Ltd v. Heller & Partners Ltd* [1964] AC 465.
23. For example, *Groom v. Crocker* [1939] 1 KB 194, 205, per Sir Wilfred Greene MR. The Court of Appeal held that the relationship between a solicitor and his client was regulated by their contract alone, and the solicitor's negligence that constituted a breach of contract with his client could not therefore ground liability in the ordinary tort of negligence. The claimant was therefore unable to recover damages for mental suffering caused by the solicitor's negligence, since these were recoverable in tort but not – at the time – in a contract claim. This rule was endorsed comparatively recently: *see* for example *Tai Hing Cotton Mill Ltd v. Liu Chong Hing Bank Ltd* [1986] AC 80, 86, per Lord Scarman.
24. *Midland Bank Trust Co Ltd v. Hett, Stubbs & Kemp* [1979] Ch 348, per Oliver J. The trend was subsequently endorsed by the House of Lords in *Henderson v. Merrett Syndicates Ltd* [1995] 2 AC 145.
25. *Midland Bank Trust Co Ltd v. Hett, Stubbs & Kemp* [1979] Ch 348, 417–18, per Oliver J. In contract, the limitation period runs from the time of breach of contract (whether or not breach was discoverable at that point), but in tort it runs from the time the claimant suffered the harm for which she sues. This discrepancy led to attempts to sue in tort rather than in contract in *Midland Bank Trust Co Ltd v. Hett, Stubbs & Kemp* [1979] Ch 348.
26. *C Czarnikow Ltd v. Koufos (The Heron II)* [1969] 1 AC 350, 385–86, per Lord Reid.

with respect to the defendant,[27] because the claimant receives an unbargained-for windfall whenever by chance the law of tort replicates a duty that the parties imposed contractually in exchange for an agreed sum.

31. The free choice rule has therefore come under increasing scrutiny, as courts attempt to find a more nuanced balance between the interests of claimants and defendants. There are recent signs of a push towards 'a rational system of law' that 'only give[s] one answer' to the question such as the extent of the defendant's liability, and not two different answers 'depending on how the claim is framed'.[28] To that end the Court of Appeal has recently concluded that the correct test of remoteness should be that required by the law of contract.[29] The law remains tolerant of concurrent liability in contract and tort, but is now less willing to allow recourse to the rules of tort – as opposed to the rules that regulate contractual claims – if this would be inappropriate in the context.[30]

§5. Contract and Quasi-contract

32. English law does not recognise a category of 'quasi-contracts', but does permit a variety of actions that the law has come to recognise as constituting a law of unjust enrichment. The aspect most relevant to contract law is the claim for restitution on the grounds of 'total failure of basis'. This describes a situation in which the claimant has made payments in expectation of receiving contracted services in exchange, but none of the services were in fact provided as agreed under the contract.

33. Provided the contract is discharged as a result of this breach, the claimant can recover the payments she made, even if the claimant has in fact made an unwise bargain and her prepayments are much more valuable than the performance she expected under the contract. However, the failure of basis must be total, in that the defendant must have performed *none* of his own contractual duties. Otherwise, the claimant has only an action for breach of contract in the ordinary way, which gives a compensatory rather than restitutionary remedy. The same is true if the claimant's own performance

27. *Henderson v. Merrett Syndicates Ltd* [1995] 2 AC 145, 185–86, per Lord Goff.

28. *Wellesley Partners LLP v. Withers LLP* [2014] EWHC 556 (Ch), [2014] PNLR 22, [212], per Nugee J; approved on appeal: [2015] EWCA Civ 1146.

29. *Wellesley Partners LLP v. Withers LLP* [2015] EWCA Civ 1146, [66], per Floyd LJ. The Court interpreted the House of Lords' decision in *Henderson v. Merrett Syndicates Ltd* [1995] 2 AC 145 as establishing only the possibility of concurrent liability, and not authoritative on the specific question of which remoteness test must apply where such concurrent liability exists.

30. One particular legal question may have to be reconsidered in light of this development. It has been held that contributory negligence is not a defence to breaches of strict contractual duties, or duties to take care that arise solely in contract and would not be imposed on the defendant in the law of tort, but that it is a partial defence if the breach of such a contractual duty also constituted a tort (*Vesta v. Butcher* [1988] 2 All ER 43, endorsing judgment of Hobhouse J; *UCB Bank Plc v. Hepherd Winstanley and Pugh* [1999] Lloyd's Rep PN 963.). As things stand, this creates a perverse incentive for defendants to argue that they were also liable in tort, and not only in contract.

took the form of some action other than the simple payment of money. Here too the claimant has only an action for breach of contract.[31]

34. Generally, therefore, where two parties have concluded a binding contract, the law regards the contract as defining what one party can recover from the other following non-performance of his contractual undertakings. The remedy for breach is therefore not the 'unmaking' of the contract through restitution of the benefits conferred by the claimant in expectation of the defendant's performance, but damages calculated to compensate the claimant for the breach, in the sense of putting her into the position that she would have occupied had the defendant performed his contractual obligations.[32] Indeed in light of this logic even the action for restitution following total failure of basis looks like an arbitrary derogation. It is not clear why prepayments of money where no return performance has been rendered, should be treated differently from ordinary breaches. The current law is therefore unprincipled, and a restitutionary remedy for breach should either be made generally available, or abolished even in the context of total failure of basis.

§6. Contract and the Law of Property

35. Although property rights are often created or transferred pursuant to a contract, property rights can be created and assigned without ever creating contractual obligations. Contractual obligations are distinguished from obligations arising under the law of property in that they are capable of binding only the parties to the contract. Whereas property rights impose duties on multiple people regardless of their specific consent to such duties, contractual duties are at least notionally the product of individuated consent. Contracting parties are unable by their own bilateral agreement to impose legal duties on third parties.

36. Their agreement may have the result of imposing legal duties on third parties where it has created a right recognised by the law of property, but the number of such rights is strictly limited by the *numerus clausus* principle. It is sometimes alleged that this principle – and with it parties' general inability to create obligations binding on parties other than themselves – amounts to a restriction of freedom of contract. This is unconvincing. Freedom of contract entails that the law will enforce the obligations parties are deemed to have undertaken. A logical corollary is that the law will generally *not* enforce obligations a party has *not* undertaken, which requires that two parties should be unable to impose binding obligations on a third.

31. Specifically reiterated in *Taylor v. Motability Finance Ltd* [2004] EWHC 2619 (Comm), per Cooke J.
32. *Robinson v. Harman* (1848) 1 Ex Rep 850, 855, 154 ER 363, per Parke B.

§7. Contract and Trusts

37. Archetypally, a trust comes into existence when a settlor transfers property to a trustee,[33] with the intention that the trustee uses and administers this property solely in the interests of another, the beneficiary (who may be the same person as the settlor). Although the trustee is necessarily the legal owner of the trust assets, equity awards the beneficiary a cause of action where the trustee exercises his common law property rights over the trust assets inconsistently with his equitable duties as trustee.

38. The creation of a trust does not necessarily entail the creation of a legal contract.[34] However, the law of contract and the law of trusts frequently interact. It is possible to contract for the creation of a trust, either in favour of one of the parties or of a third party. Likewise a contractual right can itself be made the subject of a trust.

39. Moreover, it is possible to contract for a party's services as a trustee. Where the trustee has undertaken to act as a trustee in favour of the beneficiary under a contract, there is the possibility of concurrent liability under the law of contract and the law of trusts. This will occur where the acts of the defendant trustee breach both his duties under the contract, and the equitable duties that bind him simply by virtue of his status as a trustee, independent of any contract that might exist between him and the claimant beneficiary. In principle, the claimant has her choice of actions in such situations.

40. The remedies available will differ depending on whether the claim is brought in contract or in equity.[35] While contract damages award only the claimant's expectation under the contract,[36] a claimant suing in equity can gain whatever profits the trustee has made as a result of his breach of trust. However, there are some indications that where such concurrent liability exists, 'the extent of equitable compensation should be the same as if damages for breach of contract were sought at common law'.[37]

---

33. It is also possible expressly to create a trust without effecting any transfer of property, by declaring oneself a trustee of some identified property one already owns. Trusts can also arise non-expressly, by operation of law (resulting and constructive trusts).
34. Cf for example J Langbein, 'The Contractarian Basis of the Law of Trusts' (1995) 105 Yale Law Journal 625; 'Why the rule in *Saunders v. Vautier* is wrong' in P Turner (ed), *Equity and Administration* (Cambridge University Press, 2016). While the contractarian analysis of trusts may succeed with respect to American law, it cannot account for the law in England and Wales: P Matthews, 'Why the rule in *Saunders v. Vautier* is wrong: A commentary' in P Turner (ed), *Equity and Administration* (Cambridge University Press, 2016).
35. English law has generally stringently distinguished between obligations arising under contracts and those under trusts, as being of a different juristic nature, with the latter being fiduciary, and giving rise to distinct remedies: *see* for example P Millet, 'Equity's Place in the Law of Commerce' (1998) 114 LQR 214, 255.
36. The distinction between common law and equitable remedies – especially the general non-availability of *account* in contract claims – has come under pressure, and some have suggested that trust remedies should in fact be available in contract claims: *Attorney General v. Blake* [2001] 1 AC 268, per Lord Nicholls.
37. *AIB Group (UK) Plc v. Mark Redler & Co* [2014] UKSC 58, [2015] AC 1503, [71], per Lord Toulson. *See also* Lord Neuberger in *Thanakharn Kasikhorn Thai Chamkat (Mahachon) v. Akai Holdings Ltd* [2010] HKCFA 64, [155].

§8. Good Faith and Fair Dealing

41. Under English law, contracting parties are under no general duty to negotiate,[38] perform, vary, renegotiate or enforce their contracts in good faith. In place of generally applicable duties of good faith, English contract law imposes specific standards of conduct in particular situations.[39] There has nonetheless been a sustained argument for a general duty of good faith in English contract law,[40] and indeed the law appears increasingly willing to contemplate that such a duty may arise implicitly,[41] where it can be shown that the parties would reasonably have understood their agreement to contain such an obligation.[42] This will, however, fail where the express language of the contract is inconsistent with an implied duty of good faith.[43]

§9. Style of Drafting

42. English contracts are typically long, detailed and legalistic, particularly contracts concluded between professionally advised commercial parties. In the absence of authoritative categories of 'special contracts', every contractual relationship is in principle the unique, bespoke creation of the parties' agreement. Parties cannot expect the law externally to supply an array of contract terms necessary for the efficient conduct of their contractual relationship. While this can be empowering for parties – almost every aspect of their contractual relationship is left to them individually to negotiate and design – it also behoves parties expressly to provide for every eventuality.

43. While the law will sometimes regard a specific contract impliedly to contain terms in addition to those the parties have expressly included, the threshold for implication is high, and is especially unlikely in contracts that have been professionally drafted in significant detail. The law does in some cases supply terms as default rules for certain kinds of contract, but most of these can be excluded by express language inconsistent with such terms. Commercial parties are usually keen to avoid the possibility of implied terms, since the prospect undermines prospective certainty, and will therefore try to leave as few situations undescribed – and as few risks unallocated – as possible.

---

38. It is impossible even expressly to impose such a duty, before the conclusion of a full contract: *Walford v. Miles* [1992] 2 AC 128. The parties can, however, impose a duty to *perform* in good faith by expressly including a term to this effect in their contract.
39. *See Interfoto Picture Library Ltd v. Stiletto Visual Programmes Ltd* [1989] QB 433, 439, per Bingham LJ.
40. For example, R Brownsword, 'Good Faith in Contracts Revisited' (1996) 49 Current Legal Problems 111 and generally R Brownsword, *Contract Law: Themes for the Twenty-First Century*, 2nd edn (Oxford University Press, 2006)
41. *Yam Seng Pte Ltd v. International Trade Corp Ltd* [2013] EWHC 111, [2013] 1 Lloyd's Rep 526, [144], [152].
42. This logic is somewhat circular. For the parties to understand an agreement silent on the question of good faith impliedly to contain such a duty is reasonable only if such a duty is regarded as a normal incident of commercial contracts.
43. *Yam Seng Pte Ltd v. International Trade Corp Ltd* [2013] EWHC 111, [2013] 1 Lloyd's Rep 526, [131]. *See also* for example, *Carewatch Care Services Ltd v. Focus Caring Services Ltd* [2014] EWHC 2313, [108]-[112].

§10. Sources of the Law of Contract

44. There is no single repository of the legal rules relevant to the law of contract in England and Wales, which are instead found in various legislative and non-legislative sources.

45. English contract law is comprised mostly of doctrines created and refined by the courts. English law adheres to a strict principle of precedent, or *stare decisis*. The precise logical nature of precedent is jurisprudentially contentious,[44] but it is at least clear that lower courts are not bound only to replicate the outcomes of authoritative prior decisions. More specifically, they are required to adjudicate consistently with the legal logic that the previous court adopted in order to reach its own decision, commonly known as the *ratio decidendi*.[45]

46. As a general rule, decisions of law bind all courts lower in the judicial hierarchy.[46] Moreover, decisions of the Court of Appeal are binding also on the Court of Appeal itself.[47] Traditionally, the House of Lords – then the final appellate court for England and Wales – also considered itself bound by its own former decisions. This was changed in 1966, and the new Supreme Court has inherited from the House of Lords the convention that, while it can depart from its own former decisions, it will be cautious in doing so.[48] In this way particular legal doctrines can accumulate significant momentum, such that even the Supreme Court is seldom willing to abolish outright the creations of old judges, even when these doctrines are regarded as anachronistic and impractical.

47. Legislative sources of relevant law include specific primary legislation designed to reform individual aspects of contract law doctrine, where Parliament (or, in practice, the Law Commission) believes these doctrines lead to injustice, inefficiency, or other disadvantageous results. Legislation at the EU level has a comparatively small direct influence on the core doctrines of English private law, compared to its influence

---

44. An interesting theoretical analysis is to be found in S Perry, 'Judicial Obligation, Precedent and the Common Law' (1987) 7 Oxford Journal of Legal Studies 215.
45. Statements of law not necessary to reach the outcome of the case are referred to as *obiter dicta*, and are not authoritative, although they may prove persuasive in later cases and therefore re-emerge as *ratio* in subsequent decisions.
46. In addition to English cases, the appellate courts often consider relevant decisions from other jurisdictions, particularly from elsewhere in the Commonwealth. Such cases are not authoritative as precedent, but can be persuasive, and are most often cited to inform the development of English contract law.
47. The correct approach is unclear where, for instance, the High Court is faced with both a Supreme Court (or House of Lords) decision, and a later Court of Appeal decision that the High Court considers incompatible with the Supreme Court decision that preceded it. Some cases suggest the High Court must follow the Court of Appeal (for example *Miliangos v. George Frank (Textiles) Ltd* [1976] AC 443, 478) but there are prominent examples of the opposite approach, such as the Court of Appeal's decision in *Great Peace Shipping Ltd v. Tsavliris (International) Ltd* [2002] EWCA Civ 1407, [2003] QB 679 to depart from its own prior decision in *Solle v. Butcher* [1950] 1 KB 671, on the basis that it was inconsistent with prior House of Lords authority.
48. *Cassel & Co Ltd v. Broome* [1972] AC 1027, 1054, per Lord Hailsham LC; *Kay v. Lambeth London Borough Council* [2006] UKHL 10, [2006] 2 AC 465, [42].

in other areas. However, UK primary or secondary legislation will sometimes incorporate or reproduce EU measures relevant to the law of contract.[49]

48. The writings of legal scholars also influence the development of the law. Their role is less direct than in some other jurisdictions, since the nature of common law adjudication requires judges themselves thoroughly to explain the legal logic behind their decisions. Since identifying, refining and applying legal principles is the duty of the judge herself, there is a comparatively narrow role for academic lawyers in the development of English law. Nonetheless it is increasingly common for the works of eminent living authors to be cited in courts, and it is not uncommon for the Supreme Court particularly, to rely on academic commentary in developing the common law.

49. For instance, Part 2 of the Consumer Rights Act 2015 re-implements Directive 93/13/EC on consumer rights.

Part I. General Principles of the Law of Contract

Chapter 1. Formation

§1. Agreement and Quid Pro Quo (Reciprocity)

I. Offer and Acceptance

49. A contract comes into existence when, one party having already made an offer to enter a contract, the offeree communicates his acceptance to the offeror. Formation therefore does not simply require agreement, but specifically the valid acceptance of a valid offer.

50. This somewhat ritualised approach has been criticised as artificial. In one case, Lord Denning MR proposed instead to treat formation as involving separable, sequential, questions, namely: are the parties in a contractual relationship at all, and if so, what are the terms of their contract? This reflected a broader view of formation, according to which a contract would be formed by agreement on 'all material points', with the court supplying supplementary terms as required.[50]

51. However, his suggestion that a contract could be formed without perfect agreement on all terms is anathema to the established rules of contract formation in English law, which quickly reasserted itself in the wake of Lord Denning's experiments

50. *Butler Machine Tool Company v. Ex-Cell-O Corporation (England)* [1979] 1 WLR 401, 404. This reasoning was *obiter*, since Lord Denning MR in fact concurred with his colleagues (Bridge and Lawton LLJ) in the somewhat creative conclusion that one party had done enough reasonably to lead the other to conclude they were accepting the last set of terms communicated. The broader approach formed part of his *ratio* in *Gibson v. Manchester City Council* [1978] 1 WLR 520, 524.

in the Court of Appeal. The House of Lords rejected his broader approach to agreement,[51] and orthodoxy has been reasserted in several subsequent decisions.[52]

52. The traditional approach can indeed be considered arbitrary, in that it gives effect only to the final set of terms the parties exchanged, rather than to their wider negotiations, and therefore might tend to diverge from the underlying reality of the bargain they contemplated. The narrower and more formulistic the test for agreement, the more likely it will diverge from the true character of the parties' intended deal. Moreover, the traditional rule means that no contract is formed until comparatively late in the parties' dealings. It might also encourage cynical business behaviour, since one party can continue to send its own set of terms in the hope that the other will make a tactical error, doing something a court will later interpret as giving the recalcitrant party reasonable grounds to conclude that these terms had been impliedly accepted.[53]

53. Conversely, the traditional approach has been defended as promoting prospective certainty,[54] at least when compared with a broader, more impressionistic approach, which would make it hard to know the precise terms of the parties' contract without recourse to litigation. The rule can be applied to the majority of ordinary contracts without too much distortion of the parties' dealings,[55] and provides a clean line between the pre-contractual and contractual phases of the parties' relationship. This line is perhaps particularly crucial in the English law of contract, given its denial of any special duties between the parties before the moment of contract formation.

A. Offers and Invitations

54. The law distinguishes between true offers and proposals that are merely *invitations* to form a contract at some point in the future, sometimes called invitations to treat. To comprise a true offer, a proposal must state to an adequate degree of comprehensiveness the parties' rights and obligations, and lead the recipient reasonably and genuinely to conclude that the proposer intends a contract to come into existence immediately when the proposal is accepted. Particularly, an offer of contract terms is

51. *Gibson v. Manchester City Council* [1979] 1 WLR 294. In the Court of Appeal, Lord Denning had found agreement (and therefore contract formation) by reference to the parties' entire course of dealing: *Gibson v. Manchester City Council* [1978] 1 WLR 520. The House of Lords disagreed, on the basis that the language of the penultimate communication between the parties precluded any reasonable interpretation that it was a contractual offer.
52. For example, *Tekdata Interconnections Ltd v. Amphenol Ltd* [2009] EWCA Civ 1209, [2010] 1 Lloyd's Rep 357.
53. Although strictly formation requires the recalcitrant party genuinely to believe the other party is in true agreement with the proposed terms, the honesty of this belief is difficult to disprove.
54. *Tekdata Interconnections Ltd v. Amphenol Ltd* [2009] EWCA Civ 1209, [2010] 1 Lloyd's Rep 357, [25] per Dyson LJ.
55. In *Gibson v. Manchester City Council* [1979] 1 WLR 294, 297, per Lord Diplock, the House of Lords considered the orthodox approach problematic only in 'exceptional' cases, although the House did not indicate what these might comprise. However, negotiations by letter, which this case concerned, clearly failed to meet that threshold.

distinct from a statement as to what the terms of any future contract between the parties will be.[56]

55. In contrast, a mere invitation will generally lead to the conclusion that the proposer contemplates further negotiation prior to becoming bound by a contract. Distinguishing between the two involves interpreting the substance of the proposal and the language in which it is made in the relevant context. Considerations of policy can also sometimes affect judicial determinations about whether a proposal is an offer or a mere invitation, particularly where the proposal is implied rather than expressed in words. For instance, displaying merchandise on shop shelves,[57] and placing advertisements in newspapers,[58] have both been considered invitations to treat, rather than true offers.[59]

56. However, the precise phrasing and context of a proposal can make an offer of what would otherwise be a mere invitation, or an invitation of what might otherwise be construed as an offer. For instance, the issuing of an invitation to submit tenders for contracted works will generally be a mere invitation to treat,[60] but if the terms of the communication make clear that a contract will be formed on the receipt of the lowest bid, it will be held to be an offer,[61] accepted by the submitter of the lowest bid.[62]

57. Particular rules have emerged concerning auctions. Advertisements by auctioneers will generally be mere invitations to treat. It is therefore the bidders who make offers, and the auctioneer accepts whichever offer is highest.[63] Likewise the law has settled on some conventions concerning transactions involving machines, such as vending machines and parking meters. It is the machine's owners who make the offer

---

56. For example, *Harvey v. Facey* [1893] AC 552 distinguished between a statement of price from a true offer to sell at that price.
57. *Pharmaceutical Society of Great Britain v. Boots Cash Chemists (Southern) Ltd* [1953] 1 QB 401. It is therefore the customer that makes the true offer, by taking the items from the shelves and presenting them to the cashier. The same has been held for window displays: *Timothy v Simpson* (1834) 6 C & P 499, 172 ER 1337; *Fisher v. Bell* [1961] 1 WLR 394.
58. *Partridge v. Crittenden* [1968] 2 All ER 421. It is possible that advertisements are more likely to be construed as offers, rather than mere invitations, if their terms propose a unilateral rather than bilateral contract: *Carlill v. Carbolic Smoke Ball Co* [1893] 1 QB 256.
59. The issue has often arisen obliquely in issues concerning criminal law and intellectual property, where it matters whether things have been 'offered' for sale in a legally relevant sense, or merely invited for negotiation: for example *C.A. Norgren Co and others v. Technomarketing and others* (1983) (unreported); *Fisher v. Bell* [1961] 1 WLR 394 (where the defendant escaped criminal liability for the offence of offering for sale an offensive weapon under Restriction of Offensive Weapons Act 1959 because the window display of a flick knife was merely an invitation to treat).
60. *Spencer v. Harding* (1870) LR 5 CP 561.
61. *Harvela Investments Ltd v. Royal Trust Co of Canada (CI) Ltd* [1986] AC 207.
62. Invitations to tender can also be held to constitute the offer of an independent, unilateral contract under which the offeror undertakes properly to consider a received bid equally with the others, an offer accepted by the submission of a bid. This will occur where there is a small pool of invitees already known to the offeror, and where the invitation contains a clear and well-established procedure for the consideration of submitted bids: *Blackpool and Fylde Aero Club Ltd v. Blackpool Borough Council* [1990] 1 WLR 1195.
63. *Payne v. Cave* (1789) 3 TR 148; *British Car Auctions v. Wright* [1972] 1 WLR 1519.

by installing the machine ready to be operated by customers, and the customer that accepts the offer by operating the machine.[64]

B. Termination of an Offer

58. An offer cannot be accepted once it has been rejected either expressly or impliedly by the supply of a counter-offer. A putative acceptance that purports to supply terms that do not match identically the terms contained in the original offer is not a true acceptance, but a counter-offer, which impliedly rejects the original offer.[65] However, an acceptance will not necessarily be construed as a counter-offer if it merely requests clarification of the terms it is accepting.[66]

59. An offer can also be terminated by the passage of time. If the offer is expressly time-sealed, it will expire automatically at the end of this period. If the offer is not expressed to be time-sealed, it will nonetheless be held to have expired after a reasonable time,[67] decided by reference to the circumstances.

60. An offer will also be terminated automatically if it expressly or impliedly contains a condition precedent to its continued validity and this condition fails.[68] In most cases, the continued survival of the offeror will be one such implied condition. This has always been recognised for contracts under which the offeror was to provide personal services to the offeree, but some cases have held an offer to survive the death of the offeror, at least where the offeree was ignorant of the death at the time the offer was putatively accepted.[69] However, the offeree's knowledge or ignorance is irrelevant if the law properly regards the offer as containing an implied condition that it endures only while the offeror is alive.[70]

C. Withdrawing an Offer

61. An offer cannot be withdrawn once validly accepted,[71] because a contract will necessarily have already been formed. Correspondingly, an offer cannot be accepted once validly withdrawn. Offerors have a general freedom to withdraw offers they have made,[72] reflecting that no special duties exist between the parties before the moment of formation. It follows that promises to keep offers open for a certain time are

---

64. *Thornton v. Shoe Lane Parking Ltd* [1971] 2 QB 163.
65. *Hyde v. Wrench* (1840) 3 Beav 334, 49 ER 132.
66. *Stevenson, Jaques & Co v. McLean* (1880) 5 QBD 346; *Gibson v. Manchester City Council* [1979] 1 WLR 294.
67. *Ramsgate Victoria Hotel Ltd v. Montefiore* (1866) LR 1 Ex 109.
68. *Financings Ltd v. Stimson* [1962] 3 All ER 386.
69. *Bradbury v. Morgan* (1862) 1 H & C 249, 158 ER 877; *Dickinson v. Dodds* [1876] 2 Ch D 463.
70. Or, in the case of offerors that are legal rather than natural persons, where the company, etc. has ceased to exist.
71. *Byrne v. Van Tienhoven & Co* (1880) 5 CPD 344.
72. Unless bound by some anterior, collateral contractual obligation to keep the offer open, such as an option contract. However, even this does not prevent valid withdrawal of the offer *per se*, it will just mean that withdrawing it makes the offeror liable for breach of the anterior contract.

ineffective, and withdrawal is effective even before the promised window has elapsed,[73] provided it is properly communicated.

62. However, the picture has become complicated in the context of offers to form unilateral contracts, namely a contract that imposes executory obligations on one party only. Typically this comprises a simple offer to pay a specified sum to the person who provides specified services for the offeror. This offer is accepted by the performance of the specified actions, thus forming the contract and placing the offeror under a contractual obligation to pay the promised sum, even though the offeree owes no obligations under the contract to the offeror. Where the offer is made to an unqualified mass of potential offerees, it is accepted by everyone who fulfils the stipulated conditions.[74]

63. An influential decision of the Court of Appeal stands for the rule that, although such an offer is not accepted until the specified actions contained are performed in full, the offeror nonetheless cannot withdraw her offer once the offeree has commenced performance of the actions in question.[75] Subsequent courts have tried to rationalise this rule by identifying an implied term in the offer to the effect that it will not be withdrawn once the offeree has begun the acts necessary to constitute acceptance.[76] This is unconvincing, since even express promises not to withdraw offers before a certain time are unenforceable.

64. The only doctrinally satisfactory account of the above rule is a highly artificial one, namely that the express offer of a unilateral contract also contains an implied secondary offer of a unilateral contract obliging the offeror not to withdraw the primary offer once the offeree begins the acts specified. The offeree accepts this implied secondary offer by commencing the acts whose completion will subsequently comprise acceptance of the primary offer.

D. Communication of Withdrawal

65. Like the offer itself, withdrawal of an offer is effective only if actually communicated to the offeree.[77] However, communication of withdrawal of an offer need not come from the offeror herself,[78] provided the source is reliable enough to lead a reasonable person in the position of the offeree to the conclusion that the offeror really had withdrawn her offer.

66. The rule that withdrawal is effective even if communicated to the offeree by a third party is inconsistent with the rule on communication of acceptance, and

73. *Routledge v. Grant* (1828) 4 Bing 653; *Dickinson v. Dodds* [1876] 2 Ch D 463.
74. *Carlill v. Carbolic Smoke Ball Co* [1893] 1 QB 256.
75. *Errington v. Errington Woods* [1952] 1 KB 290. However, this rule can be displaced by phrasing the offer to permit withdrawal even after commencement of the required acts (but of course not after their completion): *Luxor (Eastbourne) Ltd v. Cooper* [1941] AC 108.
76. *Daulia Ltd v. Four Millbank Nominees Ltd* [1978] Ch 231, 239.
77. *Byrne v. Van Tienhoven & Co* (1880) 5 CPD 344. This coheres with the focus of contract law as protecting reasonable expectations: without receipt of some notice to the contrary, the offeree is entitled reasonably to conclude that the offer is still open, and therefore that he will have formed a contract binding on the offeror by his communication of acceptance.
78. *Dickinson v. Dodds* [1876] 2 Ch D 463.

there is an argument that the rule should be reformed so as to require communication by the offeror or her agent, as for communication of acceptance. However, the rule on communication of withdrawal is consistent with wider contract theory; an offeree cannot accept an offer unless he genuinely and reasonably believes it is still open, a conclusion precluded where the reasonable person in his position receiving the communication of withdrawal would have concluded that the offeror really had changed her mind. Depending on the credibility of the source, it is quite possible that this would be the reasonable conclusion notwithstanding that the source was someone other than the offeror herself.

67. In the case of offers of unilateral contracts made to the public at large, it has been suggested that withdrawal is effective if the offeror takes reasonable steps to bring the withdrawal to the attention of potential offerees.[79]

E. Communicating Acceptance

68. A contract is formed not at the moment the offeree subjectively decides to accept the offeror's terms, but at the time this acceptance is deemed to have been communicated to the offeror. Acceptance will be deemed to have been communicated when it would reasonably be expected to come to the attention of the offeror, even if the offeror in fact failed to notice the relevant communication,[80] provided the offeree has taken reasonable steps to bring his acceptance to the offeror's attention.[81]

69. Specific rules apply where the parties will have contemplated acceptance by post. Where the offer has been sent by post and the offeree chooses to communicate his acceptance by the same means, acceptance will be deemed communicated at the moment the offeree posts the letter,[82] even if the letter never reaches the offeror, provided it was correctly addressed and properly despatched.[83] Should the offeree subsequently change his mind and decide to reject the offer verbally before the letter of acceptance arrives, the law is unclear on whether this rejection is successful.[84] Arguably, since the postal rule is designed to protect the offeree from the risk of failing to secure a contract he desired and reasonably expected would be formed, an actually communicated rejection should be allowed legal effect, since it is the offeree himself that elects to waive the protections the postal rule offers him. But that conclusion is logically inconsistent with the basis of the postal rule, namely that the act of posting a properly addressed letter of acceptance is itself a communication of acceptance. Acceptance cannot be withdrawn once the contract has been formed, and an attempt to do so will likely constitute repudiation of the contract.

70. The postal rule is typically justified on the basis that, if both parties anticipate the post might be used as a means of acceptance, by posting the reply the offeree takes

79. *Carlill v. Carbolic Smoke Ball Co* [1893] 1 QB 256.
80. *Tenax Steamship Co v. Owners of the Motor Vessel Brimnes (The Brimnes)* [1975] QB 929.
81. *Brinkibon v. Stahag Stahl* [1983] 2 AC 34.
82. *Adams v. Lindsell* (1818) 1 B & Ald 681, 106 ER 250.
83. *Household Fire Insurance v. Grant* (1878–79) LR 4 Ex D 216; *Re London and Northern Bank, ex parte Jones* [1900] 1 Ch 220.
84. There are suggestions in *Adams v. Lindsell* (1818) 1 B & Ald 681, 106 ER 250 that this rejection would be valid and cancel the posted acceptance, but this was *obiter*.

every step to communicate acceptance that the offeror can reasonably expect of him. It follows that the postal rule will not apply if the offer expressly requires actual communication of acceptance, or dictates the required method of response.[85] However, such stipulations will only sometimes be treated as a condition of acceptance, such that no contract can be formed by any other form of communication.[86] Sometimes it will instead be interpreted merely as an indication of preference, particularly as to the speed of response, such that acceptance will be held validly communicated provided some equally swift method has been used.[87] The question reduces to whether the offeree has genuinely and reasonably interpreted the offer as being capable of acceptance by the means he elects to use.

71. This will be affected by business practice and the circumstances of the case, but there are some general conventions: for example, a stipulation that acceptance should come by registered post will not generally be held a condition that disbars acceptance by regular post.[88] Conversely, even in the absence of express stipulation for actual communication, courts will deem the postal rule inapplicable if it would lead to results absurd in the context. Most importantly, the postal rule applies only where the parties have reasonably contemplated that acceptance might be received by post,[89] so its role has dramatically reduced with the declining importance of the post in business dealings. The rule does not apply to modern forms of instant communication,[90] since the sender can tell instantly whether the communication has been properly received, and therefore merely sending the communication is not all reasonably necessary to bring acceptance to the notice of the offeror. Rather, the offeree must keep trying until the message is properly conveyed.

72. Where an offeror makes an offer of a unilateral contract, it has been held that she waives the requirement that acceptance be communicated.[91] The offer will be accepted by the fulfilment of the stipulated conditions, without any requirement that the offeree notify the offeror of their commencement of these conditions. It follows from this understanding of unilateral contract formation that the offeror's obligations are triggered only when the relevant actions – the actions constituting acceptance by the offeree – are fully complete, because it is only at that moment that a contract is formed. In fact there have been some doubts about the point at which a unilateral offer is accepted.

73. Some sources reason that acceptance occurs when the offeree *begins* performance of the relevant actions, even before they are complete, but this is contrary to principle.[92] Clearly even after beginning performance of the stipulated actions, the

85. *Holwell Securities v. Hughes* [1974] 1 WLR 155, 157.
86. *Compagnie de Commerce et Commission SARL v. Parkinson Stove Co Ltd* [1953] 1 Lloyd's Rep 532.
87. *Tinn v. Hoffman & Co* (1873) 29 LT 271.
88. *Yates Building Co Ltd v. Pulleyn & Son (York) Ltd* (1975) 237 EG 183.
89. *Henthorn v. Fraser* [1892] 2 Ch 27, 33.
90. *Entores Ltd v. Miles Far East Corporation* [1955] 2 QB 327, 333; *Domb and another v. Isoz* [1980] Ch 548; *Brinkibon v. Stahag Stahl* [1983] 2 AC 34.
91. *Carlill v. Carbolic Smoke Ball Co* [1893] 1 QB 256.
92. In *Errington v. Errington Woods* [1952] 1 KB 290, Lord Denning acknowledged that there was no acceptance of a unilateral offer until performance was complete, but withdrawal was nonetheless barred at commencement of performance.

offeree is under no obligation to complete them, and the offeror has no cause of action against the offeree if she subsequently abandons the task before completing it. Likewise until the task is complete, the offeree cannot sue for the reward. It seems strange to treat an offer as having been accepted, and therefore a contract as having been formed, at a point in time where neither party would have any cause of action in contract against the other.

74. Acceptance can only be validly communicated by a person who genuinely and reasonably interpreted the offer as addressed to himself,[93] or by an agent acting on the authorisation of that person. It is insufficient for the offeror to be notified of the offeree's acceptance by an unconnected third party.[94] This rule protects the offeree from becoming bound into unwanted contracts or bound earlier than he had anticipated thanks to the acts of a third party, and gives the offeror greater certainty.

75. Communication of acceptance need not be verbally explicit, but can be communicated impliedly.[95] However, total silence or inaction on the part of the offeree can never communicate acceptance, even if the terms of the offer purport to treat silence as acceptance.[96] This rule is defended on the basis that silence is inherently equivocal in its meaning, and that it limits the apparent acceptance of unwanted contracts.

76. Actions can communicate acceptance when those actions are such that the reasonable person in the position of the offeror would understand them to mean the offeree had accepted. This is particularly important in the context of the 'battle of the forms', a situation that arises primarily in dealings between commercial enterprises, where there has been a purported acceptance which in fact is phrased to be 'subject to' a set of terms that is contained in the putative acceptor's standard terms of business, which in turn differ from the terms of the offer.

77. English law contains no special doctrine for resolving these impasses,[97] which instead fall to be resolved according to the normal rules of offer and acceptance. This insists that a contract is formed only when there is perfect acceptance of an offered set of terms. But because such acceptance can be communicated impliedly, for instance by commencing performance, courts will usually find a contract to have been formed in a commercial context where one party has commenced performance of some kind, on the basis that such performance constitutes implied acceptance of the last set of terms communicated.[98] These will be held to have constituted the offer, which was impliedly accepted by performance.

93. *Boulton v. Jones* (1857) 2 H & N 564.
94. *Powell v. Lee* (1908) 99 LT 284.
95. *Butler Machine Tool Company v. Ex-Cell-O Corporation (England)* [1979] 1 WLR 401.
96. *Felthouse v. Bindley* (1862) 11 CB NS 869, 142 ER 1037.
97. This is the context in which orthodox offer and acceptance analysis has been most challenged, in cases such as *Butler Machine Tool Company v. Ex-Cell-O Corporation (England)* [1979] 1 WLR 401.
98. In *Tekdata Interconnections Ltd v. Amphenol Ltd* [2009] EWCA Civ 1209, [2010] 1 Lloyd's Rep 357, [21], Longmore LJ implied that the traditional approach may be displaced where the parties have had a prolonged course of dealing, but this is likely to be a demanding threshold.

F. Objectivity

78. Although the formation of a contract requires the acceptance of an offer, English law does not require there to have been genuine subjective agreement between the parties. The law instead requires only the objective appearance of genuine agreement. English contract law does not require the defendant's genuine subjective agreement in order to hold him liable in contract; he can also be held to obligations he did not subjectively intend to undertake.

79. When the claimant tries to sue the defendant to enforce the contract that the claimant believes they have agreed, the defendant may object that he did not in fact agree to the terms that the claimant is attempting to enforce. Depending on which party is held to have made the offer and which the acceptance, this will involve the defendant submitting either (i) that he intended to accept terms different from those the claimant intended to offer and on which the claimant now sues, or (ii) that the claimant misunderstood the terms of the offer he intended to make her, and therefore that she never accepted the offer he actually intended to make.

80. If the law required genuine subjective agreement for the creation of a binding contract, no such contract could exist where the terms the offeror believed she was offering did not match the terms the recipient believed he was accepting. However, in English law such a defendant will not be allowed to deny having agreed to the terms the claimant is trying to enforce, provided the defendant's words or conduct led the claimant genuinely and reasonably to believe that the defendant *did* subjectively assent to the claimant's understanding of the terms. The rule was succinctly expressed in the important case of *Smith v. Hughes*: 'If, whatever a man's real intention may be, he so conducts himself that a reasonable man would believe he was assenting to the terms proposed by the other party...the man thus conducting himself would be equally bound as if he had intended to agree to the other party's terms.'[99]

81. In order to hold the defendant to an apparent intention that in fact was not his subjective intention, the claimant must have believed that the apparent intention did in fact match the defendant's subjective intention. This belief must be genuinely

99. *Smith v. Hughes* (1871) LR 6 QB 597, 607, per Blackburn J. *See also* 609, per Hannen J. Crucially, the defendant's objectively apparent intent is not important only because it gives evidence of his subjective consent. Rather this objective intention can found liability even if it could be conclusively shown to be inconsistent with his true intentions at the time of contracting. The point was perhaps put best in an American decision: 'A contract is an obligation attached by the mere force of law to certain acts of the parties, usually words, which ordinarily accompany and represent a known intent. If, however, it were proved by twenty bishops that either party, when he used the words, intended something else than the usual meaning that the law imposes upon them, he would still be held...': *Hotchkiss v. National City Bank of New York*, 200 F 287, 293 (SD NY 1911), per Learned Hand J.

held,[100] and must have been a reasonable conclusion to draw from the defendant's words and conduct in the circumstances.[101]

82. To decide whether this is the reasonable inference from the defendant's words and conduct, the court will interpret these from the perspective of the reasonable person in the position of the addressee,[102] equipped with all the knowledge 'reasonably available to the parties' at the time of putative contract formation.[103] Moreover, it must not be because of her own negligence that the claimant thought the defendant's manifested intention matched his subjective intention.[104] This results from the requirement that the belief be reasonable in light of all the knowledge the claimant had at the time the belief was formed: the objectivity rule does not avail the claimant when the discrepancy between the defendant's apparent and subjective intentions was due to the claimant's own negligence, because the reasonable person in the claimant's position would know of her own negligence, and therefore could not reasonably conclude – without checking first – that the defendant's apparent intention represented his subjective intention.

83. In other words, the objective intention rule means that a party's intention is deemed at law to be the intention that the reasonable person in the other party's position would have understood it to be.[105] It follows that the objectivity rule described above will not assist the claimant when the claimant's own words and conduct also led the defendant to the genuine and reasonable conclusion that the claimant shared *his* understanding of the terms of their agreement, an understanding according to which

100. The claimant cannot hold the defendant to the outward appearance of his intentions if the claimant had actual knowledge that the defendant's apparent intentions did not reflect his subjective intentions: *Paal Wilson & Co A/S v. Partenreederei Hannah Blumenthal (The Hannah Blumenthal)* [1983] 1 AC 854, 924, per Lord Brightman.

101. *Hartog v. Colin & Shields* [1939] 3 All ER 566. This case concerned an attempt to 'snap up' an offer that contained an error so obvious that any reasonable recipient should have concluded that the terms that appeared on its face were not the terms the defendant had really intended to offer.

102. *Centrovincial Estates Plc v. Merchant Investors Assurance Co* [1983] Com LR 158, per Slade LJ; *RTS Flexible Systems Ltd v. Molkerei Alois Miller GmbH* [2010] UKSC 14, [2010] 1 WLR 753, [45].

103. *Investors Compensation Scheme v. West Bromwich Building Society* [1998] 1 WLR 896, per Lord Hoffmann. This knowledge includes, where the claimant in fact knew it, the defendant's true subjective intention. Thus as a matter of logic it is impossible for the claimant genuinely and reasonably to believe that the defendant meant something other than the claimant knows to have been his true intention.

104. *Scriven v. Hindley* [1913] 3 KB 564.

105. The nature of English law's objective interpretation rule has proven controversial among contract scholars. *See* particularly the discourse: W Howarth, 'The Meaning of Objectivity in Contract' (1984) 100 LQR 265; JP Vorster, 'A Comment on the Meaning of Objectivity in Contract' (1987) 104 LQR 274; W Howarth, 'A note on the objective of objectivity in contract' (1987) 103 LQR 527. Nonetheless the law has rejected an entirely impersonal, 'fly on the wall' approach to the interpretation of the parties' agreement, which would have permitted courts to conclude the parties had formed a contract on terms that *neither* of them subjectively intended, something the objectivity rule deriving from *Smith v. Hughes* (1871) LR 6 QB 597 does not accommodate. Support for this unorthodox view can be found in, for example, *Solle v. Butcher* [1950] 1 KB 671, 691, per Denning LJ.

he is not bound in the way the claimant now submits. In that case neither of the parties' inconsistent understandings of the contract terms is enforceable against the other, and each is free to deny having ever agreed to the terms that are being invoked against them.

II. Intention to Create Legal Relations

84. It is contentious whether English law contains a doctrine of 'intention to create legal relations', at least as an independent requirement of contract formation. Clearly such an intention is not *sufficient* for the formation of a binding legal contract, since even a conspicuous common intention to form a legal contract will not survive the absence of a valid offer and acceptance.[106] Moreover, in light of the objectivity principle, a genuine *subjective* intention to create legal relations is unnecessary for valid contract formation. Indeed, there has been recent judicial reiteration that, where the question of intent falls to be considered, it is assessed in accordance with the orthodox objectivity principle.[107] A defendant cannot resist liability in contract by proving that, notwithstanding the reasonable conclusion to which his conduct led the claimant, he never desired to enter a legally binding arrangement.

85. Admittedly, an agreement will not create a contract if the parties' dealings fail *objectively* to demonstrate an intention to form a binding contractual relationship. But this does not support the existence of a freestanding requirement for contract formation, supplementary to offer and acceptance. The very essence of an offer – as opposed to a mere invitation to treat – is that it demonstrates objectively an intention to form a binding legal contract immediately on acceptance. It is therefore logically impossible to find the requirements of offer and acceptance to have been satisfied, but nonetheless to conclude the parties' agreement is non-contractual because of an absence of intention to create legal relations.

86. There persists, however, a body of jurisprudence that purports to treat intention to create legal relations independently of offer and acceptance, as a discrete requirement for an agreement's contractual effect. For instance, it has been held that in domestic or social contexts, the law will presume that parties do not intend their promises or agreements to create binding legal relations,[108] although this presumption can be rebutted by extraneous evidence that this is indeed what the parties intended.[109] Conversely, in commercial contexts, an intention to create legal relations will be

106. *Gibson v. Manchester City Council* [1979] 1 WLR 294.
107. *RTS Flexible Systems Ltd v. Molkerei Alois Miller GmbH* [2010] UKSC 14, [2010] 1 WLR 753, [45].
108. Concerning spouses *see Balfour v. Balfour* [1919] 2 KB 571; *Spellman v. Spellman* [1961] 1 WLR 921; *Merritt v. Merritt* [1970] 1 WLR 1211. Concerning parents and children *see Jones v. Padavatton* [1969] 1 WLR 328. Concerning friends *see Coward v. Motor Insurers' Bureau* [1963] 1 QB 259.
109. *Simpkins v. Pays* [1955] 1 WLR 975.

presumed to be present,[110] always subject to the precise language of the parties' communications.[111]

87. On one level, these presumptions can be absorbed into standard offer and acceptance analysis, since it will generally be less reasonable to interpret assent as intended to be of *legal* effect in social contexts than in commercial ones. This understanding of the above presumptions therefore confirms that meaninglessness of intoning 'intention to create legal relations' as if it were a requirement for contract formation distinct from orthodox objective offer and acceptance analysis. Really however the cases purporting to identify the above presumptions incant them in order to effectuate normative judicial opinions about whether agreements *should* be enforced if concluded in particular contexts.[112] These 'presumptions' are really attempts to police the boundaries of the law of contract further than is permitted by the – hitherto narrow – judicial prerogative not to enforce contracts that involve illegality or are contrary to public policy.[113]

III. Consideration

A. The Doctrine of Consideration

88. The presence of consideration is a 'cardinal necessity' for the formation of a valid contract not made by deed,[114] and in principle also for the valid variation of an existing contract (other than under a contractual variation clause).[115] The doctrine of consideration has existed in a recognisably modern form since at least the late eighteenth century,[116] but in recent years it has come under increasing attack, and has been substantially weakened in many respects. Nonetheless, the doctrine's core proposition

110. *Edwards v. Skyways* [1964] 1 QB 349, 355.
111. *Jones v. Vernon Pools Ltd* [1938] 2 All ER 626.
112. Indeed the reasoning of both the first instance judge and the Court of Appeal in *Balfour v. Balfour* [1919] 2 KB 571 was explicitly focused on the policy questions concerned in deeming the parties' agreement to be of a legal as opposed to a merely personal nature. For Atkin LJ (at 579), 'the small courts of this country would have to be multiplied one hundredfold if these arrangements were held to result in legal obligations'.
113. The reality is well demonstrated by the Supreme Court's recent consideration of the legal effect of prenuptial agreements: *Granatino v. Radmacher* [2010] UKSC 42, [2010] 3 WLR 1367. Since these are patently intended in fact to have legal effect, the question of substance for the court was whether the parties' obvious intention of legal effect should be honoured or denied in the interests of public policy. The majority were in favour of giving legal effect to a prenuptial agreement provided it was freely agreed, and did not prejudice the interests of the couple's children.
114. *Combe v. Combe* [1951] 2 KB 215, per Denning LJ. The common law will also enforce a gratuitous undertaking if made in the form of a deed and will award damages for breach. However, equitable remedies such as specific performance will not be available if the promisee provided no consideration.
115. However, the requirement of consideration in this context has been heavily diluted following *Williams v. Roffey Bros & Nicholls (Contractors) Ltd* [1991] 1 QB 1.
116. *Rann v. Hughes* (1778) 7 Term Rep 350.

survives: the recipient of a promise – the promisee – cannot enforce that promise unless he provided valuable consideration in return for the promise in question.[117]

89. There is no universally accepted definition of consideration. One influential attempt describes it as 'some right, interest, profit or benefit accruing to the [promisor], or some forbearance, detriment, loss or responsibility given, suffered or undertaken by the [promisee]'.[118] However, the essence of consideration lies not in any discernible improvement in the condition of the promisor, nor in any deterioration in the condition of the promisee, but specifically in the promisee's making of some undertaking in return for the promise in question. It is this undertaking – 'the price for which the promise of the other is bought'[119] – that empowers the promisee to hold the promisor to her undertakings. The promisee provides consideration if he undertakes to perform some action in the future; the contract can be formed by the exchange of purely executory obligations.

90. To constitute valid consideration, the promisee's act or undertaking must have been *requested* by the promisor, as the price of the promisor's own undertakings.[120] Therefore it is not sufficient that the promisee merely confers some unrequested benefit on the promisor. Indeed, the requested undertaking need not be materially beneficial to the promisor at all to constitute valid consideration,[121] provided it involves some action or forbearance on the part of the promisee.[122] While contract formation requires the exchange of undertakings of legally recognised value, the law does not investigate the 'adequacy' of the value represented by the parties' undertakings. The objective economic value of the consideration is irrelevant to contract formation.[123] Correspondingly, an undertaking can be valid consideration even if it puts the promisee to no significant

---

117. It has been suggested that, while a promise 'may appear gratuitous...the promisor expects some return in a rather more indirect way than the present doctrine of consideration recognizes.': P Atiyah, 'Consideration: A Restatement' in *Essays on Contract* (Oxford University Press, 1986). This is certainly true, but in commercial contexts the courts will strive hard to find the requirement of consideration to have been satisfied where the parties clearly intended a binding legal relationship, and it is rare for such an agreement to be denied legal effect for want of consideration.
118. *Currie v. Misa* (1875) 10 Exch 153, 162, per Lush J.
119. *Dunlop Pneumatic Tyre Co Ltd v. Selfridge & Co Ltd* [1915] AC 847, per Lord Dunedin.
120. This must be distinguished from unrequested actions in light of a gratuitous promise: In *Combe v. Combe* [1951] 2 KB 215, a husband promised to pay his estranged wife the money necessary for her subsistence, as a result of which promise the wife did not exercise her legal right to rejoin her husband. Although this was a forbearance, it was not done at the request of the husband as the 'price' of his own undertaking.
121. 'A peppercorn does not cease to be good consideration if it is established that the [promisor] does not like pepper and will throw away the corn.': *Chappel & Co Ltd v. Nestle Co Ltd* [1960] AC 87, per Lord Somervell. In this case, the majority of the House of Lords held that used chocolate wrappers formed part of the consideration supporting the promisor's undertaking, even though they were of no material use and would be disposed of immediately.
122. *Carlill v. Carbolic Smoke Ball Co* [1893] 1 QB 256, 271, per Bowen LJ.
123. *Thomas v. Thomas* (1842) 2 QB 851, 114 ER 330. English contract law does police unfair bargains, but not by denying contract formation on the basis of substantive unfairness. English law prefers to focus on unfair processes than unfair outcomes: *Hart v. O'Connor* [1985] AC 1000, 1017–1018, per Lord Brightman.

effort or inconvenience, and even if it was something the promisee might well have elected to do even if he had not made any contract with the promisor.[124]

91. Importantly, while consideration must *move from the promisee* (the party seeking to enforce the other party's undertaking),[125] it need not necessarily move *to the promisor*. The promisee provides valid consideration if he undertakes to perform some act or forbearance in favour of a third party, provided this is requested by the promisor as the price of her own undertaking.[126]

92. An undertaking will not constitute valid consideration if it has *no legally recognised* value, even if it is materially beneficial to the promisor. For instance, a promise to abandon a lawsuit against the promisor cannot be consideration for the promisor's own undertaking if the promisee knew all along that this action was without basis and guaranteed to fail.[127] Likewise acts independently required of the promisee by public law are not valid consideration.[128] However, the performance of existing *private law* duties owed to a third party is valid consideration.[129] The rule concerning public law duties expresses public policy concerns, particularly the need to prevent public officers seeking payment from private individuals for doing their public duty.[130] Therefore, undertakings to perform acts above and beyond the scope of the promisee's public law duty can constitute valid consideration.[131]

---

124. *Shanklin Pier v. Detel* [1951] 2 KB 854.
125. *Price v. Easton* (1833) 4 B & Ad 433; *Tweddle v. Atkinson* (1861) 1 B & S 393, 121 ER 762.
126. *Dunlop Pneumatic Tyre Co Ltd v. Selfridge & Co Ltd* [1915] AC 847, 853, per Viscount Haldane. However, this does not give the benefited third party a right to sue for breach.
127. *Wade v. Simeon* (1846) 2 CB 548, 564–65, 135 ER 1061, 1067. However, if the promisee genuinely but wrongly believed his suit to be valid, undertaking to abandon it can be valid consideration: *Callisher v. Bischoffshein* (1870) LR 5 QB 449, 451–452. This is so even when the promisor knew the promisee's threatened suit to be invalid: *Cook v. Wright* (1861) 1 B & S 559, 568–569, 121 ER 822, 825–826.
128. *Collins v. Godefroy* (1831) B & Ad 950, per Lord Tenterten CJ. Cf the dissenting opinion of Denning LJ in *Ward v. Byham* [1956] 1 WLR 496, 498 that the mere performance of an existing public law duty was good consideration. The other members of the Court of Appeal decided the case on orthodox reasoning, in finding that the claimant had in fact undertaken to perform actions in excess of her public law duty.
129. The most often cited authority for this proposition is *Shadwell v. Shadwell* (1860) 9 CB (NS) 159, but the facts of this case are actually best analysed as a conditional gift and not a contract at all. More relevant authority is found in, for example, *Scotson v. Pegg* (1861) 6 H & N 295, 158 ER 121; *NZ Shipping Co Ltd v. A M Satterthwaite & Co Ltd (The Eurymedon)* [1975] AC 154, 168.
130. *Glasbrook Bros v. Glamorgan County Council* [1925] AC 270, per Lord Shaw.
131. *Glasbrook Bros v. Glamorgan County Council* [1925] AC 270. Here, the House of Lords, by majority, permitted the police to make a contract with a local business owner to provide special protection during industrial unrest, despite the police's existing public law duty to maintain law and order, since the supply of services above and beyond their legally mandated minimum duties could be valid consideration to support a contract to provide such services. *See also Harris v. Sheffield United Football Club Ltd* [1988] QB 77. On this basis, the Court of Appeal in *Ward v. Byham* [1956] 1 WLR 496 (Morris and Parker LLJ) held that a mother's (implied) undertaking to ensure her child's happiness was valid consideration for the estranged father's undertaking to provide weekly support payments, because this was above and beyond the mother's public law duty to ensure the child was adequately cared for.

1. The Consideration Debate

93. There is significant academic and judicial hostility to the requirement of consideration for the formation and variation of contracts. The standard criticism is that the doctrine of consideration unacceptably denies legal effect to agreements that the parties intended to be legally enforced. As long ago as 1765, Lord Mansfield argued for the enforceability of all seriously intended undertakings, even in the absence of either a deed or valuable consideration, on the grounds that these requirements were only imposed 'for the sake of evidence' about the promisor's intention to be legally bound to the undertaking in question. Therefore, where other evidence could show the promise to have been 'entered into upon deliberation and reflection...such promises [should be] binding'.[132]

94. Notwithstanding the eminence of its many detractors, the case against consideration is probably overstated. If the parties genuinely intend to make an entirely gratuitous undertaking legally binding, this can readily be achieved through the use of a deed, which nowadays is a simple procedure. The comparative rarity of contracts in the form of a deed perhaps indicates that legal actors are less interested in binding themselves in law to unremunerated undertakings than the opponents of consideration assume. Indeed, failure to ask *anything* in return for one's promise at the very least raises doubt as to whether the promisor really wishes this promise to expose her to legal liability.

95. In emphasising the unusual cases in which the doctrine of consideration obstructs the parties' apparent intentions, its critics are perhaps examining the issue of contract formation through the wrong end of the telescope, disregarding the vast majority of cases in which consideration causes no problem, and in fact makes for a simple and secure guarantee of enforceability. While there are some complex (even archaic) rules about what can constitute valid consideration, these concern the outer fringes of the doctrine.[133] The requirement of consideration will always be satisfied by the payment of a token sum.

96. Moreover, a pure test of intention does not reflect a convincing normative justification for binding promisors to undertakings they later wish to renounce. A leading argument for abandoning the doctrine of consideration in favour of a pure test of intention appeals to the general moral importance of promise-keeping.[134] On this view, the law is justified in holding promisors to their undertakings because it is immoral to resile from a promise that one freely undertook. But advocates of this view seldom accept its logical conclusions, namely that the law should presumptively enforce *all* promises regardless of the promisor's intention to be legally bound. If we accept that the law is justified in holding people to their promises *simply* because it is immoral to break a promise, then confining legal enforceability to promises specifically intended

132. *Pillans & Rose v. Van Mierop & Hopkins* (1765) 3 Burr 1663.

133. Indeed, much of the complexity in this area of law is not because of the doctrine of consideration but of the attempts to dilute it, such as the legacies of cases such as *Williams v. Roffey Bros & Nicholls (Contractors) Ltd* [1991] 1 QB 1 and *Central London Property Trust Ltd v. High Trees House Ltd* [1947] KB 130.

134. The leading articulation is in C Fried, *Contract as Promise: A Theory of Contractual Obligation* (Oxford University Press, 1981).

to be legally binding is glaringly arbitrary. Such a limitation implies that promisors themselves can decide which of their promises are morally binding, and therefore to decide which will be legally enforceable and which will not. This hardly expresses a consistent moral vision about the inherent moral duty to keep one's promises.

97. In contrast, the doctrine of consideration endorses the moral proposition that as rational, autonomous beings, individuals have the general prerogative to change their minds, regardless of how seriously they intended a promise at the time they made it. The doctrine provides a clear answer as to why a promisee may in some cases override the promisor's general freedom to revoke her promises, namely that he has *purchased* the promisor's freedom from her in a freely negotiated exchange. Therefore, for the promisor to resile from her promise is wrongfully to appropriate an unrestricted freedom of action to which she is no longer entitled, having sold it away to the promisee in exchange for the right to constrain the promisee's own future conduct.

98. Despite these unanswered questions, opposition to the doctrine of consideration has proven highly successful, and developments in several areas of the law have undermined its integrity.

B. Gratuitous Promises

99. The doctrine of consideration does not affect the legal validity of a gratuitous transfer of property, or the unremunerated provision of a benefit to the recipient. These are not legally vulnerable simply because the recipient provided no consideration. A gratuitous undertaking (such as a promise to make an unremunerated gift) is merely *unenforceable* by the promisee in the event of the promisor's refusal or failure to perform. But if the promise is duly performed, the promisor makes a perfect gift and the promisee retains the benefit.

100. Notwithstanding the doctrine of consideration, gratuitous undertakings are enforceable if made in the form of a deed. Nonetheless, in an action for breach, the remedy will be confined to damages and no specific performance will be available if the promisee provided no consideration.

C. Absence of 'Natural Obligations'

101. English law remains committed to a bargain theory of contract formation, as described above. A contract is therefore an *exchange* of actions or undertakings, and consideration – the litmus of enforceability for prospective undertakings – does not mean simply an acceptable motive for the undertaking in question.[135] Therefore undertakings unenforceable if made only on the strength of a preexisting 'moral debt', rather than in exchange for a new undertaking from the promisee. Neither natural love and affection, nor a sense of moral obligation to the promisee, is consideration capable of supporting contract formation.

102. However, there is one qualification to the rule that actions performed in the past cannot be consideration for a new promise. The rule in *Lampleigh v. Braithwait* establishes that, where the claimant has performed some act at the defendant's request,

---

135. *Eastwood v. Kenyon* (1840) 11 Ad & E 438, 113 ER 482; *Thomas v. Thomas* (1842) 2 QB 851, 859, 114 ER 330, 333, per Patteson J.

this past action can constitute consideration for the defendant's *subsequent* promise to reward the claimant for this act.[136] However, the claimant must have performed the act at the request of the defendant, and must have made clear at the time that she expected to be remunerated in some way in the future.[137]

IV. Modifications of the Contract

103. Contracts concluded between professionally advised commercial parties generally contain mechanisms providing for variation of the contract. Even if the parties' contract does not provide for such a variation mechanism, it is nonetheless possible for the parties to vary their original contract as a matter of general common law. In that case both parties must provide valuable consideration in order to effect variation in the obligations they originally undertook. Consideration need not necessarily be provided when the contract terms are varied under a mechanism stipulated in the contract itself. Rather, the specific terms of the parties' agreed variation mechanism dictate the requirements for variation.

104. The law has traditionally maintained that the performance of one party's original contractual obligations is not valid consideration to support the other party's undertaking to increase his own obligations under the contract.[138] However, this rule has been heavily undermined by the decision of the Court of Appeal in *Williams v. Roffey Brothers*.[139] Here, a building contractor engaged a subcontractor to perform carpentry work on a series of units. The contract provided for staged payments on completion of each unit. Part way through construction, the subcontractor informed the main contractor that he would not be able to complete performance at the agreed price. They agreed to an increase in the contract price that the subcontractor claimed would permit him actually to complete performance. In fact, the subcontractor completed only some of the units, before abandoning the project. When he sued for payment for the units he had in fact completed, it was at the higher rate. The Court of Appeal unanimously held that the subcontractor had provided valid consideration to support the variation in the main contractor's duty, such that the subcontractor was entitled to be paid per unit at the high rate.

136. *Lampleigh v. Braithwait* (1615) Hobart 105, 80 ER 255.
137. *Pao On v. Lau Yiu Long* [1980] AC 614, 629, per Lord Scarman.
138. *Stilk v. Myrick* (1809) 2 Camp 317, 170 ER 1168. In this case, two sailors deserted their positions on board ship. The remaining crew members' employer offered them all extra money to complete the journey they were already contracted to undertake. The court held that the employer was not liable to pay them this extra sum following completion of the voyage. Cf *Hartley v. Ponsonby* (1857) 26 LJ QB 322, 119 ER 1471, in which the court reached the opposite conclusion, distinguishing *Stilk v. Myrick* on the basis that either (a) the mass desertion of nearly half the crew frustrated the original contract between the ship's owner and the remaining seamen, such that the subsequent arrangement that they should complete the journey in exchange for an increased rate of pay constituted an entirely fresh contract, or (b) that the desertion made continuing the journey more arduous, such that the remaining crew provided consideration for the variation by undertaking duties in excess of those they were already required to perform.
139. *Williams v. Roffey Bros & Nicholls (Contractors) Ltd* [1991] 1 QB 1.

105. The majority of the Court of Appeal interpreted the traditional rule – that one party's performance is not consideration for the other party's variation – as reflecting a rudimentary attempt to prevent unscrupulous contract parties threatening to withhold performance to force a variation in their favour.[140] Since the law now has a mature doctrine of economic duress capable of policing such behaviour,[141] the Court concluded it was appropriate to support freely negotiated variations as far as possible, by trying hard to find the necessary consideration where the parties had freely agreed on a variation.[142] The Court therefore held that the subcontractor had indeed provided consideration for the variation in the main contractor's obligations, in the form of the 'practical benefit' that the main contractor would receive as a result of the actual performance of the services he had bargained to receive – performance he would probably not receive if the contract were not renegotiated. Even though for reasons of precedent the Court maintains a notional requirement of consideration, the decision in effect permits the unilateral variation of contract terms, since ultimately the variation gave the main contractor no rights he did not have already under the original agreement.

106. Many commentators have applauded the decision in *Roffey* as reflecting the commercial need for contracts freely to evolve in accordance with the parties' changing needs. Arguably, however, commercial parties should be expected to provide for their own contractual variation mechanisms, as indeed the majority do. *Roffey* has further been praised for promoting transparency in the law, since variations have always been enforceable if unilateral in spirit as long as token consideration makes them bilateral in form. However, the decision creates its own artificiality. Unable to abolish the requirement of consideration outright, the Court of Appeal in *Roffey* fictitiously insisted that consideration had been provided even though the promisee's legal obligations remained totally unchanged. Problematically, *Roffey* reduces incentives to estimate one's costs accurately in advance.[143] Additionally, such renegotiations may be inherently closer to situations of economic duress that the Court of Appeal in *Roffey* acknowledges. For a party to warn the other that he will breach his obligations if the contractual terms are not varied is perilously close to an implied *threat* to breach unless the terms are varied.

---

140. *Williams v. Roffey Bros & Nicholls (Contractors) Ltd* [1991] 1 QB 1, per Glidewell and Purchas LLJ. In so ruling they drew on a less prominent report of the decision in *Stilk v. Myrick* (reported in 6 Esp 129, 170 ER 851), which they regarded as expressing a different *ratio* for that decision. The reporter, Espinasse, is generally regarded as having been a poor law reporter, but he nonetheless has the advantage of having acted as junior counsel in *Stilk v. Myrick* itself. However, the two reports are in fact substantially similar and the differences are more apparent than real: P Luther, 'Campbell, Espinasse and the sailors: text and context in the common law' (1999) 19 Legal Studies 526.
141. *Williams v. Roffey Bros & Nicholls (Contractors) Ltd* [1991] 1 QB 1, 21, per Purchas LJ.
142. *Williams v. Roffey Bros & Nicholls (Contractors) Ltd* [1991] 1 QB 1, 18, per Russell LJ.
143. J O'Sullivan, 'In defence of *Foakes v. Beer*' (1996) 55 CLJ 225. Indeed, this is precisely what the contractor had failed to do in *Williams v. Roffey Bros & Nicholls (Contractors) Ltd* [1991] 1 QB 1, 6.

A. A Special Case: The Variation of Debts

107. Until very recently, the logic of 'practical benefit' did not extend to a particular case of contract variation,[144] namely part payments of debts. In *Pinnel's Case*,[145] the court stated that a lesser sum cannot stand in satisfaction for a greater sum owed, so a creditor is not bound by a simple promise to accept the offered lesser sum in satisfaction for the whole debt,[146] a rule reiterated – with reluctance – by the House of Lords in *Foakes v. Beer*.[147] Such a promise is supported by consideration and therefore binding provided the debtor's obligations – and therefore the creditor's rights – change in some way other than the sum owed,[148] for example if the date of payment is brought forward. However, merely changing the form or method of payment, such as from cash to cheque, is unlikely to qualify.[149]

108. Most legal scholars felt that the rule in *Foakes v. Beer* should be reconsidered in light of the decision in *Roffey*.[150] After all, 'if the 'practical benefit' to the promisor from the performance of an existing contractual obligation can provide consideration for a *promise to pay more*, why should the same not apply to a *promise to accept*

144. It is debatable whether the question of variation of debt is actually a consideration question at all. It has been suggested that English law treats it as an issue of contract law and consideration – 'a tidy mirror image of the principle in *Stilk v. Myrick*' – as a practical means of policing debt release, which is convenient but not conceptually proper: J O'Sullivan, 'In defence of *Foakes v. Beer*' (1996) 55 CLJ 219.
145. *Pinnel's Case* (1602) 5 Co Rep 117a, 77 ER 237.
146. In fact this was *obiter*, since the part payment was made earlier than the due date for the whole debt, so there was variation of some aspect of the debtor's obligations other than the sum in question.
147. *Foakes v. Beer* (1884) 9 App Cas 605. Lord Blackburn came close to dissenting, noting (at 622) that 'prompt payment of a part of their demand may be more beneficial to [creditors] than it would be to insist on their rights and enforce payment of the whole.'
148. An exception is reaching a 'composition with creditors', under which variation is effected in the form of a deed, which avoids the need for consideration. With consent of all the creditors, the debtor amalgamates his debts and agrees partially to repay each creditor at the same proportion of the sum owed. Such arrangements are regulated by the Deeds of Arrangement Act 1914.
149. *D & C Builders v. Rees* [1966] 2 WLR 28, per Lord Denning MR.
150. *See* for example J Carter, A Phang and J Poole, 'Reactions to *Williams v. Roffey*' (1995) 8 JCL 248, 266; E Cooke, 'Working Together? Contract, estoppel and the business relationship' [2002] 1 Journal of Obligations and Remedies 5, 16.

less?'[151] Some dissenting voices defended the law's differing stances,[152] but it was ultimately clear that the law was treating analytically identical situations differently in maintaining that genuine consideration (not just some imprecise 'practical benefit') must be provided to support promises to accept less, but not promises to pay more.

109. In *Re Selectmove*, the Court of Appeal had held that, despite the logical tension between the rule in *Foakes v. Beer* and the decision in *Roffey*, it was unable to extend the logic of *Roffey* to the variation of debts, since *Foakes v. Beer* was a decision of the House of Lords; to extend the *Roffey* analysis to debt variations 'would in effect leave the principle in *Foakes v. Beer* without any application'.[153] However, the law appears at last to have yielded to the inexorable gravity of *Roffey*'s attack on the doctrine of consideration, by expanding its applicability to part payment of debts.

110. In *MWB Business Exchange Centres v. Rock Advertising*,[154] the Court of Appeal regarded an agreement to accept part payment in satisfaction of a larger debt as binding on the creditor. The Court distinguished *Re Selectmove* on the basis that there were in this case additional practical benefits to be had in varying the debt.[155] Specifically, the creditor would not be left with an unoccupied property and the resultant risks of future losses; waiving the debtor's full liability would help the creditor 'avoid a void'.[156] It was crucial therefore that the parties were in an ongoing and mutually beneficial commercial relationship that accepting part payment would help to sustain.

111. The law remains that part payment is not consideration for the creditor's promise to vary the debt if the only 'practical benefit' thus conferred by the debtor is the actual receipt of the lesser sum. If there are additional practical benefits, then the *Roffey* analysis will regard the debt variation as supported by consideration moving from the debtor. It appears therefore that in effect, the rule in *Foakes v. Beer* has been confined to one-off debts. But even in those situations, it seems possible that a sufficiently determined court could identify some remote 'practical benefit' resultant from the receipt of the lesser sum.

112. To extend the *Roffey* 'practical benefit' analysis to part payment of debts is irretrievably inconsistent with the decision in *Foakes v. Beer*, in which the House

---

151. J O'Sullivan, 'In defence of *Foakes v. Beer*' (1996) 55 CLJ 220 (the author in fact rejects the majority stance, insisting that the two cases can be distinguished).
152. For the leading defence of *Foakes v. Beer*, *see* J O'Sullivan, 'In defence of *Foakes v. Beer*' (1996) 55 CLJ 221. O'Sullivan suggests there is inherently less 'practical benefit' in the debt context than in situations such as *Roffey*, since an action for debt is not subject to limitations such as mitigation and remoteness that may make litigating meaningfully less attractive than actual performance. This is true, but it is still expensive and tedious to sue for a debt, and delay may prove fatal if the debtor's solvency is precarious. She also argues that, since money has a legally objective value, it is impossible for a creditor to benefit more from a lesser sum than from a greater sum. That too is certainly correct, but the question is not whether a lesser sum can be valued more than a larger sum, but whether the *actual receipt* of lesser sum can be valued more than a notional right to a larger one, which seems entirely possible.
153. *In re Selectmove Ltd* [1995] 1 WLR 474, 481, per Peter Gibson LJ.
154. *MWB Business Exchange Centres Ltd v. Rock Advertising Ltd* [2016] EWCA Civ 553.
155. *MWB Business Exchange Centres Ltd v. Rock Advertising Ltd* [2016] EWCA Civ 553, [47] per Kitchen LJ.
156. *MWB Business Exchange Centres Ltd v. Rock Advertising Ltd* [2016] EWCA Civ 553, [72], per Arden LJ.

of Lords denied that a lesser sum could satisfy a larger debt despite accepting that timely part payment of a debt 'may be more beneficial to [creditors] than it would be to insist on their rights and enforce payment of the whole'.[157] *Foakes v. Beer* therefore stands for the rule that practical benefit cannot provide consideration for a variation of a debt, no matter what constitutes that practical benefit.

B. Promissory Estoppel

113. Essentially a procedural rule, estoppel is of many kinds. For instance, estoppel by representation applies where one party represents facts to the other and induces the other to rely on this representation to the representee's detriment. The representor is not permitted to contradict the represented fact in litigation against the representee (whether as claimant or defendant).[158] This does not found a cause of action that would not otherwise have existed, but it can mean the success of a cause of action that would otherwise have failed, or the defeat of a claim that would otherwise have succeeded.[159] The doctrine applies only to representations of existing facts, and not to promises or statements of future intention.[160] This limitation has kept estoppel by representation out of the sphere of contract formation, because it is not an alternative means of binding people to undertakings.[161] However, largely as a reaction to the perceived inequity of the rule in *Foakes v. Beer*, another species of estoppel – sometimes called equitable or promissory estoppel – developed to enforce certain kinds of promises relating to future conduct.

114. In *Central London Property Trust v. High Trees House*,[162] a commercial tenant leased an apartment building from its owner, and sublet the rooms to residents. Due to the German bombings in London during the Second World War, the commercial tenant struggled to find willing residents. The building's owner agreed to accept half the contracted amount of rent until the end of the War. After the War, a claim was brought for the full rent liability. The court was asked whether the commercial tenant was now liable for the full annual rent, and whether in fact it had been so liable during the War, despite the owner's agreement to accept half rent, such that the tenant was liable for arrears.

115. Denning J ruled that the full rent liability could be prospectively reinstated, but the owner was bound by the promise to accept half rent during the time before reimposing full liability. Although accepting that the law of estoppel applied only to representations of existing fact and excluded future promises, Denning J nonetheless

157. *Foakes v. Beer* (1884) 9 App Cas 605, 622, per Lord Blackburn.
158. There is also estoppel by convention, which stops one party denying a state of fact or law that the parties had communicated to each other, where the parties have later contracted on the basis of that shared assumption: *Republic of India v. Indian Steamship Co Ltd (No 2)* [1998] AC 878, 913.
159. Brandon LJ observed in *Amalgamated Investment and Property Co Ltd v. Texas Commerce International Bank Ltd* [1982] QB 84.
160. *Jorden v. Money* (1854) 5 HL Cas 185, 214–215, 226–227, 10 ER 868, 881–882, 886.
161. *Central London Property Trust Ltd v. High Trees House Ltd* [1947] KB 130, 134, per Denning J: 'a representation as to the future must be embodied as a contract or be nothing.'
162. *Central London Property Trust Ltd v. High Trees House Ltd* [1947] KB 130.

identified 'cases in which a promise was made which was intended to create legal relations and which, to the knowledge of the person making the promise, was going to be acted on by the person to whom it was made and which was in fact so acted on'.[163] In cases satisfying these criteria, 'the courts have said that the promise must be honoured'.[164] The effect was that 'a promise to accept a smaller sum in discharge of a larger sum, if acted upon, is binding notwithstanding the absence of consideration'.

116. Denning J presented this rule not as an aspect of the law of estoppel, but as a direct assault on consideration as a requirement to make promises of future conduct binding. However, the resulting law of promissory estoppel has been more limited in its impact than the breadth Denning J's language might have suggested. Promissory estoppel applies between existing contract parties,[165] where one promises not to enforce some of her legal rights,[166] but the promisee provides no consideration for that promise.[167] The promise must have been 'clear and unequivocal'[168] from the perspective of the reasonable person in the position of the representee.[169] Promissory estoppel is distinct from an agreement actually to vary the terms of the contract, which continues to require consideration, albeit in a heavily diluted form.

117. Like other species of estoppel, promissory estoppel exists to prevent loss by the representee, rather than to enforce his expectations. In principle therefore the representee must have relied detrimentally on the promise in question in order for an estoppel to arise. But despite the conclusions of Denning J,[170] it is hard to see how the tenant in *High Trees* relied detrimentally on the promise to accept half rent.

118. Subsequent cases presented the reliance requirement as demanding not that the representee had incurred any detriment as a result of the promise, but simply

---

163. Denning J cited as authority the decision of Lord Cairns LC in *Hughes v. Metropolitan Railway* (1876–77) LR 2 App Cas 439: '[if the parties to a contract] enter upon a course of negotiation which has the effect of leading one of the parties to suppose that the strict rights arising under the contract will not be enforced, or will be kept in suspense, or held in abeyance, the person who otherwise might personal have enforced those rights will not be allowed to enforce them where it would be inequitable having regard to the dealings between those parties.'
164. *Central London Property Trust Ltd v. High Trees House Ltd* [1947] KB 130, 134.
165. It has also been applied where the currently existing personal obligation is due not to contract but to the operation of statute: *Durham Fancy Goods Ltd v. Michael Jackson (Fancy Goods) Ltd* [1968] 2 QB 839.
166. Some actual communication from the representor is probably necessary; the requirements are unlikely to be satisfied by mere implication, or silence: *Allied Marine Transport Ltd v. Vale do Rio Doce Novagacao SA (The Leonidas D)* [1985] 1 WLR 925, 937, per Robert Goff LJ.
167. *Ajayi v. RT Briscoe (Nigeria) Ltd* [1964] 1 WLR 1326, 1330, per Lord Hodson.
168. *Woodhouse AC Israel Cocoa Ltd SA v. Nigerian Produce Marketing Co Ltd* [1972] AC 741; *Collier v. P and M J Wright (Holdings) Ltd* [2007] EWCA Civ 1329, [2008] 1 WLR 643, per Longmore LJ.
169. *Bremer Handelgesellschaft mbH v. Vanden Avenne-Izegem PVBA* [1978] 2 Lloyd's Rep 109, 126.
170. This understanding is confirmed by his decision as Lord Denning MR in *D & C Builders v. Rees* [1966] 2 WLR 28.

that he had in some way altered his position as a result of it.[171] Some decisions were content to infer such reliance if the representation in question would have led a reasonable person to change his position in some way.[172] Most radical was the suggestion that the mere act of paying the reduced sum *would itself* constitute reliance on the promise to accept that reduced sum and not to bring an action for the whole.[173] Such reasoning is perverse, assuming that but for the representation the debtor would have paid *none* of the debt owed, and that the fact he paid even a reduced sum was attributable to the promise that he would have to pay no more.

119. This suggestion has thankfully been disavowed by the Court of Appeal in *MWB Business Exchange Centres v. Rock Advertising*, in which Kitchin LJ insisted on positive detrimental reliance of some kind; the mere payment of the lesser sum itself will not qualify.[174] The debtor's submissions concerning promissory estoppel failed for the lack of demonstrable detrimental reliance.[175]

120. Promissory estoppel is often described as merely suspensory, and not destructive, of legal rights. This cannot be strictly true, since it does indeed extinguish *past* rights in that they can never again be enforced. Although the *High Trees* decision did not consider whether an open-ended promise not to enforce legal rights that will

171. Viscount Simonds in *Tool Metal Manufacturing Co Ltd v. Tungsten Electric Co Ltd* [1955] 2 All ER; *Ajayi v. RT Briscoe (Nigeria) Ltd* [1964] 1 WLR 1326, 1330, per Lord Hodson. In *MWB Business Exchange Centres Ltd v. Rock Advertising Ltd* [2016] EWCA Civ 553, Kitchin LJ presented the requirement of reliance as wider than mere change of position. Promissory estoppel requires that the representee 'in some way relies upon' the promise, 'whether by altering his position or in any other way': *MWB Business Exchange Centres Ltd v. Rock Advertising Ltd* [2016] EWCA Civ 553, [61], per Kitchin LJ.

172. *Brikom Investments Ltd v. Carr* [1979] QB 467, 482–483, per Lord Denning MR.

173. *Collier v. P and M J Wright (Holdings) Ltd* [2007] EWCA Civ 1329, [2008] 1 WLR 643, [42], per Arden LJ: the payment itself 'is enough to make it inequitable for [the creditor]...to pursue [the debtor] for the balance'. In this Arden LJ followed Lord Denning MR in *D & C Builders v. Rees* [1966] 2 WLR 28. However, in *Collier* these statements were not authoritative, since the Court's decision was merely as to whether the facts disclosed an arguable point of law. Longmore LJ was more conservative, insisting on genuine detrimental reliance independent of the payment itself: *Collier v. P and M J Wright (Holdings) Ltd* [2007] EWCA Civ 1329, [2008] 1 WLR 643, [48].

174. *MWB Business Exchange Centres Ltd v. Rock Advertising Ltd* [2016] EWCA Civ 553. It is in retaining a requirement of meaningful reliance that the Court of Appeal saves the rule in *Foakes v. Beer* from total irrelevance. On Arden LJ's view in *Collier*, every time a creditor purports to accept part payment as satisfaction of the whole debt, he will become immediately bound by promissory estoppel without more.

175. *See* interestingly Arden LJ at [90]-[92]. She endorsed Kitchin LJ's general principles of promissory estoppel, including the need for genuine reliance. However, she suggested that such a requirement was consistent with her earlier statements in *Collier*, which cannot be correct. Kitchin LJ did not address the fact that Arden LJ's *dicta* in *Collier* are inconsistent with the need for genuine reliance.

accrue in the future could be revoked,[176] subsequent cases have confirmed that this is indeed possible.[177] In that sense, a promise founding an estoppel is merely suspensory of future rights. The representor can change her mind and prospectively reinstate full liability 'on giving reasonable notice, which need not be a formal notice, giving [the representee] a reasonable opportunity of resuming his position'.[178] For the representee to resume his position, he will have to undo whatever act of reliance founds the estoppel, to the extent necessary to become once more able to perform in full. It follows that if this is impossible, then the representor can *never* resile from her representation,[179] since no amount of notice can remove the inequity of holding the representee to his full contractual obligations.[180]

121. Denning J's reasoning in *High Trees* was wide enough to have permitted a new cause of action by virtue of the claimant's reliance on the defendant's gratuitous promise.[181] But in *Combe v. Combe*, the newly promoted Denning LJ was concerned that the *High Trees* principle would be abolished if presented as a direct challenge to the doctrine of consideration: 'it is important that [the *High Trees* principle] should not be stretched too far, lest it should be endangered'. This case confirmed that promissory estoppel 'does not create new causes of action where none existed before', but only 'prevents a party from insisting upon his strict legal rights'.[182] Subsequent courts have upheld that rule,[183] and since the Court of Appeal is bound by its own decision in *Combe v. Combe*, only a decision of the Supreme Court or an Act of Parliament can change the rule that promissory estoppel does not equip claimants to

176. Denning J let the owner prospectively reinstate full rent liability, but he tied this to the precise content of the promise originally made: 'I am satisfied that [the landlord's] promise was understood by all parties only to apply under the conditions prevailing at the time when it was made, namely, when the flats were only partially let, and that it did not extend any further than that. When the flats became fully let, early in 1945, the reduction ceased to apply.'
177. *Ajayi v. RT Briscoe (Nigeria) Ltd* [1964] 1 WLR 1326.
178. *Ajayi v. RT Briscoe (Nigeria) Ltd* [1964] 1 WLR 1326, 1330, per Lord Hodson. Active notice will not be not necessary when the promise was always time-sealed: *Central London Property Trust Ltd v. High Trees House Ltd* [1947] KB 130. This logic further condemns the suggestion that part payment of a debt can count as a sufficient act of reliance on a promise not to sue for the full amount.
179. *Ajayi v. RT Briscoe (Nigeria) Ltd* [1964] 1 WLR 1326, 1330, per Lord Hodson.
180. However, since the obligation is simply to pay a sum of money, only rarely will it be absolutely impossible for the representee to make himself able to satisfy this obligation, provided sufficient notice is given.
181. Although acknowledging that '[t]he courts have not gone so far as to give a cause of action in damages for breach of such a promise', Denning J phrased his principle broadly enough to have changed that; 'a promise intended to be binding, intended to be acted on and in fact acted on, is binding so far as it terms properly apply.': *Central London Property Trust Ltd v. High Trees House Ltd* [1947] KB 130.
182. *Combe v. Combe* [1951] 2 KB 215, 219, per Denning LJ.
183. Although sometimes unenthusiastically: In *Williams v. Roffey Bros & Nicholls (Contractors) Ltd* [1991] 1 QB 1, Russell LJ would have 'welcomed' the chance to consider the principle's application to claims for an increased contract price, but ultimately the Court declined to rule on this: *Williams v. Roffey Bros & Nicholls (Contractors) Ltd* [1991] 1 QB 1, 13, 17–18.

sue defendants for breaking an undertaking made to them.[184] For the foreseeable future therefore, the doctrine is 'to be used as a shield and not as a sword'.[185]

122. Provided promissory estoppel could be confined to the protection of detrimental reliance, allowing it to create new causes of action would not necessarily challenge contract law. While a fully constituted contract satisfying all the requirements of formation – including consideration – would remain the sole means of enforcing *expectations*, promissory estoppel could exist as a supplementary doctrine, preventing injustice by reversing detrimental *reliances* on promises that do not constitute contracts. However, there is a risk that promissory estoppel would in fact bring about the indirect enforcement of expectations, and therefore undermine the integrity of the law of contract.[186]

123. As noted above, promissory estoppel was developed largely in reaction to the rule in *Foakes v. Beer*. In *High Trees*, Denning J thought his principle meant the end of that rule in practice,[187] and the Court of Appeal has previously entertained similar thoughts.[188] However, in light of the decision in *MWB Business Centres v. Rock Advertising*, extending the *Roffey* 'practical benefit' analysis to promises to accept less than one's strict legal entitlement, perhaps promissory estoppel is of decreasing importance. Promissory estoppel, as a shield only, is confined to claims under preexisting contracts. If, after *MWB Business Centres v. Rock Advertising*, promises to accept less than one's full contractual rights can constitute binding variations of the contract itself, there seems little role for promissory estoppel.

§2. Formal and Evidential Requirements

I. Formal Requirements

124. English law generally gives full legal effect to contracts made informally, including those concluded orally. However, certain transactions are valid only if made in the form of a deed, such as 'conveyances of land or of any interest therein'.[189] To comprise a deed, a document must make clear on its face that the document is intended

184. *Baird Textiles Holdings Ltd v. Marks and Spencer Plc* [2001] EWCA Civ 274, [2002] 1 All ER (Comm) 737, [55], per Judge LJ.
185. *Combe v. Combe* [1951] 2 KB 215, 224, per Birkett LJ.
186. Indeed, American and Australian jurisprudence, in which promissory estoppel is able to found a new cause of action, in practice accepts estoppel as an alternative route to the enforcement of promises, with the remedy focusing on the claimant's expectation rather than their detrimental reliance: Restatement (Second) of Contracts, s. 90; *Waltons Stores (Interstate) Ltd v. Maher* [1988] HCA 7; *Commonwealth v. Verwayen* [1990] HCA 39.
187. *Central London Property Trust Ltd v. High Trees House Ltd* [1947] KB 130, 135, per Denning J.
188. *Collier v. P and M J Wright (Holdings) Ltd* [2007] EWCA Civ 1329, [2008] 1 WLR 643, [42], per Arden LJ and [48], per Longmore LJ.
189. Law of Property Act 1925, s 52(1).

specifically to be a deed, and signed by the party to be bound[190] in the presence of a witness who attests the signature.[191] The deed must also be 'delivered', which essentially requires some conduct by the person making the deed indicating that she intends to become bound by its terms.[192]

125. Although not requiring a deed, some contracts are only valid if made in writing, or else can only be enforced with written evidence. For instance, consumer credit contracts regulated by the Consumer Credit Act 1974 must be signed by the parties. Failure to abide by these rules means the agreement is enforceable against the debtor only by judgment of a court.[193] Several other specific examples exist.[194] Most importantly, in addition to the ordinary requirements for contractual validity,[195] contracts for the disposition of interests in land are valid only if in writing,[196] specifically a single document signed by both parties, or two identical documents signed by one party each and exchanged, incorporating all the (express) terms the parties have agreed.[197] This has come to be interpreted as including writing in digital form, and digital signature.[198]

126. Writing is also required as *evidence* of a contract of guarantee,[199] which cannot be enforced against a guarantor without such evidence. The writing can be in a simple form, such as a letter or a memorandum, provided it bears the signature of the guarantor, the names of the relevant parties and the material terms of the contract of guarantee.[200] This need not be contained in the same document.[201]

---

190. Companies incorporated under the Companies Act 2006 may substitute for a seal the signature of one director and the company secretary, or one director in the presence of a witness, or the signature of two directors: Companies Act 2006, s.44.
191. If the party herself cannot write, she can direct another to sign on her behalf, provided this is done in her presence and the presence of two witnesses: Law of Property (Miscellaneous Provisions) Act 1989, s.1. This provision simplifies the common law requirements that a deed had to be written on paper or on parchment, sealed by the individual to be bound and 'delivered' to the beneficiary with a demonstration of intention to be bound to its contents: *Goddard's Case* (1584) 2 Co Rep 4b, 5a, 76 ER 396, 399–400. In practice these requirements had already been undermined by successive decisions, to the point where a witnessed signature was regarded as equivalent to seal: *see* for example *First National Securities Ltd v. Jones* [1978] Ch 109.
192. This is usually provided by the textual language itself, such as 'signed and delivered as a deed...'
193. Consumer Credit Act 1974, s. 127.
194. For example, marine insurance contracts: Marine Insurance Act 1906, s 22.
195. *Commission for the New Towns v. Cooper (Great Britain) Ltd* [1995] Ch 259, 293, per Evans LJ.
196. Law of Property Act 1925, s. 53(1)(a). The same is true of the disposition of a currently existing interest under a trust: Law of Property Act 1925, s. 53(1)(c).
197. Law of Property (Miscellaneous Provisions) Act 1989, s. 2. This replaces the relevant provision in the Statute of Frauds 1677, although this only required writing as *evidence* of the contract in question; the new statute makes writing a requirement for the validity of the contract at law.
198. Interpretation Act 1978, sch. 1.
199. Statute of Frauds 1677, s. 4. Unlike most forms of contract requiring written proof, this was not changed by the Law Reform (Enforcement of Contracts) Act 1954.
200. It need not refer to any consideration received for the contract of guarantee.
201. Other examples include a declaration of trust over interests in land: Law of Property Act 1925, s. 53(1)(b).

A. Effect of Non-compliance

127. If a defendant denies being bound to an undertaking on the grounds that it did not satisfy the legal formality requirements, the law of estoppel sometimes may intervene where he subsequently represented to the claimant that he was bound to the undertaking – either expressly or impliedly through his conduct[202] – and the claimant has relied detrimentally on that representation. This is permitted in spite of statutory formality requirements because allowing estoppel may not always undermine the purpose of these statutory requirements. However, this depends on which aspect of formality is lacking. Although a signature requirement expresses a clear public policy rationale that equitable estoppel cannot undermine, the law of estoppel may sometimes remedy failure to comply with less crucial aspects of statutory formality rules.[203]

128. The law of estoppel has prevented defendants denying contractual obligations to make a disposition of an interest in land, despite the fact that this putative contract was not made in writing, on the basis that to allow an estoppel in appropriate cases does not undermine the purpose of the statutory provisions requiring writing for the valid disposition of interests in land.[204] However, an estoppel is less likely to be recognised in favour of commercial parties, who should be deemed to have understood the formality rules in question.[205] Likewise estoppel will not assist parties who had intended to conclude a written contract as required by the formality rules, but in fact never concluded one,[206] since such parties clearly understood the formality requirements applicable to their transaction and the consequences of failing to satisfy them.

129. It is unclear whether estoppel will interfere in the requirement that guarantee contracts be proved by writing. If so, general estoppel principles suggest the law will require an independent representation from the guarantor that he is bound by the obligation, subsequent to having undertaken that obligation in the first place.[207]

---

202. For instance, where a defendant denies being bound by an obligation because the putative deed fails the formality requirements, he can be estopped from denying liability if he nonetheless *delivered* the deed, on the basis that delivery of the (formally invalid) deed constitutes a clear representation that it was in fact valid and binding on the representor.

203. *Shah v. Shah* [2001] EWCA Civ 527, [2002] QB 35, [30] per Pill LJ. In this case the document had been signed but the signature had not been attested in the presence of the promisor, as the Act requires.

204. *Yaxley v. Gotts* [2000] Ch 162, 191, per Beldam LJ. Cf *Cobbe v. Yeoman's Row Management Ltd* [2008] UKHL 55, [2008] 1 WLR 1752, [29], per Lord Scott, who was sceptical as to whether equitable intervention here is really consistent with the absolute language of the Act.

205. *See* for example *Cobbe v. Yeoman's Row Management Ltd* [2008] UKHL 55, [2008] 1 WLR 1752.

206. *Cobbe v. Yeoman's Row Management Ltd* [2008] UKHL 55, [2008] 1 WLR 1752; *Herbert v. Doyle* [2010] EWCA Civ 1095, [2011] 1 EGLR 119, [57].

207. *See Actionstrength Ltd v. International Glass Engineering* [2003] UKHL 17, [2003] 2 AC 581. The House of Lords denied an estoppel on the facts, but the majority reasoned on the assumption it was possible as a matter of law, provided the general requirements of estoppel were present.

II. Evidential Requirements

A. *The Parol Evidence Rule*

130. When called on to interpret a contract that has been concluded in written form, the law looks only to the document itself in order to establish the parties' rights and obligations under the contract. In short, 'the bargain is the document'.[208] The parties generally cannot adduce evidence of their pre-contractual negotiations or subjective understandings of the agreement to influence the court's interpretation of the written contract.

131. This strict rule is widely considered necessary to promote legal certainty, and has been described as 'one of the great strengths of English commercial law and is one of the main reasons for the international success of English law in preference to laxer systems which do not provide the same certainty'.[209] The rule has been recently reasserted, and survives the law's marked shift towards an approach to interpretation closely focused on establishing the understanding of the contract that would have been held by reasonable persons in the parties' positions, equipped with all the knowledge available to the parties.[210]

132. However, parties may refer to pre-contractual negotiations in order to demonstrate the presence of some fact that would have constituted part of the contextual matrix in which the reasonable person in the parties' position would have interpreted the agreement.[211] The parties may also refer to negotiations to establish an estoppel by convention, or a claim for rectification. Rectification is available where one or both of the parties can establish that the written document fails to reflect the agreement they actually concluded, but this is extremely difficult in light of the great importance English law attaches to the conclusiveness of the written agreement.

133. It is also possible that something in the pre-contractual negotiations will have given rise to a collateral contract between the parties, in addition to the written contract eventually concluded.[212] To protect against this, it is common to include in commercial written contracts an 'entire agreement' clause, whose effect is to demonstrate that the parties' entire transaction is contained in the written document, and nowhere else.[213]

---

208. *Shogun Finance v. Hudson* [2003] UKHL 62, [2004] 1 AC 919, [49], per Lord Hobhouse.
209. *Shogun Finance v. Hudson* [2003] UKHL 62, [2004] 1 AC 919, [49], per Lord Hobhouse.
210. *Investors Compensation Scheme Ltd v. West Bromwich Building Society* [1998] 1 WLR 896; *Chartbrook Ltd v. Persimmon Homes Ltd* [2009] UKHL 38, [2009] 1 AC 1101.
211. *Chartbrook Ltd v. Persimmon Homes Ltd* [2009] UKHL 38, [2009] 1 AC 1101
212. *Record v. Bell* [1991] 1 WLR 853.
213. The clause may also exclude some or all implied terms, depending on its construction. However, it is possible that, although effective to exclude the incorporation of terms based on trade custom or course of dealing, such a clause might not exclude terms implied in fact or at law: *Exxonmobil Sales and Supply Corporation v. Texaco Ltd* [2003] EWHC 1964 (Comm), [2003] 2 Lloyd's Rep 686, [25]-[27].

B. Lack of a Role for Notaries

134. The English law of contract has no role for notarisation. Contracts derive their legal force purely from the parties' inherent power to bind themselves to each other personally, and the state has no role in authenticating or approving such agreements.

135. Notaries do exist in England and Wales, but they are occupied almost entirely in notarising documents already concluded – and legally binding – in England, for their use in foreign litigation, or in international transactions in legal systems that attach importance to the notarisation of private agreements.

III. Burden of Proof

136. As a matter of common law,[214] there are two standards of proof in the law of England and Wales.[215] In contrast to the strict standard required to establish guilt in criminal trials,[216] in civil litigation the facts are established on the basis of the balance of probabilities. In other words, the party with the relevant burden of proof will satisfy it merely by showing a proposition to be *more probably* true than untrue.

137. As a general principle, the party that asserts a proposition must establish its truth. The claimant therefore bears the burden of proof in establishing that each of the requirements for the defendant's liability is satisfied. Conversely, the defendant will generally bear the burden of proof in establishing any defences that may defeat *prima facie* liability. Both general principles are subject to specific derogations, for instance when there exists some presumption of fact – such as the presumption of undue influence that arises from demonstration of particular circumstantial facts – which will invert the usual burden of proof.[217] English lawyers also have a confusing tendency to describe as 'presumptions' particular *conclusions* of law produced by certain circumstantial facts, such as the 'signature rule', which conclusively deems a party signing a contractual document to have read and understood its terms in their entirety.

---

214. Other, more specific, standards can be established under statute and apply to particular areas of law.

215. In *Re B (A Child)* [2008] UKHL 35, the House of Lords confirmed that there are no intermediary standards of proof as a matter of common law. As Baroness Hale put it (at [70]), '[n]either the seriousness of the allegation nor the seriousness of the consequences should make any difference to the standard of proof to be applied in determining the facts.'

216. The criminal standard of proof is traditionally described as the prosecutor's obligation to prove the defendant's guilt 'beyond reasonable doubt', although it is now more common in practice for judges to instruct juries to convict only if they are 'sure' that all the criteria for guilt have been established.

217. In this case obliging the defendant to *dis*prove that a transaction was the result of undue influence.

§3. Liability and Negotiations

I. Pre-contractual Liability

138. English law adopts an adversarial understanding of the relationship between negotiating parties, according to which each of the parties advances his or her own rational self-interest, even at the expense of the interests of the other party. As a result of this understanding, English law recognises no general duty of cooperation or good faith between parties negotiating a contract. While parties negotiating a contract owe each other duties imposed by the general law – particularly the law of tort[218] – English law does not regard pre-contractual negotiation as a relationship imposing special obligations in the way that special obligations are necessarily imposed following contract formation. In other words, no positive duties arise between the parties simply by virtue of the fact they are negotiating towards a contract. However, the parties' conduct during negotiation can affect the legal status of the contract eventually concluded.

A. Liability for Non-disclosure

139. As a result of the absence of a good-faith requirement between negotiating parties, non-disclosure of potentially relevant facts will not generally affect the validity of the contract eventually concluded. During negotiations, English law allows the parties to withhold valuable information, even when such information would be of use or interest to the other party, or would influence the other party's decision whether to contract.[219]

140. However, duties of disclosure arise in contracts '*uberrimae fidei*' – contracts of utmost good faith. Here, failure to disclose information of the kind the specific duty demands gives the other party a right to rescind the contract. At common law, the central case of a contract of utmost good faith was an insurance contract, but statutory intervention has significantly reduced the burden of disclosure on parties negotiating for insurance coverage.[220] The common law continues to impose special duties of

---

218. Moreover, receiving confidential information during negotiations can impose an obligation of non-disclosure. This is an equitable rather than tortious duty. As an equitable duty, there is more remedial flexibility than in tort, so the wronged party can seek an injunction, or an account of any profits made due to the use of confidential information.

219. *Smith v. Hughes* (1871) LR 6 QB 597, 607, per Blackburn J: 'there is no legal [as opposed to moral] obligation on the vendor to inform the purchaser that he is under a mistake, not induced by the act of the vendor [i.e., short of misrepresentation].' *See also* Cockburn LJ at 603–604.

220. Consumers entering insurance contracts now have a duty only to take reasonable care not to make any misrepresentation to her insurer: Consumer Insurance (Disclosure and Representations) Act 2012. For non-consumers, their duty is now to give their potential insurer a 'fair presentation of the risk': Insurance Act 2015. These overturn the common law, which required a party negotiating for insurance to disclose all information he knew or ought to have known to be material to the risk the contract was intended to insure against: *Carter v. Boehm* (1766) 3 Burr 1905, 97 ER 1162; *Banque Financière de la Cité SA v. Westgate Insurance Co Ltd* [1991] 2 AC 249.

disclosure in negotiations towards contracts of partnership,[221] guarantee[222] and also in company prospectuses in which the company invites public subscriptions for shares.

141. Statute imposes stricter duties of pre-contractual disclosure in a variety of specific contexts, such as in distance selling arrangements between a trader and consumer,[223] although breach does not necessarily give automatic grounds to rescind the contract. There can also be general duties to disclose relevant information where the parties are already in a relationship on which the law imposes such heightened duties of openness, such as partnership. However, this duty of disclosure derives not from their status as negotiating parties *per se* but from their existing relationship.

142. There is generally no liability in tort for non-disclosure of relevant information, regardless of motive.[224] Only false statements are actionable. However, it is not clear whether there can be liability in tort for fraudulent non-disclosure of information that the law of contract requires to be fully disclosed in advance of contracting.[225]

B. Liability for False Statements (Independent of Contract)

143. There can be liability for misrepresentations made in advance of entering a contract. This founds a right to rescind any contract induced by the misrepresentation, and/or a claim for damages, as a matter of contract law. Misrepresentations can also independently found liability in the torts of deceit or negligence. Such tortious liability does not require a pre-contractual context, so can arise even where no contract is eventually formed. Claims in tort are usually brought following a misrepresentation that induced the claimant to enter a contract, where the claimant seeks damages to compensate her for resulting losses. In principle they can also be brought where the misrepresentation caused the claimant *not* to conclude a contract.

144. Importantly in the pre-contractual context, a representation that was true when it was made can nonetheless lead to liability for misrepresentation if the statement has been subsequently falsified by circumstantial events. The representor will commit an actionable misrepresentation if she fails to bring the new facts to the representee's attention.[226]

145. To commit the tort of deceit, the representor must make a false representation fraudulently, which means with knowledge of its falsity, without belief in its truth, or

221. *Conlon v. Simms* [2006] EWCA Civ 1749, [2008] 1 WLR 484.
222. *Hamilton v. Watson* (1845) 12 Cl & Fin 109, 8 ER 1339. This was an appeal to the House of Lords concerning Scottish law, but it is also applied in England and Wales. The duty here is more limited than the common law standard between insurer and insured, requiring only that the debtor disclose any non-standard features of the contract she is seeking to have guaranteed.
223. *See* for instance Consumer Contracts (Information, Cancellation and Additional Charges) Regulations 2013 (SI 2013/3134), implementing EU Directive 2011/83.
224. *Peek v. Gurney* (1873) LR 6 HL 377, 391, 403.
225. This was suggested by the Court of Appeal in *HIH Casualty and General Insurance Ltd v. Chase Manhattan Bank* [2001] EWCA Civ 1250, [2001] 2 Lloyd's Rep 483, [48], [164], [168], but doubted on appeal in the House of Lords: [2003] UKHL 6, [2003] 2 Lloyd's Rep 61, [75]. The idea was revived in *Conlon v. Simms* [2006] EWCA Civ 1749, [2008] 1 WLR 484, [130].
226. *With v. O'Flanagan* [1936] Ch 575.

recklessly as to its truth or falsity.[227] Mere negligence as to its truth is insufficient. The burden of proving dishonesty is on the representee.

146. The representor commits the tort of negligent misstatement where, having been under a particular duty to take reasonable care in the provision of information or advice to the representee, she failed to take the requisite care in making the representation in question, and made a representation that was in fact false. The representee has the burden of establishing that the representor owed him such a duty. Generally the duty will be recognised only where the representor knew or should reasonably have known that the information or advice would be relied on for a particular purpose,[228] without prior independent verification.[229] Moreover, it must have been reasonable for the representee to rely on the truth of the representation without independently verifying it, which will only rarely be the case between experienced and well-advised commercial parties. However, courts have recognised such liability where the representor has presented herself as the holder of specific expertise.[230]

147. Damages for tortious misrepresentations seek to put the representee in the position he would have occupied if the tort had not occurred, not the position he would have occupied had the representation in question been true. The claimant cannot recover damages representing his expectation under whatever contract the misrepresentation procured. Moreover, losses are recoverable only if the representee can establish that they were caused by the misrepresentation (or, for negligence, from the breach of duty), including any losses resulting from entering the contract where this was itself a result of the misrepresentation in question. Therefore it will be impossible to recover losses incurred before the misrepresentation was made. For fraudulent misrepresentations, the representee can recover all losses caused by the misrepresentation, whereas in the tort of negligence only losses of a foreseeable type can be recovered.[231]

II. Breakdown of Negotiations

148. English law imposes no liability – neither under the law of contract nor in tort – for breaking off negotiations before a contract is concluded, no matter how far the negotiations had progressed, even when the negotiations are broken off with the intention of inflicting harm on the other party. Until a contract is concluded, therefore, each party bears his or her own risks of the negotiations failing for any reason. In an action for breach of contract, the claimant cannot recover expenditures incurred before contract formation.[232]

149. It is possible to negotiate a preliminary agreement to displace this rule, under which one party undertakes to indemnify the other for wasted expenditure if negotiation towards the main contract fails. The parties may make such an agreement

227. *Derry v. Peek* (1889) LR 14 App Cas 337.
228. *Hedley Byrne & Co Ltd v. Heller & Partners Ltd* [1964] AC 465.
229. *Caparo Industries Plc v. Dickman* [1990] 2 AC 605, 638, per Lord Oliver.
230. For example *Esso Petroleum Co Ltd v. Mardon* [1976] QB 801.
231. *Overseas Tankship (UK) Ltd v. Morts Dock and Engineering Co Ltd (The Wagon Mound) (No 1)* [1961] AC 388.
232. Unless she is suing for reliance damages as opposed to the expectation measure.

when they want to begin a joint project as soon as possible – without waiting for the conclusion of a full set of contractual terms – but still want to protect themselves from the risk of wasted expenditure should that contract not materialise. Such agreements are often unhelpfully labelled 'letters of intent' or memoranda, but it is important to note that they are effective only if fully constituted contracts in their own right, so this cannot strictly be regarded as permitting 'precontractual' liability.

150. Contracts providing for such indemnities are enforceable, but agreements to negotiate towards a contract, or even actively to conclude one, are not. The courts maintain that such agreements are too imprecise to be legally supervised,[233] even if the agreement specifies a fixed standard of conduct required in negotiations, such as an obligation to negotiate in *good faith* towards a contract.[234] The Court of Appeal has enforced an express agreement to *renegotiate* an existing contract in certain circumstances,[235] but subsequent cases have powerfully reiterated the traditional rule that pre-contractual agreements to conclude or negotiate towards a contract in good faith are unenforceable.[236]

151. Importantly for pre-contractual liability, a party's subjective intention – for instance her intention about whether ultimately she will consent to a contractual relationship – is a question of fact,[237] so misrepresentations about one's willingness to contract can found liability in the tort of deceit, independently of whether any contract is ultimately entered, allowing recovery of losses incurred in the belief that the misrepresentor was genuinely considering entering a contract.

233. *Courtney & Fairbairn Ltd v. Tolani Bros (Hotels) Ltd* [1975] 1 WLR 297, 301, per Lord Denning MR; *Walford v. Miles* [1992] 2 AC 128, 138, per Lord Ackner.
234. *Little v. Courage* (1994) 70 P & CR 469, 476; *Walford v. Miles* [1992] 2 AC 128.
235. *Petromec Inc v. Petroleo Brasiliero SA* [2005] EWCA Civ 891, [2006] 1 Lloyd's Rep 121, [121].
236. *Georgi Velichkov Barbudev v. Eurocom Cable Management Bulgaria Eood* [2012] EWCA Civ 548.
237. After all, 'the state of a man's mind is as much a fact as the state of his digestion': *Edgington v. Fitzmaurice* (1885) 29 Ch D 459, per Bowen LJ. It is, of course, very difficult to prove the state of an individual's mind as a fact.

Chapter 2. Conditions of Substantive Validity

§1. Capacity of the Parties

I. Capacity of Minors

152. The age of majority in the United Kingdom is 18, and anyone below that age is a minor.[238] In principle a minor enjoys only limited contractual capacity. The limitations apply even if the other party was unaware of her minority.

153. Whether or not a minor has capacity depends on the type of contract in question. There are some absolute limitations. For example, a minor is never liable to repay money paid for goods ordered from her and not delivered,[239] or for instalments due under an agreement of hire purchase,[240] or for the repayment of money lent to her.[241] These rules do not render the agreement void *per se*; if the minor does in fact deliver the ordered goods, or repay the debt owed, the other party may retain them.

154. Minors have a limited capacity to enter contracts for 'necessaries'. All contracts other than for necessaries are void.[242] 'Necessaries' not only include goods required for immediate use, such as food and other consumables,[243] but also anything else required to maintain the minor's station in life. Statute now defines the goods for which minors may validly contract as those 'suitable to the condition in life of the minor and to his actual requirements at the time of sale and delivery'.[244] This protects the common law rule that even goods of a nature necessary for the maintenance of the minor's station will not be considered 'necessaries' if purchased in excessive quantity, or if they are in fact significantly in excess of the minor's requirements at the time.[245]

155. Things will not be necessaries if considered instead to be 'luxuries', but the law will distinguish 'articles of mere luxury' from 'luxurious articles of utility'.[246] The necessity of a purchase is a fact-sensitive contextual enquiry, and depends on the

238. Family Law Reform Act 1969, s. 1.
239. *Cowern v. Nield* [1912] 2 KB 419.
240. *Mercantile Union Guarantee Corporation v. Ball* [1937] 2 KB 498.
241. *R Leslie Ltd v. Sheill* [1914] 3 KB 607. In this case, the minor had obtained the loan by fraudulently misrepresenting his age. The court held that the creditor could not sue on the contract to recover the debt because of the debtor's minority, and could not sue in tort on the basis of the fraud, because this would be indirectly to enforce the contract the creditor was not permitted to enforce. The minor can only be held liable in tort if the tort liability is beyond the scope of the barred contract action, and is not merely an indirect enforcement of the contract: *Fawcett v. Smethurst* (1914) LJKB 473; *Ballet v. Mingay* [1943] KB 281.
242. Minors' Contracts Act 1987.
243. This can also cover contracts for services such as accommodation and employment.
244. Sale of Goods Act 1979, s. 3.
245. *Nash v. Inman* [1908] 2 KB 1.
246. *Chapple v. Cooper* (1844) 13 M & W 252, 153 ER 105, per Alderson B.

particular station of the minor.[247] Minors also have capacity to enter contracts under which they receive education, employment, apprenticeship or professional training of some kind, provided the contract is considered *as a whole* beneficial to the minor.[248] Even contracts for necessaries will not be binding on a minor if it contains onerous terms,[249] and a minor is anyway liable only to pay a 'reasonable price' for the goods or services received, not necessarily the full contract price.[250]

156. In some cases, such as contracts of a continuing nature, and contracts enabling the minor to acquire interests in property, a party that concluded a contract while still a minor will be bound to its terms only after ratifying the contract after attaining her majority. Alternatively, the minor may be liable during her minority but able to rescind the contract within a reasonable period of reaching majority.

157. If a contract is unenforceable against a defendant because she was a minor at the time of contracting, the court has the discretion to order the transfer of property obtained by the defendant under that contract, or property representing it, where it is just and equitable to do so.[251]

II. Mental Incapacitation

158. A contract is voidable at the election of a party who, at the time of contracting, was suffering from a mental impairment that made her incapable of understanding the agreement, provided the other party knew of this impairment at the time of contracting.[252] Some authorities suggest it is sufficient that the other party ought reasonably to have known of the incapacity, even if he in fact did not.[253] The above applies even if the incapacitation in question was the result of intoxication, provided the intoxication was apparent to the other party at the time of contracting.[254]

159. However, where a contract has been made under which an incapacitated person purchases 'necessary' goods, she is bound to pay a reasonable price for them notwithstanding her incapacitation at the time of contracting.

---

247. Items such as luxurious waistcoats (*Nash v. Inman* [1908] 2 KB 1) and gold pocket watches (*Peters v. Fleming* (1840) 6 M & W 42, 151 ER 314) can be necessaries for socially privileged undergraduates. However, there are limits. Opulent jewellery was considered not a necessary, even for a person used to moving in extremely wealthy circles: *Ryder v. Wombwell* (1868) LR 4 Ex 32.
248. The contract can still be judged overall to be for the minor's benefit even though it contains specific terms that are disadvantageous to her when looked at in isolation: *Clements v. London & North Western Railway* [1894] 2 QB 482.
249. *Fawcett v. Smethurst* (1914) 84 LJKB 473.
250. Sale of Goods Act 1979, s. 2.
251. Minors' Contracts Act 1987, s. 3(1).
252. *Imperial Loan Co v. Stone* [1892] 1 QB 599; *Hart v. O'Connor* [1985] AC 1000, 1019.
253. *Dunhill v. Burgin (Nos 1 and 2)* [2014] UKSC 18, [2014] 1 WLR 933, [25], per Baroness Hale.
254. *Gore v. Gibson* (1845) 13 M & W 621, 153 ER 260. This voidability will cease if the drunk ratifies the contract after she sobers up: *Matthews v. Baxter* (1873) LR 8 Exch 132.

III. Corporate Legal Capacity

160. The capacity of non-human legal persons in principle depends on the purposes for which they are incorporated. However, statutory intervention has reversed the rule in relation to corporations that acts outside the powers outlined in their constitutional documents.[255]

§2. Defects of Consent

I. Mistake

161. English law is said to recognise two general kinds of mistake capable of excusing contractual liability. On the one hand, the two parties may share the same mistaken belief, a situation generally referred to as 'common mistake'. On the other hand, the parties have divergent understandings of the agreement's terms, or some associated fact, a situation called 'unilateral mistake', of which there are many kinds. For instance, one party may have been mistaken as to the contractual nature of the agreement, or its terms, or the identity of the other party.

162. However, a compelling conceptual argument has been made that mistake *per se* is, irrelevant at common law. A contract will be held void for 'mistake' only if (i) an implied condition precedent prevents the contract ever coming into being (especially important in so-called common mistake), or (ii) the offer and acceptance on their true constructions are divergent.[256] To issue of so-called unilateral mistake can therefore be navigated by reference to a single question—whether the defendant is deemed to have accepted the very terms that the claimant is attempting to enforce.

A. Unilateral Mistake of Contractual Nature

163. In some cases a contract will not have been formed, despite the defendant's signature, if the defendant was sufficiently mistaken as to the nature of the document he signed. Such defendants escape liability if they can establish the defence of *non est factum*. Given the importance of the legal certainty provided by the signature rule, this defence is subject to stringent controls. The signatory challenging the contract must show that she signed under a fundamental mistake as to the character of the document in question,[257] and that the mistake was not due to her own negligence.[258]

---

255. Companies Act 2006, s. 39.
256. C Slade, 'The Myth of Mistake in the English law of Contract' (1954) 70 LQR 885.
257. *Saunders v. Anglia Building Society (Gallie v. Lee)* [1970] AC 1004. This failed to assist the challenger in this case, who correctly thought she was signing a deed of transfer; she was mistaken only as to its contents, which was held inadequate.
258. *Saunders v. Anglia Building Society (Gallie v. Lee)* [1970] AC 1004. This was fatal to the challenger in United Dominions Trust Ltd v. Western [1976] QB 513, who had signed a blank document in the expectation of the contents being filled in later by another.

B. Unilateral Mistake as to Contractual Terms

164. A mistake can prevent the formation of a valid contract only when it relates to the actual terms of the agreement. Other misapprehensions are irrelevant to contract formation, even if the other party knows of the mistake,[259] and knows that the mistaken party would not agree to the contract terms in question if the mistakes were corrected.

165. One party is under no duty to correct the other's mistake, but if the first party has induced the second party's mistake, this may constitute a misrepresentation, giving the second party the right to rescind the contract in equity. Even a mistake as to the terms of the contract will prevent formation only if the first party knows that the second holds a different understanding of the terms proposed,[260] or if the mistake is so obvious that the reasonable person would have known the mistaken party's apparent agreement was only illusory.[261]

C. Unilateral Mistake of Identity

166. English law has for some time struggled to articulate and adhere to a principled approach to cases of impersonation, where a rogue pretends to be someone else in order to induce his victim to enter a contract. In such cases there is obviously an actionable misrepresentation, so contracts thus procured will be vulnerable to rescission in equity. However, the law has struggled to decide whether such contracts are in fact void *ab initio* at common law on the basis of the mistake induced by the rogue's misrepresentation.

167. The question is crucial where the rogue has already disposed of the gains he received under the putative contract. If the contract was never validly formed at common law, then the rogue never received legal title to the assets in question and cannot transfer the title to a third party, so the initial victim may bring a claim of conversion against the innocent third party, which in practice will result in the return of the assets. But if the contract was validly formed and the rogue has already disposed of the assets, the third party will have acquired their legal title, and the court's equitable jurisdiction to rescind the contract for misrepresentation will be excluded if to rescind would adversely affect the rights of third parties.[262] In such cases, one innocent party must inevitably suffer for the misdeeds of the rogue;[263] neither party has a realistic chance of recovering her losses from the rogue himself, since petty con men seldom have significant assets of their own.

168. For many years the law on this issue has been confused. In *Phillips v. Brooks*,[264] the court held that a rogue impersonating another in order to induce the innocent party to contract is merely making an ordinary misrepresentation, for which the contract is voidable in equity but not void at law. The majority of the Court of Appeal came to the opposite conclusion in the factually similar case of *Ingram v.*

259. *Smith v. Hughes* (1871) LR 6 QB 597.
260. *Smith v. Hughes* (1871) LR 6 QB 597.
261. *Hartog v. Colin & Shields* [1939] 3 All ER 566.
262. Provided the third parties are bona fide purchasers for value without notice of the misrepresentation.
263. Cf Devlin LJ's Solomonic suggestion in *Ingram v. Little* [1961] 1 QB 31.
264. *Phillips v. Brooks* [1919] 2 KB 243.

Little,[265] ruling that the mistake of identity prevented the formation of any legal contract. Conversely, in *Lewis v. Averay*,[266] Lord Denning MR denied any meaningful distinction between impersonations and misrepresentations of other kinds, which did not prevent contract formation and only gave the power to rescind in equity. He identified a strong presumption that parties intend to contract with the person physically present.

169. The leading authority on this issue is now the decision of the House of Lords in *Shogun Finance v. Hudson*.[267] Here, the majority reasoned that, when negotiations have been conducted face-to-face, there should be a strong and only rarely rebutted presumption that the victim intends to contract with the person physically present (i.e., the rogue himself). Therefore, a contract will usually be formed despite an impersonation, but the contract will be voidable for misrepresentation.[268] Where the parties have negotiated other than face-to-face (as was the case in *Shogun Finance* itself), then the court must ask directly, 'with whom did the innocent party intend to contract?'

170. Where the parties have contracted in written form, this question is answered exclusively by interpreting the written document, and if the parties are expressly named, this will constitute conclusive evidence that the innocent party intended to contract with the person named, and with no one else, and any contrary oral evidence will be inadmissible.[269] Two dissenting members of the House considered arbitrary a rigid distinction between face-to-face negotiations and others. For the minority, the fact that negotiations were conducted face-to-face should merely be evidence for answering the fundamental question: 'to whom should the recipient party have considered the offer addressed?'[270]

171. This approach correctly bases the solution to impersonation cases in fundamental principles of contract formation. Much of the uncertainty here is resolvable by applying orthodox offer and acceptance analysis. An offer can only be accepted by a person that genuinely and reasonably believed it was addressed to him. So the relevant question becomes, 'did the rogue genuinely and reasonably interpret the victim's offer as addressed to him personally, and not conditional on his being who he said he was'. Only if the answer is yes can the rogue's putative acceptance actually form a legal contract (albeit a contract voidable in equity for misrepresentation). In many cases, the rogue may genuinely and reasonably conclude this, particularly in contexts where the specific identity of the parties is of less empirical importance. Conversely, where the offer should reasonably have been interpreted as addressed to some other specific person, it will be impossible for the rogue reasonably to interpret it as addressed to

265. *Ingram v. Little* [1961] 1 QB 31.

266. *Lewis v. Averay* [1971] 3 WLR 603.

267. *Shogun Finance v. Hudson* [2003] UKHL 62, [2004] 1 AC 919.

268. The Lords' discussion of the law on face-to-face dealings was technically *obiter* since this was a case of distance negotiations.

269. Lord Hobhouse justified this by noting the need for certainty in written contracts. However this is curious, since the parties actually named in the document – the dupe and the real person the rogue had impersonated – are obviously not in a contractual relationship; if the dupe is in any contractual relationship it can only be with the rogue, *contrary* to the terms on the face of the written document.

270. *Shogun Finance v. Hudson* [2003] UKHL 62, [2004] 1 AC 919, per Lords Nicholls and Millet (dissenting).

him personally.[271] The value of the presumptions adopted by the majority of the House of Lords in *Shogun Finance* depends on whether they are more likely to assist lower courts in answering the fundamental question of principle, or distract them from it.

II. Misrepresentation

172. An actionable misrepresentation does not by itself prevent the formation of a contract, but it will give the representee an equitable right subsequently to rescind that contract. The other contract party, or his agent, must have made the misrepresentation. If an independent third party in fact made the misrepresentation, it will nonetheless permit rescission if the contract party knew the representation had been made.[272]

173. The misrepresentation must be a statement of existing fact, which includes a statement of law.[273] Sales bluster (so-called 'mere puffs') will not support rescission if, judged objectively, they were clearly not intended to be taken seriously. Literally true statements can constitute misrepresentations in light of salient omissions, where the representor states a 'half truth' that gives a misleadingly incomplete impression of the situation.[274] Likewise, despite the lack of a general pre-contractual duty to disclose relevant information, a party will commit an actionable misrepresentation if he fails to correct a statement that was true when made but later falsified by some change of circumstances.[275]

174. Generally statements of opinion are not considered to be statements of fact. However, a misrepresentation *as to* one's opinion will in theory constitute an actionable misrepresentation of fact,[276] although it is notoriously difficult to prove that a representor lied about his subjective opinion. There is generally no actionable misrepresentation if a party merely states his honest opinion, even if the opinion is manifestly wrong.[277] However, where representor possesses some special knowledge relative to representee, even statements of opinion can constitute misrepresentations,

---

271. *Ingram v. Little* [1961] 1 QB 31, per Sellers LJ: the relevant test is 'how ought the promissee to have interpreted the promise?" For Pearce LJ, the nature of the contract dictates whether it should be interpreted as addressed only to a specific named person.
272. *Royal Bank of Scotland Plc v. Etridge (No 2)* [2002] 2 AC 773, [40].
273. *Pankhania v. London Borough of Hackney* [2002] EWHC 2441, approved in *Brennan v. Bolt Burden* [2004] EWCA Civ 1017, [2005] QB 303.
274. *Nottingham Patent Brick & Tile Co v. Butler* (1889) 16 QBD 778; *Dimmock v. Hallet* (1866) 2 Ch App 21. Here, a literally true statement that land had previously been let at a specific sum was held to create the misleading impression this was its present rental value.
275. *With v. O'Flanagan* [1936] Ch 575.
276. *Edgington v. Fitzmaurice* (1885) 29 Ch D 459, 483, per Bowen LJ. This will constitute the tort of deceit.
277. *Bisset v. Wilkinson* [1927] AC 177.

since the court may consider an express statement of opinion also to contain an implicit factual representation that the opinion was substantiated by material facts.[278]

175. Statements as to the representor's future intention are generally not statements of fact. Failing to act in accordance with one's represented intention does not make the representation actionable as a misrepresentation.[279] However, if the representor actually *undertakes* to act in a particular way in the future, this may form a term of the contract capable of supporting an action for breach.[280] Rescission is permitted even where the misrepresentation has been incorporated into the contractual terms, and even when the contract has been fully performed.[281]

176. The misrepresentation must have *induced* the contract. However, the misrepresentation need not have been the sole or principal cause of the representee's decision to contract; it must only be a factual cause.[282] In principle the misrepresentation is actionable even though it was not reasonable to be induced into contracting by the representation in question. However, if the representation would probably have influenced the reasonable person, this will lead a court to infer that it in fact influenced the representee's decision to contract,[283] and the burden is on the representor to disprove that the representation induced the representee to contract.

177. The requirement that the representation induced the contract is therefore not a serious obstacle to the representee. However, it means that a misrepresentation will not permit rescission if it in fact went entirely unnoticed by the representee, or if the representee learned that the representation was untrue before entering the contract. It is no defence that the reasonable person would not have believed the misrepresentation, or would have checked its truth before relying on it.[284]

178. Rescission of the contract is the principal remedy for all misrepresentations (fraudulent, negligent and innocent).[285] Courts have a statutory discretion to award damages in lieu of the rescission that the claimant has sought if it is equitable to do

278. *Smith v. Land & House Property Corporation* (1884) LR 28 Ch D 7. To establish when a statement of opinion will constitute a misrepresentation, the law looks to the comparative expertise of the parties. In *Bisset v. Wilkinson* [1927] AC 177, the representor gave his honest opinion as to the suitability of land for sheep farming. This was a complete guess, since the representor had no evidence or expertise on which to draw in making that estimate. The Privy Council emphasised that the representee was not justified in having taken the representation as anything other than pure opinion.
279. *Wales v. Wadham* [1977] 1 WLR 199.
280. *Kleinwort Benson Ltd v. Malaysia Mining Corp Berhad* [1989] 1 WLR 379.
281. Misrepresentation Act 1967, s. 1.
282. *Edgington v. Fitzmaurice* (1885) 29 Ch D 459; *JEB Fasteners Ltd v. Marks, Bloom & Co* [1983] 3 All ER 289.
283. *Redgrave v. Hurd* (1881) 20 Ch D 1.
284. *Redgrave v. Hurd* (1881) 20 Ch D 1. Cf tort of negligent misrepresentation, for which reliance on the misstatement must have been reasonable, and the defendant can invoke the defence of contributory negligence: *Hedley Byrne & Co Ltd v. Heller & Partners Ltd* [1964] AC 465.
285. Recently re-emphasised by the Court of Appeal in *Salt v. Stratstone Specialist Ltd* [2015] EWCA Civ 745.

so.[286] In deciding whether to do so is equitable, the court considers the nature and seriousness of the misrepresentation, the effect of rescission on the representor, and whether damages would adequately protect the representee.[287]

179. For many years it was unclear whether rescission must still be available if damages are to be awarded 'in lieu' of it,[288] but recent Court of Appeal authority confirms rescission must still be available and that if for any reason rescission is barred, the court has no power to award damages in lieu.[289]

180. A misrepresentation can also found liability in tort, where it was made fraudulently or negligently, giving an action for damages calculated to put the claimant as far as possible in the position she would have occupied had the tort not been committed.[290] In addition to actions in tort, the representee can directly claim damages from the representor under section 2(1) of the Misrepresentation Act 1967, where the representee has suffered loss as a result of entering into a contract following a misrepresentation, provided the representor would be liable in the tort of deceit if the misrepresentation had been made fraudulently. In such cases, the representor 'shall be so liable notwithstanding that the misrepresentation was not made fraudulently, unless he proves that he had reasonable ground to believe and did believe up to the time the contract was made the facts represented were true'. Liability under section 2(1) differs from liability in the tort of negligence. It applies only to representations made prior to concluding a contract.[291] Whereas in tort the representee as claimant must actively prove the representor's negligence, under section 2(1) the representor bears the burden of vindicating his conduct, which can be an onerous task.[292]

---

286. Misrepresentation Act 1967, s.2(2). This does not apply to misrepresentations by a trader that constitutes a 'misleading action' to a consumer: Misrepresentation Act 1967, s. 2(4). These are policed by secondary legislation (Consumer Protection from Unfair Trading Regulations 2008 (SI 2008/1277), amended by SI 2014/870), which gives the consumer additional remedies, such as a claim for a discount to contract price, the 'unwinding' of the contract (which has the effect of rescission), and a damages claim for consequential financial loss, distress and inconvenience or discomfort.
287. In *William Sindall Plc v. Cambridgeshire County Council* [1994] 1 WLR 1016, the Court of Appeal held there was no actionable misrepresentation, but Hoffmann LJ suggested (*obiter*) that he would have awarded damages instead of rescission, because the misrepresentation concerned an unimportant matter, because the losses that resulted were of a kind easily compensable by damages, and the cost of making good the consequences of the representation's falsity (by damages) was much less than the costs involved in rescinding the contract.
288. *Government of Zanzibar v. British Aerospace (Lancaster House) Ltd* [2000] 1 WLR 2333 held that there was no discretion under s.2(2) to award damages in lieu where rescission barred, while *Thomas Witter Ltd v. TBP Industries Ltd* [1996] 2 All ER 573 allowed damages even though rescission was barred.
289. *Salt v. Stratstone Specialist Ltd* [2015] EWCA Civ 745.
290. These are the torts of deceit and negligent misstatement, respectively.
291. Indeed, s. 2(1) applies only to misrepresentations prior to a contract, and is therefore narrower in scope than the tort of negligent misstatement.
292. In *Howard Marine and Dredging Co Ltd v. A Ogden & Sons* [1978] QB 574, the misrepresentor incorrectly stated the weight of a ship, based on the Lloyds register. The Court of Appeal held that the representee could not reasonably have relied on this statement's truth since the ship's actual weight was easily verifiable by consulting the ship's own documentation

181. Based on the language of section 2(1), the Court of Appeal in *Royscott v. Rogerson* held that the representor is liable for the same measure of damages as applies in the tort of deceit.[293] The claimant representee can therefore recover all losses, even those of an unforeseeable type. However, the House of Lords subsequently explained that the severe measure of damages in the tort of deceit has a moralistic explanation; justice apparently demands that a deliberate fraudster bears all the risk of any losses that might result from his fraud.[294] It was suggested that this policy does not apply to non-fraudulent misrepresentations, a hint that the *Royscott* 'fiction of fraud' would not survive a direct challenge in the House of Lords (now the Supreme Court).

182. The representee can seek both rescission and damages, either in tort or under section 2(1), because the two remedies operate independently. Rescission undoes the contract, while the tortious measure of damages aims to undo the effect of the misrepresentation. While rescinding the contract will often undo the effects of the misrepresentation, sometimes it will not, such as where the misrepresentation has caused consequential losses. The claimant can therefore receive damages both in lieu of the rescission she claimed, and under section 2(1), for losses consequential on the contract. However, if the claimant has received damages in lieu of rescission, these will be taken into consideration when calculating the quantum to be awarded under section 2(1).[295]

A. *Exclusion of Liability for Misrepresentation*

183. Remedies for misrepresentation may be excluded by the express terms of the contract. However, many limitations exist on the parties' freedom to exclude liability for pre-contractual misrepresentations.

184. Courts police clauses purporting to exclude liability for misrepresentation at common law, by strict approaches to their incorporation and interpretation,[296] and also under statutory review powers. The Misrepresentation Act 1967 subjects terms purporting to exclude liability for pre-contractual misrepresentation, or restrict any remedy for it, to the test of reasonableness established by the Unfair Contract Terms Act 1977.[297]

293. *Royscott Trust Ltd v. Rogerson* [1991] 2 QB 297. This was based on the apparently 'clear meaning' of 'so liable', the statutory language of s. 2(1).

294. *Smith New Court Securities Ltd v. Scrimgeour Vickers* [1996] 3 WLR 1051, per Lord Steyn.

295. Misrepresentation Act 1967, s .2(3).

296. These survived the move towards holistic and natural interpretations of contractual language, and judicial condemnations of manufacturing ambiguity in order obliquely to police the fairness of contract terms, such as in *Photo Production Ltd v. Securicor Ltd* [1980] AC 827, 851. However, the Court of Appeal has recently disavowed this practice in *Persimmon Homes Ltd v. Ove Arup & Partners Ltd* [2017] EWCA Civ 373.

297. Misrepresentation Act 1967, s. 3 and Unfair Contract Terms Act 1977, s. 8. The common law also forbids exclusion of liability for fraudulent misrepresentation: *S Pearson & Son Ltd v. Dublin Corporation* [1907] AC 351, 353–54, 362. This was confirmed in *HIH Casualty and General Insurance Ltd v. Chase Manhattan Bank* [2003] UKHL 6, [2003] 2 Lloyd's Rep 61, but this case left open the question of whether it could be possible to exclude liability for fraud by one's agent.

185. Courts will also apply this test to clauses whose effect is to prevent liability occurring, rather than to exclude liabilities that do arise. For instance, contracts may attempt to deny that any unincorporated representations have been made, or relied on. Such denials are not exclusion clauses *per se*, but protect a misrepresentor against liability through the doctrine of contractual estoppel,[298] since the representee will not be permitted subsequently to assert that a misrepresentation induced the contract. However, since the effect of such a clause is to exclude liability for misrepresentation that would arise but for the clause, the court will still assess its reasonableness. Conversely, so-called entire agreement clauses have been held outside the statutory test of reasonableness, because they are not clauses denying liability for misrepresentation.[299]

186. For consumer contracts, no clause is enforceable against a consumer if 'unfair'.[300] This broad provision applies to any clause in a consumer contract, including oblique attempts to prevent actions for misrepresentation, with a few exceptions not relevant in this context.

III. Improper Pressure

187. English law divides doctrines policing improper pressure into two, depending on the nature of the pressure applied: duress and undue influence. However, the same conduct may permit a challenge to the contract on both grounds. The presence of one or both kinds of improper pressure does not prevent contract formation, but only gives a right to rescind it in equity.[301] It is for the party seeking rescission to prove a right to rescind never for the party seeking the contract's enforcement to deny such a right.

188. Both permit rescission only if perpetrated by the other contract party or his agent, or by a third party provided the other contract party knew or ought to have known about the improper pressure when contracting with the victim.[302] Here, the victim can rescind the contract if the other party failed to take reasonable steps to ensure the transaction was the result of informed and free consent, and not the improper

---

298. *Peekay Intermark Ltd v. Australia and New Zealand Banking Group Ltd* [2006] EWCA Civ 386; [2006] 2 Lloyd's Rep 511, [57]; *Watford Electronics Ltd v. Sanderson CFL Ltd* [2001] EWCA Civ 317, [2001] 1 All ER (Comm) 696; *Springwell Navigation Corp v. JP Morgan Chase Bank* [2010] EWCA Civ 1221, [2010] 2 CLC 705.

299. *Inntrepreneur Pub Co (GL) v. East Crown Ltd* [2000] 2 Lloyd's Rep 611, 614.

300. Consumer Rights Act 2015, s. 62(1).

301. *Barton v. Armstrong* [1976] AC 104 suggests that contracts tainted by duress to the person are void, not merely voidable like contracts procured through other forms of duress.

302. *Barclays Bank v. O'Brien* [1994] 1 AC 180. This was an undue influence case, but the House of Lords has stated that its principles apply to other vitiating factors, such as duress, unconscionability or misrepresentation: *Royal Bank of Scotland Plc v. Etridge (No 2)* [2002] 2 AC 773, [40]. Both *O'Brien* and *Etridge* concerned improper pressure between a husband and wife, but the principle has been held applicable to other couples (same and opposite sex, married and unmarried) and beyond (for example, employer and employee in *Credit Lyonnais Bank Nederland v. Burch* [1977] 1 All ER 144).

pressure to which the victim has been subjected by a third party.[303] These steps must be adequate to 'bring home to [the victim] the risk she is running'.[304] This will generally require ensuring that the victim received meaningful legal advice.[305]

189. The other party will be held to have constructive notice of the improper pressure if the circumstances are such as to put him 'on inquiry'. Relevant factors include that the transaction appeared highly disadvantageous to the victim, or was of a type wherein there exists a substantial risk of having been induced to consent by improper pressure.[306] These are not rigid conditions, merely guidance in a broader enquiry into whether the other party ought reasonably to have been aware of the risk of improper pressure.[307]

190. Where traders subject consumers to duress or undue influence, this may also constitute an 'aggressive commercial practice' policed by secondary legislation, giving the consumer additional remedies, such as a claim for a discount on the contract price, the 'unwinding' of the contract,[308] and a damages claim for consequential financial loss, distress and inconvenience or discomfort.

A. Duress

191. The essence of duress is a threat made against the victim, although this need not be specific or explicit. Duress does not presuppose any prior relationship between the parties. Many kinds of threat can constitute duress, provided the threat is illegitimate. The most obvious example is a threat to the victim's person,[309] but threats of a purely economic nature can also constitute duress. The presence of consideration is not fatal to a finding of economic duress.

303. *Royal Bank of Scotland Plc v. Etridge (No 2)* [2002] 2 AC 773, [43], [87]. The third party is bound by the unconscionable conduct of the perpetrator, but does not necessarily personally commit any wrong: *Credit Lyonnais Bank Nederland v. Burch* [1977] 1 All ER 144, per Millet LJ (*obiter*); *Portman Building Society v. Dusangh* [2000] 2 All ER (Comm) 221. Cf *Credit Lyonnais Bank Nederland v. Burch* [1977] 1 All ER 144, per Nourse LJ (*obiter*).
304. *Barclays Bank v. O'Brien* [1994] 1 AC 180, per Lord Browne-Wilkinson.
305. Following *Royal Bank of Scotland Plc v. Etridge* [1998] 4 All ER 705, there is now a minimum core modicum of legal advice required. The third party (usually in practice a bank), must give the legal advisor the relevant financial information. However, the legal advisor does not need to be independent of the parties involved in the transaction.
306. *Barclays Bank v. O'Brien* [1994] 1 AC 180, per Lord Browne-Wilkinson.
307. *Royal Bank of Scotland Plc v. Etridge (No 2)* [2002] 2 AC 773. This seems similar to the test for demonstrating the presence of undue influence between the perpetrator and the victim, although in this context the focus is on the appearance of the transaction from the perspective of the reasonable person in the position of the third party.
308. This has the effect of rescission: Consumer Protection from Unfair Trading Regulations 2008 SI 2008/1277, amended by SI 2014/870.
309. Until comparatively recently this was the only kind of threat or pressure on which the doctrine of duress could operate. The doctrine was quickly expanded to include threats to property in some instances (for example *Astley v. Reynolds* (1731) 2 Str 915) but the law now also recognises threats or pressure against the victim's general economic interest: *Occidental Worldwide Investment Corp v. Skibs A/S Avanti (The Siboen and the Sibotre)* [1976] 1 Lloyd's Rep 293.

192. Particularly complex is the law's treatment of a threat to breach one's contract, which usually accompanies a demand for the contract terms to be varied.[310] Such a threat is not considered illegitimate if it constitutes only ordinary 'commercial pressure'.[311] The context in which such a threat is made is therefore highly relevant. The courts have recognised such threats as duress where, for instance, the perpetrator cynically waited until the victim had no realistic option but to capitulate to the threat and vary the contract.[312]

193. Some cases and commentators have suggested that bad faith is,[313] or should be, a prerequisite for recognising a threat to breach one's contract as duress. However, it might be more consistent with English law's strict approach to contract duties to regard threats to breach as inherently illegitimate regardless of the perpetrator's motive. English law maintains that one cannot escape liability simply because performing one's obligations becomes more expensive or onerous that was anticipated at the time of contracting.[314] This rule is greatly undermined if the law allows parties in this position to threaten to breach their contract – and thereby force a variation in their favour – provided they do so for 'legitimate' motives, such as to avoid one's own financial hardship. Requirements of bad faith have generally been denied in recent cases, which have held that 'a threat to break a contract will generally be regarded as illegitimate, particularly where the defendant must know that it would be in breach of contract if the threat were implemented'.[315]

194. In *The Universe Sentinel*, the House of Lords stated that a threat to do some otherwise lawful act could constitute duress depending on how the threat was made.[316] However, there are very few examples of such 'lawful act duress'. In *CTN Cash and Carry v. Gallagher*, one party threatened to withhold future credit in order to induce the payment of a debt they incorrectly but genuinely believed was outstanding. The credit arrangement was entirely discretionary, and could lawfully be discontinued in the future for any reason. The Court of Appeal denied that the threat constituted economic duress, but emphasised that the threat was made in good faith, due to a genuine belief that the debt was owed.[317]

---

310. *Quaere* how differently the law should treat (i) a threat to breach unless terms varied, and (ii) a warning that contract will be breached unless the terms are varied: i.e., the situation in *Williams v. Roffey Bros & Nicholls (Contractors) Ltd* [1991] 1 QB 1.
311. *Occidental Worldwide Investment Corp v. Skibs A/S Avanti (The Siboen and the Sibotre)* [1976] 1 Lloyd's Rep 293, 336; *Pao On v. Lau Yiu Long* [1980] AC 614, 635.
312. *Atlas Express Ltd v. Kafco (Importers and Distributors Ltd)* [1989] 1 QB 833.
313. *DSND Subsea Ltd v. Petroleum Geo Services ASA* [2000] BLR 530.
314. *Davis Contractors v. Fareham Urban District Council* [1956] AC 696.
315. *Kolmar Group AG v. Traxpo Enterprises Pty Ltd* [2010] EWHC 113 (Comm), [2010] 2 Lloyd's Rep 653, [92]. Cf *Huyton SA v. Peter Cremer GmbH and Co* [1999] 1 Lloyd's Rep 620, in which Mance J was openly critical of any requirement of bad faith to make a threat to breach one's contract illegitimate.
316. *Universe Tankships Inc of Monrovia v. International Transport Workers Federation (The Universe Sentinel)* [1983] 1 AC 366. This was actually a claim for restitution, not rescission of a contract, but it was declared applicable in contract in *Dimskal Shipping Co SA v. International Transport Workers Federation* [1992] 2 AC 152.
317. *CTN Cash and Carry Ltd v. Gallaher Ltd* [1994] 4 All ER 714, per Steyn LJ and Sir Donald Nicholls VC.

195. In *Borrelli v. Ting*, the Privy Council recognised duress where the perpetrator did something technically lawful but did so in bad faith, for selfish and obstructive reasons, on the grounds that 'it would offend justice' to let him have the benefit of the agreement thus induced.[318] However, it is likely to be rare for a lawful act to constitute illegitimate pressure in ordinary commercial dealings.[319] Particularly, the courts are unlikely to regard a threat not to enter a contract at all as illegitimate for the purpose of the law of duress, since this would comprise an unacceptable limitation of parties' freedom of contract.

196. For economic duress, the threat must have been a *sine qua non* cause of the contract in order to produce a right to rescind.[320] Indeed it must have been the 'decisive' cause of the victim's decision to contract,[321] not just one of many cumulative factors. However, duress to the person has been recognised where the evidence suggests the victim would have contracted even if the threat had never been made.[322] The law had adopted a policy that an aggressor should not receive the benefit of a contract he sought to obtain by threats of violence merely because, by coincidence, the victim intended to enter the contract in question anyway.

197. Rescission is available only if submission to the threat in question was a reasonable course of conduct. Generally the victim must show that she had no realistic choice but to submit.[323] In *Adam Opel v. Mitras Automotive*,[324] the victim seriously considered resisting the illegitimate pressure and instead seeking legal redress, but chose ultimately to submit to the illegitimate threat. Duress was nonetheless made out because the legal remedies available would have been too slow to assist the victim in the circumstances.

198. In addition to being a substantive requirement of relief, the reasonableness of submission to the threat, and particularly the lack of any practical alternative, provides helpful evidence that the victim's decision to contract was in fact induced by the threat.[325]

---

318. *Borrelli v. Ting* [2010] UKPC 21.
319. *CTN Cash and Carry Ltd v. Gallaher Ltd* [1994] 4 All ER 714, 719, per Steyn LJ.
320. The traditional test required the threat to have overborne the will of the victim, to the extent that the decision to contract was not truly voluntary: *Pao On v. Lau Yiu Long* [1980] AC 614, but the modern test focuses on the test of causation.
321. *Huyton SA v. Peter Cremer GmbH & Co* [1999] 1 Lloyd's Rep 620, 636.
322. *Barton v. Armstrong* [1976] AC 104.
323. *Universe Tankships Inc of Monrovia v. International Transport Workers Federation (The Universe Sentinel)* [1983] AC 366.
324. *Adam Opel GmbH v. Mitras Automotive (UK) Ltd* [2007] EWHC 3205 (QB), [2008] Bus LR D55.
325. *Pao On v. Lau Yiu Long* [1980] AC 614, per Lord Scarman. Here, the availability of an alternative course of action was treated as evidence of factual causation. It was treated similarly in *Kolmar Group AG v. Traxpo Enterprises Pty Ltd* [2010] EWHC 113 (Comm), [2010] 2 Lloyd's Rep 653, [92], per Christopher Clarke J: 'If there was no reasonable alternative, that may be very strong evidence in support of a conclusion that the victim of the duress was in fact influenced by the threat.' But not conclusive: 'even the total absence of protest does not mean that the payment was voluntary.'

B. *Undue Influence*

199. Unlike duress, undue influence requires a preexisting relationship. It does not require an identifiable threat or pressure,[326] since this doctrine operates instead on abuse of the subtle power imbalances that characterise particular personal relationships. There is often no concrete evidence of undue influence, so presumptions are frequently employed. However, the House of Lords has confirmed that undue influence comprises one single doctrine, even though its presence may validly be shown either through evidence or through presumptions.[327] Although undue influence is regarded as a wrong against the victim, it does not necessarily require conscious exploitation on the part of the perpetrator.[328]

200. A presumption of undue influence is triggered by '[p]roof that the complainant placed trust and confidence in the other party in relation to the management of the complainant's financial affairs, coupled with a transaction which calls for explanation', a presumption that must be rebutted with 'satisfactory evidence to the contrary'.[329] Certain relationships will almost always satisfy the first criterion for the presumption,[330] but generally it is a question of fact whether there was the necessary relationship of trust and confidence in this particular case, although occasionally the fact that the parties were in a relationship of trust has been inferred from the nature of the transaction they made.[331]

201. The relationships in which undue influence may potentially operate are limitless.[332] They have included a young singer and his manager,[333] an elderly man and his housekeeper,[334] a parent and adult child,[335] a solicitor and his client,[336] a bank manager and his client[337] and a religious officer and a believer.[338] However, it is hard to imagine a court would ever find two commercial parties to be in such a relationship.

202. In addition to a relationship of trust and confidence, the presumption of undue influence requires a transaction of a particular kind. The precise description has varied. Early case law looked for a transaction 'not reasonably accounted for...on ordinary motives'.[339] The court would infer that the transaction was the result of undue influence if there was no innocuous explanation for it. For a while the law favoured a

---

326. Some older cases of threats (for example, a threat to report someone to the police – *Williams v. Bayley* (1866) LR 1 HL 200) were dealt with as cases of undue influence, but would now be considered examples of duress.
327. *Royal Bank of Scotland Plc v. Etridge (No 2)* [2002] 2 AC 773.
328. *Royal Bank of Scotland Plc v. Etridge (No 2)* [2002] 2 AC 773.
329. *Royal Bank of Scotland Plc v. Etridge (No 2)* [2002] 2 AC 773, [14], per Lord Nicholls.
330. For example, doctor-patient, lawyer-client: *Royal Bank of Scotland Plc v. Etridge (No 2)* [2002] 2 AC 773, [157], [161]
331. *Credit Lyonnais Bank Nederland v. Burch* [1977] 1 All ER 144.
332. *Barclays Bank v. O'Brien* [1994] 1 AC 180.
333. *O'Sullivan v. Management Agency and Music Ltd* [1985] QB 428.
334. *In re Craig* [1971] Ch 95.
335. *Lancashire Loans Ltd v. Black* (1934) 1 KB 380.
336. *Wright v. Carter* [1903] 1 Ch 27.
337. *Lloyds Bank v. Bundy* [1975] QB 326.
338. *Allcard v. Skinner* (1887) 36 Ch D 145, 185.
339. *Allcard v. Skinner* (1887) 36 Ch D 145, 185.

more material approach, examining whether the substance of the transaction was 'manifestly disadvantageous' to the complainant.[340] The precise threshold of disadvantage was unclear; although some authorities required the disadvantage to be glaring,[341] others applied less strict criteria. However, in *Royal Bank of Scotland v. Etridge*, the House of Lords reinstated the traditional focus on the explicability of the transaction. A presumption of undue influence will arise where the transaction 'cannot be explained by reference to the ordinary motives by which people are accustomed to act'.[342]

203. Rebutting the presumption that the transaction was procured by undue influence is not easy. The coexistence of a relationship of trust and confidence and a suspicious transaction imposes on the party attempting to enforce the contract a duty to take reasonable steps to ensure the complainant's consent was in fact the product of 'free, full and informed thought'.[343] It is not enough to show that the complainant did not understand the terms of the agreement and its implications, nor to show that the complainant did not consciously 'feel' pressured to enter the contract.[344] It is also no defence that the contract is in fact advantageous to the complainant.[345]

204. The conventional way of rebutting the presumption of undue influence is to show that, prior to transacting, the complainant received independent legal advice.[346] However, the nature of the parties' relationship and the transaction in question will affect the weight of the presumption of undue influence, which is proportional to the strength of evidence needed to rebut it. So while a mere token, fleeting discussion with a solicitor will generally be inadequate,[347] in some cases the presumption may still be rebutted even though the complainant received no independent advice.[348] In other cases, even the receipt of independent advice may not suffice to rebut the presumption.[349] Legal advice is unlikely to rebut the presumption when the complainant was still subject to the influence in question at the time the independent advice was provided.[350]

340. *National Westminster Bank Plc v. Morgan* [1985] AC 686.
341. *Bank of Credit and Commerce International v. Aboody* [1990] 1 QB 923.
342. *Royal Bank of Scotland Plc v. Etridge* [1998] 4 All ER 705.
343. *Zamet v. Hyman* [1961] 1 WLR 1442, per Lord Evershed MR.
344. *Goodchild v. Bradbury* [2006] EWCA Civ 1868, [2006] All ER (D) 247.
345. *CIBC Mortgages Plc v. Pitt* [1994] 1 AC 200, 209. The terms of the contract are therefore relevant only as evidence of undue influence; there is no positive requirement that the contract terms be disadvantageous.
346. Legal advice is not a positive requirement, only evidence of rebutting presumption, albeit the conventional one. This is shown in cases like *In re Brocklehurst* [1978] Ch 14, where there was extraneous evidence that the victim acted with genuine free will, such that the presumption would have been rebutted despite absence of independent legal advice (*obiter*, since the court in fact held the parties' relationship did not raise the presumption).
347. *Goodchild v. Bradbury* [2006] EWCA Civ 1868, [2006] All ER (D) 247.
348. *R v. Attorney General for England and Wales* [2003] UKPC 22, [2003] All ER (D) 246.
349. *Royal Bank of Scotland Plc v. Etridge (No 2)* [2002] 2 AC 773, [20].
350. *Allcard v. Skinner* (1887) 36 Ch D 145. *See also Boustany v. Piggott* [1995] 69 P&CR 298 (concerning unconscionability).

205. Rescission of the contract is the only remedy available for undue influence. Some cases have awarded more creative remedies, such as an account of profits,[351] equitable compensation[352] and loss splitting,[353] but much of this creativity resulted from an understanding of undue influence now precluded by House of Lords authority.[354]

IV. Gross Disparity

206. English law does not admit of any general power to relieve against contractual liability purely on the basis of the difference in power between the parties. There were once judicial attempts to establish a general power to relieve on the basis of significant inequality of bargaining power.[355] But the House of Lords rejected this transition, defending the traditional doctrines of equity, each of which focuses on distinct inequities in the process of contract formation. The House of Lords considered the creation of a novel ground of relief focusing solely on the inequality of the parties' bargaining appropriate only for Parliament.[356]

207. Perhaps the closest English law comes to a doctrine of disparity is the equitable jurisdiction to relieve against unconscionable bargains.[357] This is invoked rarely, and is successful even less often. Rescission may be available where the complainant can prove that she was at a significant disadvantage with respect to the stronger party as a result of some weakness or disability, and that the stronger party

351. *O'Sullivan v. Management Agency and Music Ltd* [1985] QB 428. This was a fully executed contract for personal services, so rescission was highly problematic. The court ordered an account of the profits of the contract, but allowed the retention of a sum in respect of the work the perpetrator had performed for the victim.
352. *Mahoney v. Purnell* [1996] 3 All ER 61. Here, restoration of the *status quo ante* impossible, but May J, driven to 'do practical justice', awarded equitable compensation (a remedy common for breach of fiduciary duties, but not for undue influence).
353. *Cheese v. Thomas* [1994] 1 WLR 129. The court did not order full restoration of the money obtained by undue influence, but rather that the loss (due to property market deflation) should be shared between the victim and the perpetrator in proportion to their contributions.
354. *Royal Bank of Scotland Plc v. Etridge (No 2)* [2002] 2 AC 773. The House denied a substantive difference between the traditional categories of 'actual' and merely 'presumed' undue influence, declaring instead that there was only one effective doctrine of undue influence, which always indicates a moral wrong. This can, however, be demonstrated either by actual evidence (which is rare), or on the basis of a presumption triggered by a relevant relationship and transaction, which the alleged perpetrator fails to rebut. Previously it was thought that, in cases of merely presumed undue influence, the perpetrator should not be regarded as a wrongdoer, and therefore deserved a degree of leniency, such that the complainant's remedy should take account of its impact on the perpetrator.
355. *Lloyds Bank v. Bundy* [1975] QB 326, 339, per Lord Denning MR.
356. *National Westminster Bank Ltd v. Morgan* [1985] AC 686, 707–08, per Lord Scarman.
357. It derives from the equitable practice of protecting expectant heirs who assigned their inheritance rights at an undervalue: *Earl of Aylesford v. Morris* (1873) 8 Ch App 484. The doctrine expanded in the nineteenth century to the general protection of the 'poor and ignorant' who contracted at significant undervalue without independent advice: *Fry v. Lane* (1888) 40 Ch D 312, 322 per Kay J. The somewhat condescending reference to the 'poor and ignorant' were disparaged in *Cresswell v. Potter* [1978] 1 WLR 255, 257, per Megarry J.

acted unconscionably in taking advantage of the vulnerability that he knew to exist.[358] This need not be deliberate exploitation; it suffices if the stronger party merely failed to act properly in light of the other's weakness.[359]

208. The substantive unfairness of the transaction is clearly not sufficient for relief.[360] The balance of authority suggests that substantive unfairness is not even strictly *necessary* for rescission.[361] However, where there is little concrete evidence as to the stronger party's actual conduct, the court will look to the terms of the contract, on the basis that substantial unfairness implies that the contract was procured in some improper way.[362]

209. As for undue influence, the presence of independent legal advice will not always prevent a finding that the contract was obtained unconscionably. To do so, it is probable that the advice must be sufficient to be effective in the particular context.[363]

§3. Other Conditions of Validity

I. Existing and Licit Cause

210. No requirement of this kind limits the formation of valid contracts in English law.

II. Determined or Determinable, Possible and Licit Object

211. Even where the parties appear to have reached an agreement of some kind, the law will not consider an enforceable contract to exist if its terms lack sufficient certainty. For instance, the presence of clauses which necessitate further negotiation between the parties themselves – such as an express agreement subsequently to agree on the price – will generally mean no contract has yet been formed.[364] However, like

358. *Boustany v. Piggott* [1995] 69 P&CR 298.
359. *Hart v. O'Connor* [1985] AC 1000, per Lord Brightman.
360. *Hart v. O'Connor* [1985] AC 1000; *Boustany v. Piggott* [1995] 69 P&CR 298.
361. *Blomley v. Ryan* [1956] HCA 81, (1956) 99 CLR 362.
362. For example, *Boustany v. Piggott* [1995] 69 P&CR 298. Here, the transaction's substantive unfairness was relevant in inferring unconscionable conduct, since the victim refused to give evidence.
363. *Boustany v. Piggott* [1995] 69 P&CR 298. The transaction was held voidable despite the victim's receipt of independent legal advice because, at the time of the advice, she was still subject to the continuing influence of the perpetrator, which robbed the advice of its effect. This suggests that legal advice is not a formulaic requirement, but only an evidential indicator concerning whether the transaction was freely made, albeit one on which great weight is placed.
364. Cf total silence on the issue of price, in which case statute will sometimes avoid the conclusion that the parties had not yet formed a binding legal contract by implying-in a term setting the price at a reasonable sum: for example Sale of Goods Act 1979, s. 8 (likewise for contracts for services: Supply of Goods and Services Act 1982, s. 15 for non-consumer situations; Consumer Rights Act 2015, s. 51 for consumer situations).

the putative doctrine of 'intention to create legal relations', this does not belong so much as a freestanding requirement for contract formation, but instead collapses into the crucial issue of offer and acceptance.

212. This includes whether the proposal in question is such as to lead the addressee genuinely and reasonably to interpret it as an offer of legally binding contractual terms, rather than an arrangement without legal effect. Vagueness will generally militate against this finding.[365] But the law has a predisposition to find adequate certainty where the proposal was clearly a *contractual* offer, in that it gave the reasonable impression of offering a legally binding relationship.[366] The rules of certainty also echo the distinction between true contractual offers and mere invitations to treat, and the question of whether the reasonable person in the position of the addressee should have interpreted a particular proposal as being a true offer rather than a mere invitation.

213. This accounts for the fact that the court may still find a contract formed notwithstanding that some of the parties' obligations were still uncertain at the moment of agreement, provided by the time performance fell due they would *become* certain as a result of something other than the parties' own further negotiation. Examples include an agreement to sell at the market price at a particular future moment,[367] or at a price to be determined by an independent third party.[368] Neither of these terms prevents the formation of a contract since neither is inconsistent with holding the proposal to be a true offer rather than just an invitation to treat, as would a caveat envisaging further negotiations by the parties themselves.

III. Initial Impossibility

214. It is entirely possible under English law to impose binding contractual obligations that are in fact impossible to achieve, or are entirely beyond the control of the party undertaking them. Despite the increasing influence of promise-based conceptions of contract, a contractual obligation in English law is best understood not as a promise, but as an assumption of liability for non-performance.

215. However, generally no contract will be formed if both parties believed something to be possible at the time of contracting, but this shared belief was in fact

365. Some courts have made the link expressly: for example *British Steel Corp v. Cleveland Bridge and Engineering Co Ltd* [1984] 1 All ER 504, in which the court suggested that severe gaps in the agreement mean non-enforceability specifically because they indicate the parties had no intention to be bound at that stage.

366. *See* for example *Tang v. Grant Thornton International Ltd* [2012] EWHC 3198 (Ch), [2014] 2 CLC 663, [56]-[61]. This also explains the distinction between cases such as *May & Butcher v. R* [1934] 2 KB 17 (no enforceable contract) and *Foley v. Classique Coaches Ltd* [1934] 2 KB 1, where an enforceable contract was found. Here, the court took the parties impliedly to have agreed a 'reasonable price' term, in light of clear contextual evidence that they intended a binding contract to be formed at this point.

367. *Brown v. Gould* [1972] Ch 53.

368. *Lloyds Bank Ltd v. Marcan* [1973] 1 WLR 1387. However, at least in the context of sales of goods, the contract is void if this third party in fact 'cannot or does not make the valuation' required: Sale of Goods Act 1979, s.9.

mistaken—so-called common mistake.[369] In *Bell v. Lever Bros*, the House of Lords held that a contract would be void for a common mistake as to some quality without which the obligations undertaken were 'essentially different'. The mistake must relate to the 'essence' of the contract.

216. In *Great Peace Shipping v. Tsavliris Salvage,*[370] the Court of Appeal looked to the law of frustration – regulating when obligations are discharged by subsequent impossibility – to refine the doctrine of common mistake. Relief on the grounds of common mistake, including as to the possibility of performance, requires (i) a false but shared belief at the time of contracting as to a state of affairs, (ii) the absence of any warranty as to the correctness of this belief, such that the contract itself does not itself expressly or impliedly allocate the risk of the belief's falsity, (iii) that the falseness of the belief is neither party's fault and (iv) that as a result of the falseness of the belief, the performance of the parties' obligations is impossible.

217. Despite adopting the impossibility criterion from the law of frustration, the Court of Appeal suggested that courts should be slower to find contracts void for common mistake than to find them frustrated on the grounds of subsequent impossibility of performance. That is because, in mistake cases, it is possible in advance to verify the assumption in question, so the contract will generally impliedly allocate responsibility for the correctness of the belief on which the parties have contracted, which will therefore exclude the possibility that the contract is void for common mistake.

218. It is unclear how strictly the 'impossibility' test should be applied. In *Great Peace* itself, the Court of Appeal appears not to have taken its own test entirely seriously.[371] In *Brennan v. Bolt Burdon*,[372] Maurice Kay LJ applied the impossibility threshold literally and strictly, but Sedley LJ doubted whether actual impossibility should always be a requirement (and moreover stated that impossibility should not be a requirement for the voiding of contracts for common mistakes of law). In *Kyle Bay Ltd*,[373] the *Great Peace* impossibility test was interpreted as entailing only that the performance in fact rendered would be a thing 'essentially and radically different' from the obligation undertaken.[374]

219. *Great Peace* emphasised that the contract cannot be voided for common mistake if the non-existence of the assumed state of affairs is attributable to the fault of either party, but the test for fault remains uncertain. In *Associated Japanese Bank v. Credit du Nord*,[375] Steyn J presented the requirement of fault as entailing only that

---

369. The qualifying mistake can be one of fact or of law: *Brennan v. Bolt Burden* [2004] EWCA Civ 1017, [2005] QB 303.

370. *Great Peace Shipping Ltd v. Tsavliris (International) Ltd* [2002] EWCA Civ 1407, [2003] QB 679.

371. The parties' actual *contractual obligations* related only to the charter of a ship, which remained entirely possible despite the mistake in question; it was only the charterers' *purpose* in making the contract that was impossible to achieve.

372. *Brennan v. Bolt Burden* [2004] EWCA Civ 1017, [2005] QB 303.

373. *Kyle Bay Ltd (T/A Astons Nightclub) v. Underwriters* [2006] EWHC 607 (Comm), [2006] Lloyd's Rep IR 718.

374. *Associated Japanese Bank (International) Ltd v. Credit du Nord SA* [1989] 1 WLR 255, per Steyn J.

375. *Associated Japanese Bank (International) Ltd v. Credit du Nord SA* [1989] 1 WLR 255, per Steyn J.

the party alleging voidness for common mistake held the mistaken belief unreasonably. But in *McRae v. Commonwealth Disposals Commission*,[376] the High Court of Australia required that a party held her mistaken belief unreasonably, and had herself induced the other party to hold the same belief. The Court of Appeal in *Great Peace* suggested that these clearly divergent understandings of fault were in fact the same, so it is unclear what understanding of fault *Great Peace* actually adopts.

220. The law on common mistake is contentious, and it is debatable how the voidness of such contracts is best rationalised. Some understand it as representing a sui generis rule of law, providing that a contract is void where a sufficiently fundamental shared assumption proves false. Others attribute the result of a shared assumption's falsity to the precise agreement the parties have struck, and particularly to the terms that are implied into it, in fact and at law.[377]

221. On this view, where the parties have apparently contracted and one party subsequently alleges the contract is void for common mistake, the contract will stand unless an express or implied term in the offer and acceptance makes formation conditional on the truth of a particular shared assumption.[378] This approach finds support in Lord Atkin's alternative ratio in *Bell v. Lever Bros*, in which he asked whether the parties' agreement expressly or impliedly provides for the contract's voidness should the assumption in question prove false.[379] Likewise Lord Thankerton's reasoning in that case focused solely on the construction of the agreement the parties had made. Other decisions too, such as *Couturier v. Hastie* – often cited as establishing a positive rule of law that the non-existence of contractual subject matter renders the contract void – actually turn on the interpretation of the parties' particular agreement.[380]

222. In *Great Peace*, the Court of Appeal criticised the interpretive approach to common mistake on the grounds that actual contracting parties generally do not consider the outcome of their shared assumptions proving false, so it is fictitious to impute intentions regarding this eventuality. However, the interpretive process, of which the implication of terms in fact forms an integral part,[381] is not concerned with whether or not the actual human beings in question pondered what they wished to

376. *McRae v. Commonwealth Disposals Commission* [1951] HCA 79. Australian case but approved in *Great Peace Shipping Ltd v. Tsavliris (International) Ltd* [2002] EWCA Civ 1407, [2003] QB 679.
377. This is the same dispute that concerns frustration of contracts due to subsequent impossibility of performance.
378. The classic articulation of this view is found in C Slade, 'The Myth of Mistake in the English law of Contract' (1954) 70 LQR 885.
379. Such a term will be implied only where necessary, which accounts for Lord Atkin's determination that a mistake must be 'essential'.
380. In this case, the question was whether the buyer had 'bought the adventure', i.e., assumed the risk of the goods' non-existence. Lord Cranworth explicitly stated that the case turned on the construction of the contract, which is how this case has been subsequently understood by the High Court of Australia: *McRae v. Commonwealth Disposals Commission* [1951] HCA 79. While the parties' agreement, properly interpreted, will often entail its own voidness if the contracted-for property in fact does not exist, this is not a positive rule of law.
381. *Attorney General of Belize v. Belize Telecom Ltd* [2009] 1 WLR 1988, [17]-[27], per Lord Hoffmann; Cf the majority of the Supreme Court in *Marks and Spencer Plc v. BNP Paribas Securities Services Trust Company (Jersey) Ltd* [2015] UKSC 72.

happen should a shared assumption prove false.[382] It looks in this case to whether the contract they have in fact agreed is, properly interpreted, absolute or conditional on the shared assumption's truth.

223. Therefore the optimal approach, if the contract does not expressly provide for the falsity of the shared assumption, is to assess first whether a term to this effect falls to be implied in fact. Failing that, the court should look to the terms that fall to be implied at law. For instance, in a contract of sale, generally the seller is deemed at law impliedly to have warranted that the goods in question exist. However, the terms of a specific contract may expressly or by necessary implication provide for a different result, such as to place the risk of non-existence on the buyer, or to provide that there is no liability if the goods are revealed not to exist.

224. At one point the law appeared to have developed a supplementary jurisdiction to rescind contracts in equity for common mistakes fundamental to the contract, even when the contract would not be held void at common law. This was proposed by Denning LJ in *Solle v. Butcher*,[383] who imagined the House of Lords in *Bell v. Lever Bros* to have inadvertently overlooked this equitable jurisdiction. However, the Court of Appeal later denied any such equitable power,[384] and departed from Denning LJ's reasoning in *Solle v. Butcher* on the basis that it was irreconcilable with the decision of the House of Lords in *Bell v. Lever Bros*. That conclusion is surely correct, since the equitable jurisdiction asserted in *Solle v. Butcher* would allow contracts to be unworked in situations where the House of Lords in *Bell v. Lever Bros* stated they should endure.[385] There is clearly no room for rescission in equity on an interpretive understanding of the effect of common mistake. Once the contract is interpreted to reveal its reaction to the assumption proving false, there is no justification for allowing this reaction to be overridden in equity. To allow this would be to permit the court to rewrite the parties' contract to make it a substantively fairer bargain, precisely what Denning LJ achieved in *Solle v. Butcher*.

IV. Illegality and Public Policy

225. Some contracts are prohibited by statutory rules. In such cases the statute will determine what, if any, legal effects flow from the contract.[386] Contracts can also be denied legal force by the common law illegality doctrine, often expressed in the

---

382. *Shirlaw v. Southern Foundries (1926) Ltd* [1939] 2 KB 206, 227, per Mackinnon LJ. The court engages in a hypothetical thought experiment, assessing what the parties would have replied had they been asked about the term's inclusion. Whether or not they in fact considered it is immaterial.
383. *Solle v. Butcher* [1950] 1 KB 671.
384. *Great Peace Shipping Ltd v. Tsavliris (International) Ltd* [2002] EWCA Civ 1407, [2003] QB 679.
385. It is contentious whether the Court of Appeal may validly depart from its own previous ruling by invoking a prior decision of the House of Lords.
386. A severance clause will mean the remainder of a contract is upheld even if one or more of its terms are held unlawful.

Latin maxim '*ex turpi causa non oritur actio*'.[387]Historically the doctrine was intimately concerned with the defeat of morally unacceptable actions, such as suits arising under contracts linked to sexual immorality[388] and blasphemy. The doctrine's obsession with personal morality has for some time been in remission, as more recent judicial *dicta* emphasise the need for some kind of unlawfulness as opposed to mere immorality.[389]

226. A contract affected by the illegality principle can still have legal effect. It can still support a transfer of title to property even if the contractual purpose was unlawful,[390] and may support an action for restitution of a sum paid on the grounds of total failure of basis. The illegality doctrine merely prevents a claimant advancing what would otherwise be a valid private law action, such as a claim for breach of contract.

227. The operation of the illegality doctrine has changed significantly in recent years. For many years, the Court of Appeal favoured an openly moralistic approach, with courts speculating whether the 'public conscience' would be affronted by the success of the claim at hand,[391] paying close attention to 'the relative moral culpability of the parties'.[392] The House of Lords subsequently disavowed this approach in *Tinsley v. Milligan*, instead adopting a narrow and dispassionate understanding of the illegality doctrine.[393] The majority held that a claimant would be 'entitled to recover if he is not forced to plead or rely on the illegality'.[394]

228. However, the recent Supreme Court decision in *Hounga v. Allen* catalysed an open resurgence in the wide and discretionary understanding of the illegality doctrine, uniformly applicable across the private law spectrum. The claimant took up unlawful employment in the UK as a live-in domestic servant for the defendant. She was severely mistreated, and eventually dismissed. She sued the defendant for unlawful discrimination on grounds of her non-UK citizenship. In the Supreme Court, Lord Wilson held that the public policy considerations in favour of barring the claim had to be weighed against those in favour of allowing it,[395] concluding that this balancing exercise decisively favoured allowing the claim.[396]

---

387. Usually traced to the judgment of Lord Mansfield in *Holman v. Johnson* (1775) 1 Cowp 341, 343; 98 ER 1120, 1121.
388. A classic example is *Pearce v. Brooks* (1866) LR 1 Exch 213, in which the court refused to enforce an action for the price of a carriage that had been supplied in the knowledge that the buyer would use it for her work as a prostitute.
389. For example, *Les Laboratoires Servier v. Apotex Inc* [2014] UKSC 55, [2014] 3 WLR 1257, [28], per Lord Sumption, insisting that acts only engage the illegality doctrine if criminal or 'quasi-criminal'.
390. *Tinsley v. Milligan* [1994] 1 AC 340.
391. *Saunders v. Edwards* [1987] 1 WLR 1116, 1132, per Nicholls LJ.
392. *Saunders v. Edwards* [1987] 1 WLR 1116, 1127, per Kerr LJ. *See also* Kerr LJ's judgment in *Euro-Diam v. Bathurst Ltd* [1988] 2 WLR 517.
393. *Tinsley v. Milligan* [1994] 1 AC 340. Although a trusts decision, *Tinsley*'s ratio soon expanded outside equity. It was declared applicable in tort in *Moore Stephens v. Stone & Rolls Ltd (in liquidation)* [2008] EWCA Civ 644, a point confirmed on appeal: [2009] UKHL 39, [2009] 1 AC 1391, [97], per Lord Scott.
394. *Tinsley v. Milligan* [1994] 1 AC 340, per Lord Browne-Wilkinson.
395. *Hounga v. Allen* [2014] UKSC 47, [2014] 1 WLR 2889, [42].
396. *Hounga v. Allen* [2014] UKSC 47, [2014] 1 WLR 2889, [52].

229. In *Jetivia v. Bilta*, the Supreme Court held that the crimes of a company director also constituting a breach of duty to the company cannot be attributed to the company when the company sues that director for breach of duty.[397] The Court's reasoning, however, was divided according to the Justices' distinct understandings of the illegality doctrine. In Lord Sumption's view, the case fell to be decided by the ordinary principles of corporate attribution. However, Lords Toulson and Lord Hodge decided the case by reference to the illegality principle.[398] The critical issue was simply 'whether it is contrary to public policy' that the claim should succeed.[399]

230. In *Patel v. Mirza*, the claimant had transferred a large sum to the defendant on the understanding that he would use it to bet on the price of shares using special insider knowledge he expected to obtain, constituting the crime of insider dealing. In fact, the project was abandoned due to factors beyond the parties' control. When the claimant sued for the return of the money, the defendant invoked the illegality rule in his defence. The Court of Appeal allowed recovery by invoking the so-called *locus poenitentiae* principle – presented as a supplement to the illegality doctrine – that prevents the defeat of a claim where the illegal project was abandoned before it commenced.[400]

231. However, Gloster LJ provided an alternative *ratio*, allowing recovery simply because there were no 'considerations of public policy [which] require that [the claimant] has to forfeit the funds'.[401] It was this approach that found most favour in the Supreme Court, which confirmed that the effect of illegality on a private law claim is to be resolved by a policy-balancing enquiry calculated to promote justice and the public interest. The majority Justices thought it important to avoid 'incongruous results in legal and moral terms',[402] and actively to 'strive for the most desirable policy outcome'.[403] To achieve this, a court must 'tak[e] into account a range of factors', to establish 'whether the public interest...should result in denial of the relief claimed'.[404] The Court declined 'to lay down a prescriptive or definitive list' of the relevant considerations,[405] although Lord Toulson suggested these would 'include the seriousness

397. *Jetivia SA v. Bilta (UK) Ltd* [2015] UKSC 23, [7], per Lord Neuberger.
398. *Jetivia SA v. Bilta (UK) Ltd* [2015] UKSC 23, [120]. This echoes Lord Toulson's lone dissent in *Les Laboratoires Servier v. Apotex Inc* [2014] UKSC 55, [2014] 3 WLR 1257, [62], which endorsed the Court of Appeal's willingness to 'take into account a wide range of considerations in order to ensure that the [illegality] defence only applies where it is a just and proportionate response to the illegality involved in the light of the policy considerations underlying it.': [2012] EWCA Civ 593, [2013] RPC 21, [73].
399. *Jetivia SA v. Bilta (UK) Ltd* [2015] UKSC 23, [166].
400. The Court held that this was engaged even though the project was abandoned because it became impossible, rather than because the claimant underwent a change of heart, denying any requirement of 'genuine repentance': *Patel v. Mirza* [2014] EWCA Civ 1047, [2015] 1 Ch 271, [44]-[45] per Rimer LJ.
401. *Patel v. Mirza* [2014] EWCA Civ 1047, [2015] 1 Ch 271, [76]. The illegality doctrine was therefore not engaged at all, so recourse to the supplementary *locus poenitentiae* exception was unnecessary.
402. *Patel v. Mirza* [2016] UKSC 42, [127], per Lord Kerr.
403. *Patel v. Mirza* [2016] UKSC 42, [91].
404. *Patel v. Mirza* [2016] UKSC 42, [109].
405. *Patel v. Mirza* [2016] UKSC 42, [107], per Lords Toulson and [173], per Lord Neuberger.

of the [claimant's] conduct, its centrality to the contract, whether it was intentional and whether there was marked disparity in the parties' respective culpability'.[406]

232. The majority of the Supreme Court was keen to integrate the presence of illegality into the assessment of whether the claim should be allowed, even though reference to that illegality was unnecessary in establishing a complete cause of action. This openly abandons the central aspiration of *Tinsley*,[407] namely to distinguish between (i) illegality *constitutive* of the claim at hand, and (ii) illegality that is merely a part of the history and irrelevant to the application of the law between the parties. It remains likely that a claim for restitution on grounds of failure of basis will still succeed despite the contract's unlawful purpose, since the Supreme Court in *Patel* regarded public policy as unlikely to prevent recovery in such situation (as opposed to an action to enforce the primary obligations under such a contract).

233. The rise of the discretionary policy-balancing approach to the illegality doctrine may eventually expand the kinds of action on which it operates. Its restriction to acts of a criminal or quasi-criminal character – therefore requiring some unlawfulness and not just immorality – was allied to a narrow view of the illegality doctrine that did not permit judicial discretion. With the re-emergence of a discretionary and moralistic approach, a broader range of actions may once again come to engage the rule, leaving it to the court to decide whether, all things considered, the contractual claim should be permitted. Cases may no longer be outside the doctrine just because they concern mere immorality and no actual unlawfulness.

V. Other Unenforceable Contracts

234. An agreement may be unenforceable for many reasons concerned with its substance, such as illegality and uncertainty, discussed elsewhere. Additionally, contracts are presumptively unenforceable if they operate in restraint of trade. Such contracts are enforceable only to the extent that the party seeking enforcement can show the scope and duration of the restriction to be reasonable in relation to the public interest.[408]

235. Common law regulates both restraints imposed on employees and restraints imposed on sellers of businesses. The first category of restraint typically purports to restrict the freedom of former employees to engage in certain activities despite leaving the employment of the other party.[409] To justify such a clause, a former employer must demonstrate some proprietary interest in need of special protection from former employees, such as commercial secrets or goodwill.[410] The restriction must only be wide enough to protect against damage to these interests.[411] The second category of

406. *Patel v. Mirza* [2016] UKSC 42, [107].
407. This involved the majority actually departing from *Tinsley v. Milligan* [1994] 1 AC 340: *Patel v. Mirza* [2016] UKSC 42, [114].
408. *Nordenfelt v. Maxim Nordenfelt Guns and Ammunition Co Ltd* [1894] AC 535.
409. This includes indirect restrictions: *Bull v. Pitney Bowes Ltd* [1966] 2 All ER 384 (concerning forfeiture of pension rights on involvement in any activity competing with the former employer's business).
410. Particular business structures or methods of organisation will not suffice.
411. *Commercial Plastics Ltd v. Vincent* [1964] 3 WLR 820.

restraint is enforceable only if no wider than necessary to protect the buyer's interests in the goodwill she will acquire in the purchase of the business. Such restraints must therefore relate to the actual business operated and be within its scope.[412]

§4. The Consequences of a Defect of Consent or a Lack of Substantive Validity

I. Avoidance of the Contract

236. English law distinguishes between contracts void at law, and contracts merely voidable in equity. To find a contract void is to declare that, contrary to appearances, the parties were never truly in a contractual relationship at all. A voidable contract, in contrast, satisfies the requirements for contract formation, and takes effect in law as a valid contract. Nonetheless the law awards a party the right subsequently to rescind the contract, as a result of some factor that taints its formation. The distinction becomes acutely important when third parties claim to have derived rights contingent on the validity of the original contract.

237. A voidable contract will create rights and obligations that endure unless and until the contract is rescinded. However, rescission will not be permitted if to do so would prejudice the rights of third parties. Therefore, if a third party, prior to the rescission, purchases goods obtained under a voidable contract, provided those parties purchased in good faith, for value and without notice of the grounds for rescission of the original contract, the contract can no longer be rescinded and the third party's title to the goods is secure.

238. Conversely, if the original contract is void, it creates no true rights or obligations. In light of the rule that a transferor cannot assign something she does not herself have –*nemo dat quod non habet* – she is therefore unable to pass any legal rights to the third party. A victim can therefore sue the third party in the tort of conversion.[413] It will therefore often be in the interests of a victim to show the contract was not merely voidable in equity, but void at law. This has influenced the development of the law relating to contracts obtained by impersonation.

II. Retroactive Effect of Avoidance or Nullity

239. Although rescission in equity does not deny that a contract arose at law, its effect is to reinstate the parties' positions before contracting by restoration of the

412. *British Concrete Co v. Schleff* [1921] 2 Ch 563.
413. In the absence of a direct reivindicatory action, English law asserts property rights in these circumstances through a tort claim, particularly in the tort of conversion. The claimant sues for damages equal to the value of the thing the defendant has dealt with in a way inconsistent with the rights of the owner. The award of damages will extinguish the original title to the thing: Torts (Interference with Goods) Act 1977, s. 5. It is possible to order delivery of the thing instead of damages (s. 3), but this is not common.

status quo ante. Its effect is therefore both prospective and retrospective. On rescission, all the parties' executory obligations are discharged, and their already executed obligations are reversed. Rescission must therefore be strictly distinguished from termination of a contract, the effect of which is prospective only and does not affect obligations that have already fallen due at the time termination occurs.[414]

240. Rescission is available at the election of the victim and does not require a court order. The victim must simply give notice to the other party that she is exercising her equitable right to rescind the contract. If the issue is subsequently litigated, the court will treat rescission as having occurred at the time the victim gave this notice. Such notice can be express, or implied, when the victim communicates clearly through her conduct that she wishes to rescind. Sometimes the actual communication of notice to the other party is impossible. Where this is so, the victim has only to take all reasonable steps to communicate her intention to rescind.[415]

241. There are numerous grounds on which a court will refuse rescission even where grounds to rescind exist. Rescission is barred where restoration of the *status quo ante* is impossible.[416] This is because rescission does not merely seek to prevent disadvantage to the victim or enrichment of the other party. Rather, it seeks to reverse the *actual performances* rendered pursuant to the rescinded contract. Thus rescission will in principle be barred where the other party no longer possesses the goods received under the contract, although there is room for flexibility,[417] particularly where the goods in question are fungible.[418]

242. The right to rescind will also be extinguished if the victim, while aware of her right to rescind the contract,[419] instead chose to affirm it. The victim must have made it unequivocally clear to the other party that she had elected not to exercise her right to rescind the contract, either by express communication or by conduct inconsistent with a desire to set the contract aside. Affirmation is to be distinguished from mere

414. Confusingly, some commentators and courts refer to both termination and rescission by the latter term, even though their legal consequences are very different.

415. *Car and Universal Finance v. Caldwell* [1965] 1 QB 525 (for example, reporting the fraud in question to the police).

416. This applies in duress too: *Halpern v. Halpern* [2007] EWCA Civ 291, [2008] QB 195.

417. *Erlanger v. New Sambrero Phosphate Co* (1878) 3 App Cas 1218: The requirement of restoring the *status quo ante* is not absolute or literal. Rescission will be available provided the parties can be returned substantially to their original positions.

418. *Smith New Court Securities Ltd v. Scrimgeour Vickers* [1996] 3 WLR 1051. Here, shares purchased under the contract had been sold on and could therefore not be returned since this would interfere in the rights of the innocent purchasers. The House of Lords noted the need for flexibility where restoration of the *status quo* was literally impossible. Lord Browne-Wilkinson (*obiter*) reasoned that, since shares are fungible, even though the *specific* shares purchased could not be restored, others could be, so rescission should be possible.

419. In the case of duress or undue influence, affirmation is possible only after the pressure founding the duress, or the undue influence, has ended.

delay,[420] which is not an independent bar to rescission, although it may provide evidence of an implied affirmation. Rescission will also be barred if it would prejudice the rights of innocent third parties, who acquired such rights in good faith, for value, and without notice of the fact that the original contract was vulnerable to rescission.

III. Damages

243. No damages are available where the contract is void for mistake, since no contract on which to found an action for damages ever exists. Damages are available for misrepresentation, and may also be awarded in lieu of the rescission that the victim seeks. For other vitiating factors such as duress and undue influence, rescission of the contract is the only remedy, and no damages are available. However, subjecting another to duress may independently constitute the tort of intimidation, giving the victim an action against the perpetrator that will compensate with damages the losses resulting from the perpetrator's actions.[421]

420. *Salt v. Stratstone Specialist Ltd* [2015] EWCA Civ 745. This disavows *Leaf v. International Galleries* [1950] 2 KB 86, in which a misrepresentation had emerged by chance five years after the contract was concluded, whereupon the victim immediately sought rescission. Denning LJ in the Court of Appeal held rescission was barred simply by the passage of time, and that a misrepresentee is under a duty to verify representations made to him within a reasonable time.

421. *Rookes v. Barnard* [1964] AC 1129. As a tortious action for damages, this claim is not affected by the bars to rescission, so survives affirmation of the contract by the victim.

Chapter 3. The Contents of a Contract

§1. The Different Clauses

I. Ascertaining the Express Terms

244. It is important to distinguish the parties' actual contractual *undertakings* – the obligations whose non-fulfilment sustains an action for breach – and mere representations that are not incorporated into the contract itself.[422] The answer in all cases is in principle yielded by objective offer and acceptance analysis. However, this analysis functions differently with regard to written and oral contracts.

245. In written contracts, 'entire agreements clauses' are common, particularly in commercial contracts, and exclude a finding that the contract incorporates any terms or representations other than those contained in the contractual text. In oral contracts the question must be asked specifically of each specific putatively incorporated representation: did the party alleging the incorporation of the representation in question genuinely and reasonably interpret it as a *term* of the contract the parties were agreeing to enter? The reasonableness of a conclusion that the other party was in fact undertaking an obligation in line with the representation in question will depend on its significance to the contract itself. Such an interpretation will generally be reasonable where the party alleging the term's incorporation had made it clear to the other party that the issue discussed was central to his willingness to contract.[423]

246. Also relevant is the context and manner in which the representation was made, especially if it was made (or repeated) immediately before final contract formation.[424] The parties' relative knowledge as to the substance of the representation will also be important; it will be more reasonable to interpret the representation as a contractual undertaking if the representor has superior expertise.[425] Conversely, where the representor has no particular relevant knowledge, it is unlikely that the reasonable representee would think the representor intended to bind himself contractually to the representation.[426]

422. Unincorporated representations are relevant since they may allow rescission for misrepresentation. The division between incorporated and unincorporated representations is sometimes affected by statute. For instance, representations made by traders to consumers prior to contract formation are likely to be deemed terms of the contract: Consumer Rights Act 2015.

423. *Couchman v. Hill* [1947] KB 554.

424. *Heilbut, Symons & Co v. Buckleton* [1913] AC 30, 43, 49.

425. *See* for example *Dicke Bentley Productions Ltd v. Harold Smith (Motors) Ltd* [1965] 1 WLR 623.

426. *Oscar Cess Ltd v. Williams* [1957] 1 WLR 370, 376.

A. *Incorporation of Other Terms*

247. Where a contract is formed in a context in which the reasonable person would understand the full contract terms to include rights and obligations other than those expressly stated, other express terms may have been incorporated 'by reference' to an extraneous document in which these terms appeared,[427] even if one party did not in fact read the document in question. This results from orthodox offer and acceptance analysis, since the offeror will act reasonably in interpreting the other party's acceptance as applying also to the additional terms, provided she was given reasonable notice of these terms' existence before accepting.[428] The nature of the notice drawn to additional terms is relevant in deciding whether the offeror's conclusion that the other party assented to them was reasonable.[429]

248. Additional express terms can also be incorporated on the basis of a course of dealing between the parties. For instance, a defendant could in principle rely on an exclusion clause contained in his standard business terms even if he did not provide the claimant a copy of the relevant terms prior to the formation of the contract in question.[430] The court will decide whether the defendant was reasonably entitled to conclude that the claimant assented to the term in question. This may be a reasonable conclusion, notwithstanding the fact that the claimant never saw the term in question on this particular occasion, where the parties have dealt on substantially identical terms with a high degree of regularity and consistency.[431]

249. Such terms can even be incorporated even where the claimant has never been presented a copy of the defendant's standard terms, provided those standard terms reflect a widespread industry norm, since it may be reasonable for the defendant to conclude the claimant was assenting to the terms on which all actors in the relevant

427. *Thompson v. London, Midland and Scotland Railway Co* [1930] 1 KB 41. Reference is immaterial if contract formation has already occurred at the time of reference: *Olley v. Marlborough Court Ltd* [1949] 1 KB 532. In this case, the claimant booked a room at a hotel, and items were stolen from her baggage. The hotel was unable to invoke a notice excluding liability for theft that had been affixed to the rear of the bedroom door, since the exclusion clause was not incorporated into the parties' contract, which had already been formed at the hotel reception.

428. *Parker v. South Eastern Railway* (1877) 2 CPD 416. However, terms will not have been successfully incorporated where the offeror actually knew the other party in fact did not agree to them: *Harris v. Great Western Railway Co* (1876) 1 QBD 515, 530–32, per Blackburn J, or if the offeror reasonably should have known the other party did not subjectively agree to their incorporation: *Scriven v. Hindley* [1913] 3 KB 564.

429. *Chapelton v. Barry Urban District Council* [1940] 1 KB 532: The reasonable recipient of a receipt would not think it held contractual terms.

430. *McCutcheon v. David MacBrayne Ltd* [1964] 1 WLR 165.

431. *McCutcheon v. David MacBrayne Ltd* [1964] 1 WLR 165 (unsuccessful); *Hardwick Game Farm v. Suffolk Agricultural and Poultry Producers' Association* [1966] 1 WLR 287 (successful, where the parties had contracted on the same terms over 100 times). Incorporation by course of dealing is more likely in commercial than in consumer contexts: *Hollier v. Rambler Motors (AMC)* [1972] 2 WLR 401.

industry did business.[432] However, this will generally be a reasonable conclusion only where both parties are active in the same industry and therefore familiar with the industry's standard business terms.[433]

250. Where the parties have transacted on one party's standard terms, and these terms contain specific obligations highly onerous to the other, the other is bound to the particularly onerous terms only if he was made specifically aware of it prior to communicating his assent to the standard terms as a whole.[434]

B. Signature

251. However, a party will be bound by all the other party's standard terms, however onerous, if he was supplied a copy of them and indicated acceptance by signature. Subject to the narrow defence of *non est factum*, a signatory is deemed conclusively to have agreed to all the terms included in the written document.[435] This is true even if no reasonable person in the position of the other party could have believed the signatory was genuinely consenting to the onerous terms, and even if the other party knows that the signatory has not read the terms and therefore cannot know their contents.[436]

252. The signature rule is therefore a significant exception to the ordinary rules of offer and acceptance, and it has been rejected in some other leading common law jurisdictions.[437] The rule is generally justified by reference to commercial convenience; it is apparently essential for business practice that signatures be legally unchallengeable evidence of assent.[438]

---

432. *British Crane Hire Corp Ltd v. Ipswich Plant Hire Ltd* [1975] QB 303. Here, Lord Denning MR emphasised that incorporation by course of dealing is distinct from incorporation by trade custom, but that the two can be cited together to show incorporation where it could not be established by reference to one alone.
433. Lord Denning MR in *British Crane Hire Corp Ltd v. Ipswich Plant Hire Ltd* [1975] QB 303 held that incorporation by trade custom could occur only where the parties had an 'equality of bargaining power'. This language is misleading and has given rise to some confusion. Lord Denning MR was speaking not of economic bargaining power, but informational equality; both parties must know the terms under which the industry functions.
434. *Spurling v. Bradshaw* [1956] 1 WLR 461, 466, per Denning LJ: 'the more unreasonable a clause is, the greater the notice which must be given of it.' Likewise in *Thornton v. Shoe Lane Parking* [1971] 2 QB 163, which held that unusual or onerous clauses in standard terms require special attention to be drawn to them before they will be held incorporated. *See also Interfoto Picture Library Ltd v. Stiletto Visual Programmes Ltd* [1989] 2 QB 433.
435. *Harris v. Great Western Railway Co* (1876) 1 QBD 515, 530. However, the signatory will not be bound by a specific term if he was misled about its meaning or effect before signing: *Curtis v. Chemical Cleaning* [1951] 1 KB 805.
436. *L'Estrange v. Graucob* [1934] 2 KB 394, 403, per Scrutton LJ: 'it is wholly immaterial whether he has read the document or not.'
437. *See* for example the Ontario Court of Appeal in *Tilden Rent-a-Car Co v. Clendenning* (1978) 83 DLR (3d) 400.
438. *Peekay Intermark Ltd v. Australia and New Zealand Banking Group Ltd* [2006] EWCA Civ 386, [2006] 2 Lloyd's Rep 511, [43] per Moore-Bick LJ.

II. Implied Terms

253. A contract can be deemed to contain terms that the parties themselves did not expressly include in their written document or oral agreement. English law divides such implied terms into those implied 'in fact' and those implied 'at law'. The former are terms implied into a specific contract only, variously by reference to the presumed intentions of the parties, or the term's necessity for the operability of the contract.

254. Although the conceptual basis on which terms are implied into specific contracts is contentious, English law has long insisted that terms will be implied into a contract only when such implication is in some way necessary, and not merely because to do so is 'reasonable'.[439] The courts have adopted two tests for whether this demanding threshold is satisfied in a particular case.

255. In *The Moorcock*, the court ruled that terms could only be implied into a contract to 'give such business efficacy to the transaction as must have been intended... by both parties',[440] allowing implication only if the contract could not realistically function in the way the parties had intended without the addition of the term in question. *Shirlaw v. Southern Foundries* adopted a different formula, namely the so-called officious bystander test. A term could be implied into a contract only if it was 'something so obvious that it goes without saying; so that, if, while the parties were making their bargain, an officious bystander were to suggest some express provision for it in their agreement, they would testily suppress him with a common "Oh, of course!"'.[441] Crucially, the court must be convinced that *both* parties would have thought the proposed term went without saying.

256. The relationship between these tests has never been precisely clear, nor has it been conclusively established whether a term must satisfy just one or both tests before it can be implied into a contract. Nonetheless both tests have been recently and authoritatively endorsed by the Supreme Court, in *Marks and Spencer v. BNP Paribas*.[442] In this case the Court unanimously refused to imply a term into a commercial lease since it was not 'necessary for business efficacy'.[443] In refusing implication, the key considerations appeared to be (i) that the parties negotiated in light of, and had not expressly excluded, a well-established legal convention to the contrary of the term

439. *Liverpool City Council v. Irwin* [1977] AC 239. The House of Lords was in fact discussing terms implied in law, which are analytically distinct from terms implied in fact. The House's requirement of necessity therefore really means that the terms considered for implication at law must be equally applicable to all contracts of the type in question, regardless of the identities or circumstances of the actual parties: J Stapleton, 'Duty of care and economic loss: a wider agenda' (1991) 107 LQR 249, 290–291). Nonetheless this case is widely cited as authority for the necessity requirement for terms implied in fact.

440. *The Moorcock* (1889) LR 14 PD 64, per Bowen LJ.

441. *Shirlaw v. Southern Foundries (1926) Ltd* [1939] 2 KB 206, 227, per Mackinnon LJ.

442. *Marks and Spencer Plc v. BNP Paribas Securities Services Trust Company (Jersey) Ltd* [2015] UKSC 72, [21]. Lord Neuberger believed the traditional tests provided a 'clear, consistent and principled' approach to the law on implied terms. He suggested that only one of the traditional tests would need to be satisfied to permit implication of a specific term, although it was his opinion that in most cases a proposed term would satisfy either both or neither of these tests.

443. *Marks and Spencer Plc v. BNP Paribas Securities Services Trust Company (Jersey) Ltd* [2015] UKSC 72, [37].

that the claimant sought to have implied, and (ii) the agreement was a very detailed and professionally drafted commercial contract.[444] Lord Neuberger also suggested that a term's fairness was necessary (but not sufficient) to permit its implication.[445] Nonetheless he disavowed any express requirement of 'reasonableness and equitableness'.[446]

257. The most interesting aspect of the Supreme Court's decision in *Marks and Spencer* is its reflections on the conceptual basis behind the implication of contract terms. In *Attorney General of Belize v. Belize Telecom*, Lord Hoffmann had described the implication 'in fact' of contract terms as simply an aspect of contractual construction: 'the implication of the term is not an addition to the instrument. It only spells out what the instrument means'.[447] 'Implied terms' are therefore not judicially *supplied* in order to salvage what would otherwise be an unworkable contract, but only judicially *revealed*, in that these terms from the beginning formed an integral part of the parties' agreement.

258. In *Marks and Spencer*, however, the Supreme Court disparaged Lord Hoffmann's analysis in *Belize*. This is regrettable, since *Belize* represents a major improvement in English law's understanding of the implication of terms in fact. Crucially, it provides a logical doctrinal justification for why courts may ever legitimately consider a contract to contain terms the parties did not expressly agree. Specifically, 'implication' is a valid undertaking only because it is an integral aspect of deducing what liabilities the parties (objectively) intended to undertake. However, some judges appear strongly opposed to this understanding of implication, probably because they fear that it will make implication easier, with damaging consequences for prospective legal certainty.[448] English law is in need of a single, authoritative test for the implication of terms that simultaneously protects the certainty the strict traditional rules provide, and reflects an interpretive understanding of the process of implication.

259. In addition to terms implied 'in fact', terms can also be implied 'at law'. These are general default rules imposed on all contracts satisfying certain criteria,[449] and can be imposed either by common law or by statute. They are therefore distinct from terms implied in fact, and the implication of a term at law will not be precluded

444. *Marks and Spencer Plc v. BNP Paribas Securities Services Trust Company (Jersey) Ltd* [2015] UKSC 72, [7], [16] and [38], per Lord Neuberger. Interestingly, these two apparently crucial factors are not really relevant to a test for implication based on the *necessity* of the term proposed.

445. *Marks and Spencer Plc v. BNP Paribas Securities Services Trust Company (Jersey) Ltd* [2015] UKSC 72, [21].

446. That requirement was once advocated by Lord Simon in *BP Refinery v. Shire of Hastings* (1977) 52 ALJR 20, 26.

447. *Attorney General of Belize v. Belize Telecom Ltd* [2009] 1 WLR 1988, [17]-[27].

448. The authorities in *Belize Telecom*'s wake have consistently ruled that it did not dilute the necessity threshold: J McCaughran, 'Implied terms: the journey of the man on the Clapham omnibus' (2011) 70 CLJ 607. In *Marks and Spencer*, Lords Clarke and Carnwath correctly considered Lord Hoffmann's *Belize* judgment to have authoritatively declared the conceptual basis of implication, but insisted that it left the necessity threshold unaffected: *Marks and Spencer Plc v. BNP Paribas Securities Services Trust Company (Jersey) Ltd* [2015] UKSC 72, [66], per Lord Carnwath and [77], per Lord Clarke.

449. Sometimes unconvincingly attributed to the intentions of the parties: *Hardwick Game Farm v. Suffolk Agricultural and Poultry Producers' Association* [1966] 1 WLR 287, 339, per Diplock LJ.

simply because the same term would not satisfy the test for implication in fact.[450] Some terms implied at law can be excluded by the parties' agreement. Others cannot, and operate to restrict the parties' freedom of contract in pursuit of some particular public policy objective.

260. Courts have repeatedly ruled that the common law will imply terms at law only if 'necessary',[451] language that tends to cause confusion with the process of implying terms in fact. Prominent examples of terms implied at law include those implied by the Sale of Goods Act 1979, which imply business contracts terms concerning the title of the goods sold.[452] It is impossible to exclude liability for breach of this implied term.[453] The Act also imposes implied terms that goods will correspond with their description,[454] that they will be of satisfactory quality,[455] and that they will be fit for any purpose that the buyer made known to the seller.[456] Liability for breach of these terms can be excluded only if such exclusion satisfies a statutory requirement of reasonableness.[457]

III. Standard Terms and Exemption Clauses

261. Contracts in standard form are perfectly valid,[458] although they are subject to particular scrutiny when purporting to subject contracting parties to highly onerous terms, particularly exclusion clauses. Exclusion clauses and clauses contained in standard terms are also subject to statutory powers of review. For consumer contracts, these powers are contained in the Consumer Rights Act 2015. For non-consumer contracts, the most relevant legislation is the Unfair Contract Terms Act 1977.

262. The Unfair Contract Terms Act 1977 regulates attempts by contract or notice to exclude or limit liability due to things done in the course of business, or due to the occupation of premises used for business purposes. It is impossible to exclude liability for death or personal injury as a result of negligence.[459] Any term excluding or limiting liability for breach of contract in contracts concluded on one's 'written standard terms of business',[460] are enforceable only so far as they satisfy the requirement

---

450. *Scally v. Southern Health & Social Services Board* [1992] 1 AC 294.
451. *Liverpool City Council v. Irwin* [1977] AC 239.
452. Sale of Goods Act 1979, s. 12. The same term is implied into contracts of hire-purchase by the Supply of Goods (Implied Terms) Act 1973, s. 8.
453. Unfair Contract Terms Act 1977, s. 6(1)(a) and (b).
454. Sale of Goods Act 1979, s. 13(1).
455. Sale of Goods Act 1979, s. 14(2).
456. Sale of Goods Act 1979, s. 14(3).
457. Unfair Contract Terms Act 1977, ss. 6–7.
458. And indeed necessary for commercial convenience, since they save time negotiating, allow easy comparisons based on price, and increase prospective certainty because their terms quickly gain authoritative interpretations: *Federal Commerce and Navigation Co Ltd v. Tradax Export SA (The Maratha Envoy)* [1978] AC 1, 8, 13–14, per Lord Diplock:
459. Unfair Contract Terms Act 1977, s. 2. This includes tort, breach of a contractual duty to take care, or breach of the 'common duty of care' occupiers owe to lawful visitors under the Occupiers' Liability Act 1957; Unfair Contract Terms Act 1977, s. 1(1).
460. Unfair Contract Terms Act 1977, s. 3(1).

of 'reasonableness'. The court will examine the substance of the term in order to decide if it excludes liability.

263. If a term's effect is the exclusion or restriction of liability that would otherwise exist, it is treated as an exclusion clause and subjected to the reasonableness test.[461] The statute also contains its own anti-avoidance provisions, targeting clauses purporting to modify or exclude the duty itself, as opposed to liability for its breach, and clauses purporting to restrict particular remedies.[462]

264. To be considered reasonable, the term must be 'a fair and reasonable one to be included having regard to the circumstances which were, or ought reasonably to have been, known to or in the contemplation of the parties when the contract was made'.[463] Schedule 2 of the statute gives guidelines for the application of the reasonableness test. The court should consider the parties' relative bargaining power, whether there was an inducement to accept the term, and whether the party putatively bound by the term had the opportunity to contract elsewhere without being subject to a similar term.[464] It is the responsibility of the party seeking to rely on the term to show that it is reasonable.[465] The term is either enforceable or it is not; the court has no power to alter it to make it reasonable, or to enforce its effect only as far as is reasonable.[466]

265. The Consumer Rights Act 2015 regulates contracts concluded between a 'trader' and a 'consumer'.[467] Certain liabilities cannot be excluded. For instance, it is impossible for a trader to exclude liability for death or personal injury as a result of negligence.[468] Any term purporting to exclude liability for breach of the terms implied into contracts for goods, services or digital content by Part 1 of the Act are not binding on the consumer,[469] although the consumer may rely on such terms.[470]

266. All other terms, and not just exclusion clauses, are not binding on the consumer if they are 'unfair'.[471] An unfair term is that 'contrary to the requirement of good faith...causes a significant imbalance in the parties' rights and obligations under the contract to the detriment of the consumer'.[472] This test is to take into account 'the nature of the subject matter of the contract'[473] and 'all the circumstances existing when

461. *Phillips Products Ltd v. Hyland* [1987] 1 WLR 659.
462. Unfair Contract Terms Act 1977, ss. 3(2)(b) and 13(1).
463. Unfair Contract Terms Act 1977, s. 11.
464. Strictly this schedule applies only to Clauses purporting to restrict the implied terms in goods contracts (Unfair Contract Terms Act 1977, ss. 6–7) but it has been judicially extrapolated as guidance for all the Act's restrictions on exclusion of liability.
465. Unfair Contract Terms Act 1977, s.11(5).
466. *Stewart Gill Ltd v. Horatio Myer & Co Ltd* [1992] QB 600. Cf language of the Unfair Contract Terms Act 1977 itself ('*in so far as*...the contract term satisfies the requirement of reasonableness.')
467. As defined by the Unfair Contract Terms Act 1977, s. 2.
468. Consumer Rights Act 2015, s. 65. As for the Unfair Contract Terms Act 1977, this means breach of contractual duty to take care, tortious negligence, or breach of the 'common duty of care' occupiers owe to lawful visitors under the Occupiers' Liability Act 1957: Consumer Rights Act 2015, s. 65(4).
469. Consumer Rights Act 2015, ss. 31 (goods), 57 (services), 47 (digital content).
470. Consumer Rights Act 2015, s. 62(3).
471. Consumer Rights Act 2015, s. 62(1).
472. Consumer Rights Act 2015, s. 62(4).
473. Consumer Rights Act 2015, s. 62(5)(a).

the term was agreed and to all of the other terms of the contract or any other contract on which it depends'.[474] The court must consider a term's fairness wherever relevant to the disposition of the case, even if the parties have not raised the issue.[475] The court cannot assess for fairness the terms specifying the contract's main subject matter, or the price in relation to the goods, services or digital content supplied,[476] which has been broadly interpreted.[477] If one term of the contract is held unenforceable on the grounds of unfairness, the wider contract continues in effect.[478]

267. In addition, traders are under a general duty to ensure their written terms are legible and that they are in plain and intelligible language.[479]

IV. Penalty Clauses

268. English law is supportive of liquidated damages clauses, namely clauses that provide in advance the quantum of liability that results from a specific breach. Such clauses increase prospect certainty, and are advantageous to claimants because an action for the recovery of such a sum is not subject to the duty to mitigate and the remoteness rules that affect claims for unliquidated damages. Conversely, penalty clauses are unenforceable in English law.

269. The dividing line between liquidated damages clauses and penalty clauses is notoriously vague, because both are secondary obligations to pay a specified sum in the event of a breach.[480] If judged to be a penalty clause, a clause is automatically unenforceable and the court has no power to amend or reduce the quantum of liability to a satisfactory level.[481] In the joined appeals of *Cavendish Square Holding BV v. Makdessi* and *ParkingEye Ltd v. Beavis*,[482] the Supreme Court doubted that the penalty rule, which restricts freedom of contract and reduces certainty,[483] would have been

474. Consumer Rights Act 2015, s. 62(5)(b).
475. Consumer Rights Act 2015, s. 71.
476. Consumer Rights Act 2015, s.64.
477. *Office of Fair Trading v. Abbey National Plc* [2009] UKSC 6, [2010] 1 AC 696 (decided under the Consumer Rights Act 2015s precursor provisions, the Unfair Terms in Consumer Contracts Regulations 1999 (SI 1999/2083)).
478. Consumer Rights Act 2015, s. 67.
479. Consumer Rights Act 2015, s. 68.
480. The penalty doctrine can also police clauses denying entitlements to sums that would be due but for breach: *Cavendish Square Holding BV v. Talal El Makdessi* and *ParkingEye Ltd v. Beavis* [2015] UKSC 67, [2015] 3 WLR 1373.
481. Any clause judged to be a penalty is unenforceable automatically and entirely; there is, apparently, 'no exercise of discretion at all': *Else (1982) Ltd v. Parkland Holdings Ltd* [1994] 1 BCLC 130, 144, approved by Lords Neuberger and Sumption in *Cavendish Square Holding BV v. Talal El Makdessi* and *ParkingEye Ltd v. Beavis* [2015] UKSC 67, [2015] 3 WLR 1373, [9].
482. *Cavendish Square Holding BV v. Talal El Makdessi* and *ParkingEye Ltd v. Beavis* [2015] UKSC 67, [2015] 3 WLR 1373.
483. *Cavendish Square Holding BV v. Talal El Makdessi* and *ParkingEye Ltd v. Beavis* [2015] UKSC 67, [2015] 3 WLR 1373, [3].

invented today.[484] However, under the weight of precedent,[485] the Supreme Court declined to abolish this controversial rule.[486] Nonetheless, the Court comprehensively restated the test by which the law identifies a penalty clause. Most freely agreed clauses providing for significant sums on breach of contract will now be judged to be non-penal, and enforceable. The Supreme Court presented the penalty doctrine as concerning two sequential questions: 'In what circumstances is the rule engaged at all? And what makes a contractual provision penal?'[487]

A. What Kind of Clauses can be Reviewed under the Penalty Rule?

270. According to Lords Neuberger and Sumption, '[t]he penalty rule regulates only the remedies available for breach of a party's primary obligations, not the primary obligations themselves'.[488] The Court suggested that in some circumstances a term disentitling a party in breach to money otherwise due to him – as opposed to the more usual obligation to pay money on breach – could constitute a penalty.[489] Nonetheless, the court asserted a 'fundamental difference between a jurisdiction to review the fairness of a contractual obligation and a jurisdiction to regulate the remedy for its

484. *Cavendish Square Holding BV v. Talal El Makdessi* and *ParkingEye Ltd v. Beavis* [2015] UKSC 67, [2015] 3 WLR 1373, [36].
485. Equity has long taken the view that a claimant should not be allowed to sue for more than her actual loss: *Peachy v. Duke of Somerset* (1720) 1 Strange 447; *Sloman v. Walter* (1784) 1 Bro Ch 418.
486. Lord Mance demanded 'the strongest reasons for so radical a reversal of jurisprudence', and saw a continued justification for the penalty rule in the widespread use of standard form contracts: *Cavendish Square Holding BV v. Talal El Makdessi* and *ParkingEye Ltd v. Beavis* [2015] UKSC 67, [2015] 3 WLR 1373, [162].
487. *Cavendish Square Holding BV v. Talal El Makdessi* and *ParkingEye Ltd v. Beavis* [2015] UKSC 67, [2015] 3 WLR 1373, [11], per Lords Neuberger and Sumption.
488. *Cavendish Square Holding BV v. Talal El Makdessi* and *ParkingEye Ltd v. Beavis* [2015] UKSC 67, [2015] 3 WLR 1373, [13] (a distinction with which Lord Hodge agreed at [241]). Primary obligations are those contractual undertakings whose non-fulfilment grounds an action for breach: *Photo Production Ltd v. Securicor Ltd* [1980] AC 827, 848–49, per Lord Diplock.
489. Lord Sumption and Neuberger were content to assume this without actually deciding the point: *Cavendish Square Holding BV v. Talal El Makdessi* and *ParkingEye Ltd v. Beavis* [2015] UKSC 67; [2015] 3 WLR 1373, [73]. Lords Mance and Hodge declared this decisively (at [154]) and also approved the penalty rule's application to clauses requiring the breaching promisor to transfer property of 'money's worth' (at [157] and [230]).

breach'.[490] Therefore, if a clause's effect (not merely its form[491]) is to 'define the primary obligations of the parties... the penalty rule will not apply', because it is 'not a proper function of the penalty rule to empower the courts to review the fairness of the parties' primary obligations'.[492]

271. However, it is not clear why parties' freedom of contract should be more constrained with respect to their secondary obligations than their primary obligations. Both the moral case for recognising freedom of contract and the moral case for constraining it in some circumstances surely apply with equal force to primary and secondary obligations alike. The Supreme Court provided no intellectually satisfying answer for why the law treats primary and secondary obligations differently in this respect.

B. *What makes a Clause 'Penal'?*

272. Much twentieth century case law assumed a clause providing for the payment of a sum on breach of contract to be a penalty clause if it could not be considered a genuine pre-estimate of the losses likely to be suffered by the innocent party as a result of breach.[493] However, recent jurisprudence has preferred a more flexible approach, sensitive to commercial reasonableness of clauses designed to do something other than compensate the victim of a breach.[494] The Supreme Court has

490. *Cavendish Square Holding BV v. Talal El Makdessi* and *ParkingEye Ltd v. Beavis* [2015] UKSC 67, [2015] 3 WLR 1373, [13]. The court acknowledged (at [14]) that restricting the penalty rule to clauses affecting secondary obligations allows it to be sidestepped by building extravagant deterrents into the parties' *primary* obligations instead of their secondary obligations. Nonetheless the court declined to follow the High Court of Australia's controversial decision in *Andrews v. Australia and New Zealand Banking Group Ltd* [2012] HCA 12, in which it asserted an equitable jurisdiction to relieve against onerous provisions contingent on occurrences other than breach. Particularly, it was thought improper judicially to extend a doctrine that interferes with freedom of contract.

491. *Cavendish Square Holding BV v. Talal El Makdessi* and *ParkingEye Ltd v. Beavis* [2015] UKSC 67, [2015] 3 WLR 1373, [15].

492. *Cavendish Square Holding BV v. Talal El Makdessi* and *ParkingEye Ltd v. Beavis* [2015] UKSC 67, [2015] 3 WLR 1373, [73]. Clauses that alter certain primary obligations on breach of other primary obligations show the distinction between primary and secondary obligations to be perilously thin. Classifying such a clause is liable to be teleological, influenced strongly by whether a judge thinks it should ultimately be regarded as penal.

493. The dichotomy – which Lord Hodge described as a 'straightjacket' at [225] – was attributed to a misreading of the speech of Lord Dunedin in *Dunlop Pneumatic Tyre Co Ltd v. New Garage & Motor Co Ltd* [1915] AC 79.

494. *Murray v. Leisureplay Plc* [2005] EWCA Civ 963, [2005] IRLR 946, especially [105], per Clarke LJ, and [118], per Buxton LJ. Here, the Court of Appeal stressed the importance of the commercial context in upholding a clause requiring payment in excess of damages recoverable at common law, even where there would have been no undue difficulty in assessing those damages in advance. This decision was approved in *Cavendish Square Holding BV v. Talal El Makdessi* and *ParkingEye Ltd v. Beavis* [2015] UKSC 67, [2015] 3 WLR 1373, [150], per Lord Mance

finally rejected the traditional assumption,[495] reasoning that 'commercial interests may justify the imposition upon a breach of contract of a financial burden which cannot... be related directly to loss caused by the breach',[496] and has little to do with compensation for loss.[497]

273. Lords Neuberger and Sumption held that a clause could be commercially justified even though intended to deter – although not *punish* – breach.[498] The party seeking to enforce a deterrent clause must, however, show 'a legitimate interest in performance extending beyond the prospect of pecuniary compensation flowing directly from the breach'.[499] Lords Neuberger, Sumption and Mance considered relevant not only the claimant's own interests in promoting compliance, but also those of parties with whom the claimant enjoyed an independent contractual relationship.[500]

274. It seems that a deterrent clause can be (prima facie) legitimated by the general social utility of the enterprise in question, which places an enormous burden on parties alleging a clause to be penal. According to Lords Neuberger and Sumption, a clause is penal if the deterrent is 'out of all proportion' to the claimant's legitimate interests in securing performance.[501] Lord Toulson thought it 'impossible to lay down abstract rules' for what this test in practice requires, 'because it depends on the particular facts'.[502] Lord Hodge admitted that 'ultimately [it is] a value judgment for the court'.[503]

275. In light of this decision, a clause intended to *punish* breach of contract remains penal, and therefore unenforceable, because punishment is not a legitimate

495. *Cavendish Square Holding BV v. Talal El Makdessi* and *ParkingEye Ltd v. Beavis* [2015] UKSC 67, [2015] 3 WLR 1373, [31], per Lords Neuberger and Sumption.
496. *Cavendish Square Holding BV v. Talal El Makdessi* and *ParkingEye Ltd v. Beavis* [2015] UKSC 67, [2015] 3 WLR 1373, [145].
497. *Cavendish Square Holding BV v. Talal El Makdessi* and *ParkingEye Ltd v. Beavis* [2015] UKSC 67, [2015] 3 WLR 1373, [152], per Lord Mance.
498. *Cavendish Square Holding BV v. Talal El Makdessi* and *ParkingEye Ltd v. Beavis* [2015] UKSC 67, [2015] 3 WLR 1373, [28].
499. *Cavendish Square Holding BV v. Talal El Makdessi* and *ParkingEye Ltd v. Beavis* [2015] UKSC 67, [2015] 3 WLR 1373, [28], per Lords Neuberger and Sumption. Lord Hodge thought that the court must examine 'the legitimate interests, *commercial or otherwise*, which the innocent party has sought to protect' (at [44]). However, all the interests the court identified in approving the deterrent clauses in *Cavendish* and *ParkingEye* were commercial, and only Lord Hodge hinted that non-commercial interests may have relevance.
500. According to Lord Mance, the parking charge was non-penal because it was 'an understandable ingredient of a *scheme serving legitimate interests*': *Cavendish Square Holding BV v. Talal El Makdessi* and *ParkingEye Ltd v. Beavis* [2015] UKSC 67, [2015] 3 WLR 1373, [199].
501. *Cavendish Square Holding BV v. Talal El Makdessi* and *ParkingEye Ltd v. Beavis* [2015] UKSC 67, [2015] 3 WLR 1373, [32].
502. *Cavendish Square Holding BV v. Talal El Makdessi* and *ParkingEye Ltd v. Beavis* [2015] UKSC 67, [2015] 3 WLR 1373, [293].
503. *Cavendish Square Holding BV v. Talal El Makdessi* and *ParkingEye Ltd v. Beavis* [2015] UKSC 67, [2015] 3 WLR 1373, [287].

interest.[504] However, if the clause is intended merely to *deter* breach, it will be non-penal if its severity is proportionate to a legitimate interest in incentivising performance.[505]

V. Arbitration Clauses

276. At common law, the court in principle had an inherent jurisdiction to stay actions brought in contravention of a contractual undertaking to settle disputes other than through litigation,[506] but the law nonetheless remained in many ways hostile to contractual arbitration clauses.

277. Predictably, the court would not respect a contractual arbitration clause[507] if it considered the contract itself to be contrary to public policy and unenforceable on that basis, any more than the court would enforce a direct action for breach of such a contract.[508] However, the common law subjected arbitration clause to particular scrutiny even where the contract was otherwise unobjectionable and enforceable. The common law maintained that a clause was contrary to public policy – and unenforceable – if it purported to oust the court's inherent jurisdiction to adjudicate on legal disputes.

278. In principle, a clause would be upheld if no more than an undertaking between the parties that they would attempt to resolve their disputes through arbitration *prior* to litigating. Such clauses were understood not as ousting the court's jurisdiction over legal disputes, but as defining the point at which a cause of action arose under the contract.[509] The clause therefore would not prevent a court adjudicating an action for breach brought in defiance of the arbitration clause, but bringing such an action would itself constitute a breach of contract, for which the defendant could bring a successful counterclaim.[510]

279. Conversely, clauses would not be enforced if their putative effect was to exclude the court's jurisdiction to review an arbitrator's decision for errors of law,[511] or to undermine such review, for instance by permitting arbitrators to decide according

504. *Cavendish Square Holding BV v. Talal El Makdessi* and *ParkingEye Ltd v. Beavis* [2015] UKSC 67, [2015] 3 WLR 1373, [32], per Lords Neuberger and Sumption.

505. Establishing the purpose of the clause is not subject to the parol evidence rule. The parties can adduce evidence of pre-contractual negotiations, and the understanding of the term in question subjectively held by the parties: *Dunlop Pneumatic Tyre Co Ltd v. New Garage & Motor Co Ltd* [1915] AC 79, 81 and 92, per Lord Atkinson; *Clydebank Engineering and Shipbuilding Co Ltd v. Yzquierdo y Castaneda* [1905] AC 6. In *Robophone Facilities Ltd v. Blank* [1966] 1 WLR 1468, external factors such as the state of the market for telephone rentals was considered material to the characterisation of the clause.

506. *Channel Tunnel Group Ltd v. Balfour Beatty Construction Ltd* [1993] AC 334.

507. Nor a putative arbitral award under it: *Soleimany v. Soleimany* [1999] QB 785, 799.

508. *Soleimany v. Soleimany* [1999] QB 785, 797.

509. *Scott v. Avery* (1855) 5 HLC 811.

510. *Doleman & Sons v. Osset Corporation* [1912] 3 KB 257, 267.

511. *Czarnikow v. Roth Schmidt & Co* [1922] 2 KB 478. Clauses declaring arbitrators' awards to be 'final' or 'conclusive' may not prevent review of the decision for error of law: *Jones v. Sherwood Computer Services* [1992] 1 WLR 227.

to something other than law, such as their own conceptions of what was fair or practical.[512]

280. Statute has intervened in the common law rules, in order to expand the parties' freedom 'to agree how their disputes are to be resolved', subject to 'such safeguards as are necessary in the public interest'.[513] The Arbitration Act 1996 preserves the court's power to decline to recognise an arbitral award on public policy grounds,[514] but generally requires a court to stay proceedings brought in contravention of an arbitration agreement, provided this was concluded in written form,[515] and is not for whatever reason 'void...or incapable of being performed'.[516] In a change to the common law rule, the Act requires the court to stay proceedings even if the claimant seeks summary judgment on the grounds that the claim advanced is beyond dispute, admitting of no realistic defence.[517]

281. The Act permits the parties to exclude by agreement the court's jurisdiction to review arbitrators' decisions for errors of law.[518] The court retains the power to hear appeals from arbitral awards on points of law,[519] but this requires either the consent of both parties or the permission of the court,[520] and is anyway possible only on satisfaction of several statutory requirements.[521]

282. The appeal must relate to a point of law that (i) the arbitrator was actually required to decide and (ii) will substantially affect the rights of one or both of the parties. The arbitrator's decision on this question must either have been 'obviously wrong', or must at least be 'open to serious doubt' and moreover raising an issue of 'general public importance'. It must, moreover, be 'just and proper for the court to determine the question' notwithstanding the fact that the parties themselves preferred the issue to remain with the arbitrator. A particularly influential consideration is the extent to which having the issue authoritatively decided by the court 'would add significantly to the clarity and certainty of English commercial law'.[522] This is most likely where the issue is a generally important question of contract law doctrine,[523] or

512. *Home and Overseas Insurance Co Ltd v. Mentor Insurance Co (UK) Ltd* [1989] 1 Lloyd's Rep 473, 485. However, clauses could validly empower arbitrators to interpret the contractual language other than based on strict legal canons of construction: *Home and Overseas Insurance Co Ltd v. Mentor Insurance Co (UK) Ltd* [1989] 1 Lloyd's Rep 473. Sometimes the court would salvage arbitration clauses by severing the aspects that purported to free arbitrators to reason and decide other than according to law: *Home Insurance Co v. Administrata Asigurarilor* [1983] 2 Lloyd's Rep 674, 677.
513. Arbitration Act 1996, s. 1(b).
514. Arbitration Act 1996, s. 81(1)(c). The central case might be an award whose effect was to enforce a contract the court considered offensive to the illegality rule.
515. Arbitration Act 1996, s. 5(1).
516. Arbitration Act 1996, s. 9(4).
517. *Halki Shipping Corporation v. Sopex Oils Ltd* [1998] 1 WLR 726.
518. Arbitration Act 1996, ss. 45(1) and 69(1).
519. Arbitration Act 1996, s. 69.
520. Arbitration Act 1996, s. 69(2).
521. Arbitration Act 1996, s. 69(3).
522. *Pioneer Shipping Ltd v. BTP Tioxide Ltd (The Nema)* [1982] AC 724, 743.
523. *Clea Shipping Corporation v. Bulk Oil International Ltd (The Alaskan Trader)* [1983] 1 Lloyd's Rep 315.

the determination of the case requires the interpretation of a standard form industry contract,[524] or the facts giving rise to the dispute are likely to affect a large number of commercial contracts.[525]

283. A written arbitration clause does not bind a consumer claiming against a defendant who acted in the course of business,[526] unless that consumer is claiming more than GBP 5,000.[527] The clause will, however, bind the party who contracted in the course of business. Other statutes render arbitration clauses unenforceable in certain contexts.[528]

§2. Interpretation

284. English law has largely – but not entirely – abandoned technical rules of construction in favour of a unified and contextual approach to the interpretation of contracts. Old, discrete 'canons' of interpretation were largely unworked by a succession of influential decisions, culminating in a holistic 'Restatement' of the principles of contract interpretation at the hands of Lord Hoffmann. In the important case of *Investors Compensation Scheme v. West Bromwich Building Society*, Lord Hoffmann identified a 'fundamental change' that had occurred in the law of contract interpretation,[529] the result of which had been to 'assimilate the way in which [contracts] are interpreted by judges to the common sense principles by which any serious utterance would be interpreted in ordinary life'.

285. The consequence of this change was the abandonment of the old, formalistic rules that had dictated the courts' approach to the interpretation of particular kinds of contractual term. To interpret a contract is in principle simply to deduce 'what the parties using those words against the relevant background would reasonably have been understood to mean'. Crucially, the court does not seek the understanding that the parties subjectively held at the time of contracting, but 'the meaning which the instrument would convey to a reasonable person having all the background knowledge which would reasonably be available to the audience to whom the instrument is addressed'.[530]

286. To arrive at this meaning, the contract is interpreted in light of the 'absolutely anything which would have affected the way in which the language of the document would have been interpreted by a reasonable man', provided this would have been

524. *Italmare Shipping Co v. Ocean Tanker Co Inc (The Rio Sun)* [1981] 2 Lloyd's Rep 489.
525. *Pioneer Shipping Ltd v. BTP Tioxide Ltd (The Nema)* [1982] AC 724.
526. Arbitration Act 1996, ss. 89–91 (as amended by Consumer Rights Act 2015, sch. 4, paras 30–33). Consumers in this context can be legal or human persons.
527. Arbitration Act 1996, s. 91; Unfair Arbitration Agreements (Specified Amounts) Order 1999 (SI 1999/2167).
528. Employment Rights Act 1996, s. 203; Equality Act 2010, s. 144.
529. *Investors Compensation Scheme Ltd v. West Bromwich Building Society* [1998] 1 WLR 896, 912.
530. *Attorney General of Belize v. Belize Telecom Ltd* [2009] 1 WLR 1988, [16], per Lord Hoffmann. In that sense the interpretation of contract terms is intrinsically linked with questions of contract formation: on what terms, if any, are the parties deemed to have entered a binding legal contract?

reasonably available to the parties.[531] Particularly relevant will be the commercial context, in light of the law's 'shift from literal methods of interpretation towards a more commercial approach'.[532]

287. Courts will resolve ambiguity in the contractual language in line with the more commercially sensible multiple possible interpretations.[533] This preference accords with a focus on the parties' intentions, since 'a commercial construction is more likely to give effect to the intention of the parties'.[534] Sensitivity to the background and the commercial context in which the contract was agreed may in rare cases mean that the text is held to mean something other than what its language would mean if taken in isolation; the process of interpretation 'does not require judges to attribute to the parties an intention which they plainly could not have had'.[535] However, this will occur only rarely, since the law assumes that contracting parties do not generally fail to express their meaning in words.[536]

288. Connected with the idea of interpretation as focused on the parties' reasonable understanding of the agreement is that rule that courts cannot *alter* the substance of the contract to make it more commercially sensible,[537] even when the alternative is an absurd outcome, if they find that the term in question is unambiguous.[538]

289. However, courts sometimes stray from resolving ambiguity in favour of commercial common sense into transparent attempts to doctor the agreement to promote its effectiveness. In *Schuler v. Wickman Machine Tool Sales*, Lord Reid considered that: '[t]he more unreasonable the result the more unlikely it is that the parties can have intended it, and if they do intend it the more necessary it is that they shall make that intention abundantly clear'.[539] In this case, the clear meaning of the contractual language entailed a degree of liability 'so unreasonable that it must make me search for some other possible meaning of the contract'. Lord Reid would acknowledge the literal meaning of the contractual language 'only if that is the only possible interpretation'.[540] For Lord Wilberforce in dissent, to suggest the clause in question was unreasonable was 'to assume, contrary to the evidence, that both parties to this contract adopted a

531. *Investors Compensation Scheme Ltd v. West Bromwich Building Society* [1998] 1 WLR 896, per Lord Hoffmann.
532. *Sirius International v. FAI Insurance Ltd* [2004] UKHL 54, [19], per Lord Steyn.
533. *Rainy Sky SA v. Kookmin Bank* [2011] UKSC 50, [2011] 1 WLR 2900; *Arnold v. Britton* [2015] UKSC 36, [2015] AC 1619.
534. *Manai Investment Co Ltd v. Eagle Star Life Assurance Co Ltd* [1997] AC 749, 771, per Lord Steyn.
535. *Investors Compensation Scheme Ltd v. West Bromwich Building Society* [1998] 1 WLR 896, per Lord Hoffmann.
536. *Investors Compensation Scheme Ltd v. West Bromwich Building Society* [1998] 1 WLR 896, 912, per Lord Hoffmann.
537. *Megaro v. Di Popolo Hotels Ltd* [2007] EWCA Civ 309, [2007] All ER (D) 210, [19] per Chadwick LJ.
538. *Skansa Rashleigh Weatherfoil Ltd v. Somerfield Stores Ltd* [2006] EWCA Civ 1732, [2007] CILL 2449 at [21] per Neuberger LJ.
539. *Schuler AG v. Wickman Machine Tool Sales Ltd* [1974] AC 235.
540. Other authorities also expressly suggest manipulating language into a commercially sensible construction where its natural construction means a commercially perverse result: *Antios Compania Naviera SA v. Salen Referierna AB* [1985] AC 191, 201, per Lord Diplock.

standard of easygoing tolerance rather than one of aggressive, insistent punctuality and efficiency'.

290. The recent Supreme Court decision in *Arnold v. Britton* demonstrates the enduring ideological division among judges on this issue.[541] In that case, a literal reading of the contract term in question led to a result that was commercially perverse and highly disadvantageous for one party. However, the majority of the Supreme Court emphasised that the meaning of the contract is fixed at the moment of formation, and the process of interpretation therefore must not be influenced by the court's awareness of subsequent events. Although the term in question led to commercially unpalatable results in the circumstances that in fact transpired, its meaning and role in the parties' contractual relationship was clear, and there was no inherent ambiguity to resolve. The majority denied outright any judicial power to *seek out* ambiguity in order to prefer a commercially sensible interpretation. Lord Carnwath in dissent felt that the court had interpretive flexibility unless the contractual language was insurmountably unambiguous.

291. Although the law generally interprets in light of all the contextual knowledge available to the parties at the time of contracting, this is subject to an important exception, namely the parol evidence rule. The parties can neither adduce evidence of their pre-contractual negotiations to affect the interpretation of the contract, nor of their own subjective understandings of the text at the time of contract formation.[542] This exception arises out of judicial policy, not legal principle.[543]

292. In light of Lord Hoffmann's 'Restatement' of the rules of interpretation in *Investors Compensation Scheme v. West Bromwich Building Society*, the law has generally ceased to treat particular categories of contract terms as subject to distinct

541. *Arnold v. Britton* [2015] UKSC 36, [2015] AC 1619.
542. *Investors Compensation Scheme Ltd v. West Bromwich Building Society* [1998] 1 WLR 896, 912–913, per Lord Hoffmann; *Chartbrook Ltd v. Persimmon Homes Ltd* [2009] UKHL 38, [2009] 1 AC 1101. Here, the House of Lords refused to depart from the general rule that evidence of pre-contractual negotiations is inadmissible when seeking to interpret a contract, even in light of the principle that interpretation is an exercise in establishing the meaning that the reasonable persons in the position of the parties would have taken in light of all the context that was or ought to have been known to the parties (*Investors Compensation Scheme Ltd v. West Bromwich Building Society* [1998] 1 WLR 896). However, the parol evidence rule does not exclude reliance on pre-contractual negotiations in order to establish that a fact which may be relevant as background was known to the parties at the time of contracting, or to support a claim for rectification or estoppel by convention.
543. The standard justification for this exception is an appeal to the importance of legal certainty. *See* for example *Shogun Finance v. Hudson* [2003] UKHL 62, [2004] 1 AC 919, [49], per Lord Hobhouse: 'The rule that other evidence may not be adduced to contradict the provisions of a contract contained in a written document is fundamental to the mercantile law of this country; the bargain is the document; the certainty of the contract depends on it...This rule is one of the great strengths of English commercial law and is one of the main reasons for the international success of English law in preference to laxer systems which do not provide the same certainty.'

interpretive approaches, a position reiterated in the Supreme Court's decision in *Arnold v. Britton*.[544]

293. Some remnants of the older approach have remained, with courts sometimes insisting that particularly explicit language is required before a party will be held to have surrendered legal rights.[545] A party who seeks to exclude certain liabilities, such as for misrepresentation, 'cannot be mealy-mouthed' but must instead 'bring it home that he is limiting his liability for falsehoods'.[546] Nonetheless the Court of Appeal has recently emphasised that, at least in commercial contracts between parties of equal bargaining power, exclusion clauses should be understood as part of the freely negotiated allocation of risk, and therefore interpreted naturally without artificial levels of strictness.[547]

544. In *Arnold v. Britton* [2015] UKSC 36, [2015] AC 1619, Lord Neuberger refused to regard service charges as having any special rule of interpretation. The court must award contracts the meaning they would have conveyed to the reasonable person in the position of the parties, at the time of contract formation.
545. *Bank of Credit and Commerce International v. Ali* [2002] 1 AC 251, [10], per Lord Bingham: 'in the absence of clear language, the court will be very slow to infer that a party intended to surrender rights and claims of which he was unaware and could not have been aware'. This is despite *dicta* to the effect that courts should not strain the rules of interpretation in order to permit oblique control of contractual freedom (for example *Photo Production Ltd v. Securicor Ltd* [1980] AC 827, 851). Cf Lord Hoffmann (*Bank of Credit and Commerce International v. Ali* [2002] 1 AC 251,[38] and [55]) in dissent, declining to read down the natural meaning of the term in question in service to an artificial 'rule of construction' aimed at protecting rights. Such would be justified only 'if it is necessary to remedy a widespread injustice' ([60]).
546. *Thomas Witter Ltd v. TBP Industries Ltd* [1996] 2 All ER 573, 595–96, Jacob J. The clarity required successfully to exclude a particular liability seems to be proportional to the onerousness of the exclusion, including the severity of the breaches for which it purports to exclude liability: *Photo Production Ltd v. Securicor Ltd* [1980] AC 827, 850.
547. *Persimmon Homes Ltd v. Ove Arup & Partners Ltd* [2017] EWCA Civ 373.

Chapter 4. Privity of Contract

§1. The Rule of Privity of Contract

I. Third Parties and the Contract

294. The creation of a contract can in some ways affect the private law rights and obligations of people other than the contracting parties. For instance, there is liability in tort for intentionally and without reasonable justification inducing another to breach a contract of which the tortfeasor is aware.[548] It is also possible that a contract party will owe duties to a third party in tort as a result of having undertaken to provide contracted services.[549]

295. However, no one can be subject to *contractual* obligations by virtue of any contract to which she is not a party. Traditionally, English law also maintained that third parties could never enforce the terms of a contract concluded between others, even when the contracting parties had intended that a particular third party should have the right to enforce their agreement.[550] This was described as a 'fundamental' aspect of English contract law in *Dunlop Pneumatic Tyre v. Selfridge*, when the House of Lords insisted that 'only a person who is a party to the contract can sue on it'.[551]

296. Although there are no true exceptions to the privity rule at common law, there exist several methods of circumventing its effects, giving third parties causes of action in other ways. A promisee could undertake an identical obligation in favour of the third party in the form of a deed, enforceable notwithstanding the absence of consideration. The parties could also enter collateral contracts with the third party intended to be able to enforce the terms contained in the parties' own agreement. In

548. *Lumley v. Gye* (1852) 2 El & Bl 216, 118 ER 749; *OBG Ltd v. Allan* [2007] UKHL 21, [2008] 1 AC 1.

549. *White v. Jones* [1995] 2 AC 207.

550. *Tweddle v. Atkinson* (1861) 1 B & S 393, 121 ER 762. Here, a man's father and father-in-law agreed that the father-in-law should give a sum of money to the young man in question, stating that the young man should have the right to sue either of the two parties. The son consented to this arrangement. After the father-in-law's death, the young man sued his executor to enforce the agreement. The court declared the young man unable to enforce the promise.

551. *Dunlop Pneumatic Tyre Co Ltd v. Selfridge & Co Ltd* [1915] AC 847, 853, per Lord Dunedin. This rule was powerfully reiterated in, for example, *Scruttons Ltd v. Midland Silicones Ltd* [1962] AC 446; *NZ Shipping Co Ltd v. A M Satterthwaite & Co Ltd (The Eurymedon)* [1975] AC 154, 166; *White v. Jones* [1995] 2 AC 207, 252, 266. The position was less certain before the nineteenth century: *see* for example *Dutton v. Poole* (1678) 2 Lev 210; *Martyn v. Hind* (1776) Cowp 437. For an exploration of the development of the privity rule, *see* V Palmer, *The Paths to Privity: the History of Third Party Beneficiaries in English Law* (Austin & Winfield, 1992).

some cases third parties have been awarded actions in tort that are tantamount to a right to enforce the contract in question.[552]

297. It is also possible to create a trust of the promisee's cause of action in favour of the third party. Here, the promisee holds the right to sue on the contract as a trustee for the third party, and may be compelled in equity to exercise this in order to enforce the promisor's undertaking.[553] The promisee sues for the losses suffered by the third-party beneficiary, for whom the damages will be held on trust. However, for the courts to recognise a trust of the promise, there must have been an express and irrevocable intention to create one.[554] The court will not infer an intention to create a trust of the promise merely from the parties' shared intention that a third party should benefit under the contract.[555]

298. Where there is a trust of the promise, the contracting parties cannot alter the terms of the contract without the consent of the third-party beneficiary.[556] If the third-party beneficiary sues the promisee for breach of trust for failing to enforce the contract at law against the promisor, the action is unaffected by defences that the promisor would have been able to raise against the promisee, such as exclusion clauses in the contract.

A. The Case for Reform

299. The privity rule attracted increased hostility as the prevailing understanding of the basis for contractual liability changed from bargain to intention. Where contracting parties intended their agreement to be enforceable by a third party, many reasoned that third-party enforcement should be permitted.[557]

300. There was also a widespread impression that the privity rule caused injustice to third parties, since a third party with an expectation of receiving a benefit under a contract would have no remedy if the promisee were unwilling or unable to sue the defaulting promisor. In *Beswick v. Beswick*, a husband contracted with his nephew that, after the husband's death, the nephew would provide regular payments to support his widow. The husband died and his unscrupulous nephew stopped the payments to the widow, who sued the nephew to enforce the contract made in her favour between the nephew and her late husband. The House of Lords, with some reluctance and implicit support for reform,[558] ruled that a third party, even one that the contract was concluded specifically to benefit, was unable to enforce the contract.[559] Many believed

552. *White v. Jones* [1995] 2 AC 207. In this case compensatory damages in tort in effect awarded the third party's expectation.
553. In some instances the third-party beneficiary can bring an action directly in the trustee's name: *Vandepitte v. Preferred Accident Insurance Corporation of New York* [1933] AC 70, 79.
554. *In re Sinclair's Life Policy* [1938] 3 All ER 124.
555. *In re Schebsman* [1944] Ch 83.
556. This is one reason that the use of trusts of the promise survives the radical relaxation of the privity rule in the Contracts (Rights of Third Parties) Act 199; it gives the third party rights even stronger than those bestowed under the Act.
557. *Darlington Borough Council v. Wiltshier Northern Ltd* [1995] 1 WLR 68, 76, per Steyn LJ.
558. *See* particularly the speech of Lord Reid.
559. Luckily for Mrs Beswick, she was also the administratrix of her husband's estate, and was able to enforce the contracts he had made before death in this special capacity.

the privity rule meant injustice for third parties with 'reasonable expectations of having the legal right to enforce the contract'.[560]

301. However, it is not clear that it is 'reasonable' for a third party to expect the power to enforce another's contract, in light of a (formerly) firm rule that only the supply of valuable consideration gives one the right to enforce another's future undertakings.[561] A more compelling criticism of the privity rule was that, where the whole purpose of the contract was the conferral of a benefit on a third party, it produced a lacunae in liability. A defaulting promisor would escape liability because the person with the cause of action would suffer no substantial loss, so would recover only nominal damages, while the party suffering substantial loss would have no standing to sue.[562]

302. However, the privity rule makes irresistible doctrinal sense in a system of contract law that demands consideration for the enforcement of others' undertakings. Indeed, privity is more a manifestation of the consideration rule than a freestanding doctrine in its own right.[563] Their symbiosis is revealed in the *ratio* of leading decisions.[564] The doctrine of consideration dictates that the right to hold another to an undertaking must be *purchased* from him in a negotiated exchange. It therefore tells the third party that she cannot sue the promisor, because she has not bought the right to sue him. Privity, ultimately, tells the third party the very same thing. While the right to sue the promisor has been bought, it has not been bought by the person who now seeks to compel the promisor to perform his undertaking.

303. As discussed below, statutory reform has largely abolished the classical rule on privity of contract in England and Wales. However, in light of the enduring requirement of consideration, it is incoherent to award enforcement rights to third parties. It is inexplicable that third parties, who have provided no consideration with

560. A Burrows, 'Reforming privity of contract: Law Commission Report No. 242'(1996) Lloyd's Maritime and Commercial Law Quarterly 467, 468.

561. R Stevens, 'The Contracts (Rights of Third Parties) Act 1999' (2004) 120 LQR 292, 296.

562. However, the problem here could have been addressed by reform of the law of damages, rather than privity, for instance by allowing the promisee to recover substantial losses on the third party's behalf.

563. Some commentators insist that consideration and privity can be disentangled: 'A father might, for example, promise his daughter to pay GBP 1,000 to anyone who married her. A man who married the daughter with knowledge of and in reliance on such a promise might provide consideration for it, but could not enforce it, as it was not addressed to him.': E Peel, Treitel on the Law of Contract (14th ed), (Sweet & Maxwell, 2015), 699. However, if the promise was not addressed to the groom, he *cannot provide consideration* in the legally meaningful sense (a thing of legal value *moving from the promisee*) because he is *not the promisee*; this is not a case of a unilateral offer made to all young men, capable of acceptance by performing the requested action of marrying the daughter, but rather a promise *to the daughter*, which no one but the daughter can accept and for which no one but the daughter can provide consideration in the true sense.

564. *Tweddle v. Atkinson* (1861) 1 B & S 393, 121 ER 762, per Crompton J: the son cannot enforce the contract between his father and father-in-law because he was a 'stranger to the consideration', which 'must move from the party entitled to sue upon the contract.' In other words, one becomes a party to a contract *by providing consideration*. If someone wishes to enforce an informal contract, 'consideration must have been given by him to the promisor or to some other person at the promisor's request': *Dunlop Pneumatic Tyre Co Ltd v. Selfridge & Co Ltd* [1915] AC 847, 853, per Viscount Haldane.

which to buy the promisor's undertaking, can enforce an undertaking that the *promisee himself* would not be able to enforce if he provided no consideration in return. The framers of the reform acknowledge the tension with the doctrine of consideration,[565] and hint that it should be resolved by the abolition of the doctrine of consideration itself.[566]

II. Contracts for the Benefit of a Third Party

304. Despite sustained judicial hostility to the doctrine of privity, judges typically considered it so fundamental to English contract law that only legislation could legitimately reform it.[567] That legislative intervention has now materialised, in the form of a 'general and wide-ranging exception' to privity.[568]

305. Following the recommendation of the Law Commission,[569] Parliament enacted the Contracts (Rights of Third parties) Act 1999. This statute enables a third party to enforce terms of the contract 'in his own right' where certain requirements are satisfied.[570] This includes the ability to invoke an exclusion clause contained in the contract to defend against a claim by one of the contract parties.[571] The Act does not affect burden privity, and parties remain unable by contract alone to impose binding obligations on third parties.

306. A third party can enforce a specific contract term if (a) the contract 'expressly provides that he may',[572] or (b) 'the term purports to confer a benefit on him'.[573] This second limb is subject to a caveat; it will not apply if 'on a proper construction of the contract it appears that the parties did not intend the term to be enforceable by the third party'.[574] The second limb thus creates a rebuttable presumption that the parties intended a third party to be able to enforce a term that purports to confer a benefit on

565. A Burrows, 'Reforming privity of contract: Law Commission Report No. 242'(1996) Lloyd's Maritime and Commercial Law Quarterly 467, 483; Law Commission Report No. 242, [6.17].
566. A Burrows, 'Reforming privity of contract: Law Commission Report No. 242'(1996) Lloyd's Maritime and Commercial Law Quarterly 467, 468.
567. *Scruttons Ltd v. Midland Silicones Ltd* [1962] AC 446, 473, per Lord Reid. There was, however, increasing judicial willingness to attack the doctrine of privity: *Beswick v. Beswick* [1968] AC 58, 72, per Lord Reid; *Woodar Investment Development Ltd v. Wimpey Construction UK Ltd* [1980] 1 WLR 277, 300, per Lord Scarman.
568. Law Commission Report No. 242, [5.16]. *See also* A Burrows, 'Reforming privity of contract: Law Commission Report No. 242'(1996) Lloyd's Maritime and Commercial Law Quarterly 467, 484. However, the Act's effect has been referred to as the abolition of the privity doctrine in leading judicial dicta; *Alfred McAlpine Construction Ltd v. Panatown Ltd* [2001] 1 AC 518, 544, per Lord Goff.
569. Law Commission Report No. 242. This followed an earlier unsuccessful attempt at initiating legislative dilution of the privity rule in 1937 (Law Revision Committee's Sixth Interim Report, Cmd. 5449, s. D).
570. Contracts (Rights of Third Parties) Act 1999, s. 1(1).
571. Contracts (Rights of Third Parties) Act 1999, s. 1(6).
572. Contracts (Rights of Third Parties) Act 1999, s. 1(1)(a).
573. Contracts (Rights of Third Parties) Act 1999, s. 1(1)(b).
574. Contracts (Rights of Third Parties) Act 1999, s. 1(2).

her.[575] Importantly, the Act does not give enforcement rights to third parties who suffer loss due to a breach of the term in question if that term is not such as to confer a benefit on the third party if performed.

307. It is not clear what exactly is required before a term is deemed to 'confer a benefit' on a third party. The cases adopt differing approaches. In *Prudential Assurance v. Ayres*,[576] Lindsay J interpreted this as essentially a factual question. The presumption would be engaged if the effect of the term was the conferral of a benefit on the third party, whether or not this was the sole or even predominant purpose of the contract. The third party need not be the only person to benefit from the performance of the term in question. But in *Dolphin Maritime & Aviation Services v. Sveriges Angfartygs Assurans Forening*,[577] the court held that a term does not 'purport to confer a benefit' on a third party simply because that party will benefit from its performance. The language of 'conferral' suggests that the benefit to a third party must have been one of the purposes of the parties' agreement, and not merely an incidental consequence of performance.[578]

308. Authoritative settlement of the issue in the Supreme Court is anxiously awaited. When drafting contracts, it is presently safest to assume that a term will be prima facie enforceable by third parties that stand to derive even incidental benefits from its performance, and therefore expressly to exclude such enforcement rights.

309. If the presumption of third-party enforceability is engaged, it is difficult to rebut. The Law Commissioner responsible for the Act anticipated that it would usually be rebutted only by an express term in the contract that was inconsistent with the third party having the right to enforce.[579] Neutrality as to third-party enforcement will not be sufficient to rebut the presumption.[580]

310. The third party must be 'expressly identified in the contract by name, as a member of a class or as answering a particular description'.[581] However, there is no need for the third party to be in existence at the time the contract is formed. The Act therefore includes human persons born (or legal persons incorporated) after the contract was made,[582] provided such persons are suitably identified in the contract.

311. The contracting parties can remove or vary the third party's rights, but this will require the third party's consent if she has communicated her assent to the original terms, or has relied on the original terms, provided the promisor actually knew of this reliance or could reasonably have foreseen it.[583] However, the contract may provide

575. The Act does not give third parties the right to enforce the contract *as a whole* third-party enforceability is assessed discretely for each individual term.
576. *Prudential Assurance Co Ltd v. David Monroe Ayres & Christopher Grew* [2007] EWHC 775 (Ch), [2007] All ER (D) 43.
577. *Dolphin Maritime & Aviation Services Ltd v. Sveriges Angfartygs Assurans Forening* [2009] EWHC 716 (Comm), [2009] 2 Lloyd's Rep 123.
578. *Dolphin Maritime & Aviation Services Ltd v. Sveriges Angfartygs Assurans Forening* [2009] EWHC 716 (Comm), [2009] 2 Lloyd's Rep 123, per Christopher Clarke J.
579. A Burrows, 'Reforming privity of contract: Law Commission Report No. 242' (1996) Lloyd's Maritime and Commercial Law Quarterly 467, 473.
580. *Nisshin Shipping Co Ltd v. Cleaves & Co Ltd* [2003] EWHC 2602, [2004] 1 Lloyd's Rep 38.
581. Contracts (Rights of Third Parties) Act 1999, s. 1(3).
582. Contracts (Rights of Third Parties) Act 1999, s. 1(3).
583. Contracts (Rights of Third Parties) Act 1999, s. 2(1).

that the parties may vary or remove the third party's rights, notwithstanding communication of assent, or reliance.[584] In some circumstances, the court may also permit the parties to remove the third party's rights without her consent.[585]

312. The third party's own enforcement right is independent from that of the promisee, and does not remove the promisee's own right to enforce the promisor's obligations.[586] Likewise, the third party can sue even if the promisee has already sued the defaulting promisor for breach of the same term. However, where the third party sues the promisor for breach after the promisee has already sued for breach of the same term and recovered damages in respect of either (i) the third party's loss or (ii) the promisee's own costs incurred in making good the promisor's default to the third party, the court must reduce the third party's own damages 'to such extent as it thinks appropriate to take account of the sum recovered by the promisee'.[587] If the promisee's action against the promisor failed, then the third party's damages will not be reduced in this way.

313. This provision is intended to protect the promisor from double liability for the same breach. However, the language of the Act only requires the adjudicating court to reduce the third party's damages 'to such extent as it thinks appropriate'. It is therefore possible that the promisor's total liability after both actions will be greater than it would have been after a single action by the promisee alone. There is also a risk that this procedure leaves the third party under-compensated. Since both litigants (the promisee and the third party) will be suing for their own independent expectation interest, it makes little sense from a compensatory perspective to reduce one claimant's damages by reference to the other's.

314. Like the promisee's own action against the promisor, the third party's action is subject to other relevant contract terms, such as exclusion clauses and time bars.[588] It is also subject to the same ordinary rules of remoteness and mitigation. The third party has available to her any remedy that would have been available had she been a party to the contract.[589] In an action brought by the third party, the promisor can invoke any defence he would have had in an action brought by the promisee,[590] as well as any terms specifically dealing with claims by third parties.[591]

315. The Act does not affect any rights the third party in question might enjoy by virtue of one of the common law circumventions of the privity rule,[592] which continue to be widely used even in preference to enforcement rights available under the Contracts Act.

584. Contracts (Rights of Third Parties) Act 1999, s. 2(3).
585. Contracts (Rights of Third Parties) Act 1999, ss. 2(4) and 2(5).
586. Contracts (Rights of Third Parties) Act 1999, s. 4.
587. Contracts (Rights of Third Parties) Act 1999, s. 5. Reduction of the third party's damages is not triggered if the promisee sues successfully for specific performance of the promisor's obligations. However, where this occurs, the third party will have received the benefit of the contract, so will not be able to demonstrate any actionable loss.
588. Contracts (Rights of Third Parties) Act 1999, s. 1(4).
589. Contracts (Rights of Third Parties) Act 1999, s. 1(5).
590. Contracts (Rights of Third Parties) Act 1999, s. 3(2).
591. Contracts (Rights of Third Parties) Act 1999, s. 3(3).
592. Contracts (Rights of Third Parties) Act 1999, s. 7.

§2. Transfer of Contractual Rights

316. Parties can in principle transfer their contractual rights to others,[593] a process known as assignment, although they cannot assign their contractual obligations.[594] Assignment can occur voluntarily or by operation of law. For instance, on death, one's contract rights pass to personal representatives, who are able to sue for breach of these rights or recover sums due on any contracts to which the deceased was a party. The representatives may also perform outstanding executory obligations and claim the payment due.

317. Assignment is the transfer of an existing right, not the creation of a new one. Assignment does not alter the extent of the promisor's liability, but only to whom he is liable. The law imposes rules to prevent debtors being prejudiced by an assignment of the right held against them. For instance, assignees receive their rights subject to whatever claims at law or in equity subsisted against the assignor. The assignee will have the same remedies as the assignor would have had,[595] and her claims will be subject to any defences as would have existed against the assignor. An assignee cannot recover a greater quantum of damages than the assignor would have been able to recover.

318. The central means by which a promisee will assign her rights is a statutory mechanism provided by section 136(1) of the Law of Property Act 1925,[596] which provides that: 'Any absolute assignment by writing under the hand of the assignor... of any debt or other legal thing in action, of which express notice in writing has been given to the debtor...is effectual in law.' There is no need to provide consideration for the assignment.[597] Where assignment is successful, the assignee can sue the promisee in her own name; there is no need to join the assignor as co-claimant. It is possible to assign primary contract rights or only secondary ones.

319. The statutory reference to any 'other legal thing in action' is widely construed. It is possible to assign in this way legal rights arising other than under a contract, including rights generated by statute.[598] It includes rights other than to a sum of money,[599] and rights that the promisor will forbear from certain actions rather than perform certain actions.[600] Nonetheless it is not possible in this way to assign purely equitable rights, such as interests under a trust. Additionally assignment can only transfer rights currently in existence; it is impossible to 'assign' rights that will arise

593. Although generally not their contractual obligations: *Tito v. Waddell (No 2)* [1977] Ch 106, 291.

594. *See* for example *Linden Gardens Trust Ltd v. Lenesta Sludge Disposals Ltd* [1994] 1 AC 85, 103, per Lord Browne-Wilkinson. Cf novation, a process under which both the benefits and burden are transferred (although really this is the making of a new contract rather than the assignment of the rights and obligations under an existing one).

595. A claim for damages by the assignee will remedy his losses and not those of the assignor: *Dawson v. Great Northern and City Railway Company* [1905] 1 KB 260.

596. Largely replicating the earlier provision to this effect in Judicature Act 1873, s. 25(6). This itself replaced the old common law rules on legal assignment.

597. *Harding v. Harding* (1886) 17 QBD 442.

598. *Dawson v. Great Northern & City Railway* [1905] 1 KB 260.

599. *Torrington v. Magee* [1902] 2 KB 427.

600. *Jacoby v. Whitmore* (1883) 49 LT 335.

in the future, although an attempt to do so may constitute a contract to assign the right in question in the future, provided this undertaking satisfies the general rules for contract formation.

320. Assignment under section 136(1) is effective only if absolute, and not if the assignor purports to retain some interest in the substance of the contract.[601] This mechanism will therefore exclude a putative assignment of half of a debt.[602] Likewise assignment as a charge to secure a debt to the assignee may not be absolute.[603]

321. The promisor must be given notice in writing of the assignment. This need not come from the assignor, and may come from the assignee instead, but it is insufficient for the debtor to learn that a putative assignment has occurred through independent means.[604] Notice must be given before the action is brought against the promisor,[605] but not necessarily at the time of assignment.

322. Putative assignments that do not meet the criteria for statutory assignment may still operate as an equitable assignment. Equitable assignment of a purely equitable right – such as a beneficial interest under a trust – must be made in writing and signed by the assignor,[606] although equitable assignment of a right recognised at common law may be done orally.[607] The promisor must still be given notice of the assignment, but this may be merely oral.[608]

323. Contractual rights cannot be assigned either at law or in equity if the contract creating those rights expressly or impliedly shows that the original parties intended the rights to be non-assignable.[609] The court will presume that the parties intended to permit assignment of a right where it would not matter to the promisor to whom he rendered performance. However, this is subject to any contrary intention that the agreement as a whole may demonstrate.[610] Obligations presumed not to be assignable include contracts of employment, and contracts involving personal confidences. Public policy imposes further restrictions unrelated to the intentions of the parties.[611]

---

601. This is because in that case, it may prove necessary to have the assignor before the court as a party in a dispute concerning the contract, so it would be undesirable to allow the assignee to bring the action alone, without the assignor as co-claimant, which is the effect of s. 136(1) assignment.
602. *Forster v. Baker* [1910] 2 KB 636; *Raiffeisen Zentralbank Osterreich AG v. Five Star General Trading LLC (The Mount I)* [2001] EWCA Civ 68, [2001] 1 Lloyd's Rep 597, [74].
603. *Durham Bros v. Robertson* [1898] 1 QBD 765. However this depends on the precise formulation of the assignment. Some assignments by way of mortgage (i.e., containing a proviso that the debt should be reassigned back to the assignor if the debt to the assignee is repaid) have been held to be absolute: for example, *Tancredo v. Delagoa Bay* (1889) 23 QBD 239.
604. *Hercules Piling Ltd v. Tilbury Construction Ltd* (1992) 61 Build LR 107.
605. *Walker v. Bradford Old Bank* (1884) 12 QBD 511.
606. Law of Property Act 1925, s. 53(1)(c).
607. Unless the contract terms specify that assignment must be done according to some particular formality.
608. *Ex parte Agra Bank* (1868) LR 3 Ch App 555.
609. *Helstan Securities Ltd v. Hertfordshire County Council* [1978] 3 All ER 262. Indeed, an attempt to do so will generally constitute a breach of contract. However, the secondary right to damages for breach of such a primary obligation is not necessarily personal and can therefore be assigned.
610. *Don King Productions Inc v. Warren* [2000] Ch 291, 318–19.
611. For example, Pensions Act 1995, s. 91.

§3. The Special Case of a 'Sub-contract'

324. Subcontractors are not exempt from privity, and they remain unable directly to enforce terms contained in the contract between the client and the main contractor.[612] To circumvent the resultant difficulties, commercial parties usually rely on collateral contracts. This is particularly effective in bringing subcontractors within the scope of exclusion clauses agreed between the client and the main contractor.[613] A collateral contract describes the situation where a contract between two parties is accompanied by a contract between one (or each) of those parties and a third party in respect of the subject matter of the main contract. A collateral contract must satisfy the normal requirements for contractual validity, such as the requirement for valuable consideration moving from the promisee.[614]

325. In *Scruttons v. Midland Silicons*, Lord Reid hypothesised that a subcontractor may in some circumstances be able to invoke an exclusion clause contained in the contract between the main contractor and the client to defend against a claim in tort brought by the client. This would require that (i) the clause in the main contract was clearly intended to apply also to the subcontractor, (ii) the main contractor could plausibly be regarded as having acted both in his personal capacity to form a contract with the client, and as agent for the subcontractor in a collateral unilateral contract between the client and the subcontractor and that (iii) the requirement that the subcontractor should provide consideration to support the direct contract with the client were somehow 'overcome'.

326. This was confirmed, and rationalised, in *The Eurymedon*. The law treats the main contractor as having simultaneously contracted personally with the client, and as agent for the subcontractor in a direct collateral contract between the client and the subcontractor, a contract composed essentially of a single exclusion clause.[615] The question of agency is generally not probed too deeply; the courts are willing to overlook the issue in order to uphold a slightly artificial but commercially useful arrangement.[616] The contract between the main contractor and the client, in stating that its exclusion clause should also cover subcontractors,[617] is thus regarded as simultaneously comprising an offer of a unilateral contract with the client, which the subcontractor accepts by

612. *Scruttons Ltd v. Midland Silicones Ltd* [1962] AC 446. Such arrangements generally exclude the Contracts (Rights of Third Parties) Act 1999 and navigate instead by the familiar – if complex – collateral contracts.

613. They may also be used where the main contractor requires the subcontractor to undertake direct 'collateral warranties' in favour of the main contractor's clients, or others who may be interested in suing them over their performance (such as residents).

614. *Charlock v. Liverpool Corporation* [1968] 1 WLR 1498. Cf collateral contracts imposed by statute, such as by the Consumer Contracts Act 2015, s. 30, which gives consumers purchasing goods contractual rights against a guarantor (usually the manufacturer), even though the ordinary requirements of contract formation are not met.

615. *NZ Shipping Co Ltd v. A M Satterthwaite & Co Ltd (The Eurymedon)* [1975] AC 154, 167–68, per Lord Wilberforce.

616. *See* for instance *Great Atlantic Insurance Co v. Home Insurance Co (The New York Star)* [1981] 1 WLR 138, 144, per Lord Wilberforce.

617. So-called 'Himalaya clauses', named after the vessel in *Adler v. Dickson* [1955] 1 QB 155.

performing the requested services. The subcontractor provides consideration by becoming suable by the client.

§4. Actio Pauliana

327. Courts have the statutory power to set aside a transaction that was made in order to defraud the transferor's creditors.[618] This is particularly important in the context of insolvency and bankruptcy proceedings, during which applications for the setting aside of certain transactions may be made by the transferor's creditors, or by the trustees in bankruptcy in the interests of the transferor's creditors as a whole. However, the application can be made outside formal insolvency proceedings, and the transferor need not be insolvent for an application to be brought.[619]

328. The power in question applies only to transactions made at an undervalue,[620] and with the intention either to put the assets beyond the reach of one's creditors,[621] or in some other way to prejudice a creditor's interests.[622] It is not enough that this is merely the incidental effect of the transaction, if this was not the transferor's purpose in making it. However, the defrauding of one's creditors does not have to be the transferor's sole purpose, but only one substantial purpose of the transaction.[623] The requisite intention can be inferred from the circumstances of the transaction,[624] or proved by positive evidence in the usual way.

329. An application can be brought by any 'victim of the transaction' in question,[625] even if that victim was not a creditor that the transferor specifically intended to defraud

618. The modern rules are contained in Part XVI of the Insolvency Act 1986, which replaces Part IX of the Law of Property Act 1925. This itself replaced the Fraudulent Conveyances Act 1571 (13 Eliz 1, c 5).
619. Insolvency Act 1986, s. 424(1).
620. Insolvency Act 1986, s. 423(1). The act defines transactions at an undervalue as those made for no consideration, or for consideration of significantly less monetary value than the thing transferred. The Act does not define what is meant by 'significantly less', and the cases take differing stances on when a difference in monetary value will be significant: compare for example *In re Marini Ltd* [2004] BCC 172 and *Gil v. Baygreen Properties Ltd* [2004] EWHC 1732 (Ch), [2005] BPIR 95.
621. Defined as 'a person who is making, or may at some time make, a claim' against the transferor: Insolvency Act 1986, s. 423(3).
622. Insolvency Act 1986, s. 423(3). Provided this specific intention is shown, it is not necessary furthermore to show the presence of fraud.
623. *Royscott Spa Leasing v. Lovett* [1995] BCC 502; *Inland Revenue Commission v. Hashimi* [2002] EWCA Civ 981, [2002] BCC 943. The presence of reasons behind this purpose (such as the understandable desire to protect one's family home from one's creditors) does not alter the 'purpose' of the transaction within the meaning of the Act: *Arbuthnot Leasing International Ltd v. Havelet Leasing Ltd (No 2)* [1990] BCC 636.
624. *Moon v. Franklin* [1996] BPIR 196.
625. Insolvency Act 1986, s. 424(1). However if the defendant individual or company is in liquidation or bankruptcy, such claimants must obtain the permission of the court to bring an action: Insolvency Act 1986, s. 424(1)(a).

by her transaction. However, once an application is brought, it is deemed to have been brought on behalf of all the victims of the transaction.[626]

330. The court may make whatever order it thinks fit in order to restore the transferor to the position she would have occupied had she not made the transaction in question, and to protect the interests of victims prejudiced by the transaction.[627] The court does not have to make any order whatsoever, and it may refuse to interfere in the transaction if this would cause unacceptable hardship to the transferor.[628] But such reticence is rare,[629] and the usual result of a successful application is for the court to have the transferred property revested in the transferor, so that individual creditors can recover from her in the normal way.[630]

331. The court may alternatively choose to set aside the transaction only in part.[631] The court may also make orders providing for the protection of third parties liable to be adversely affected by orders made against the transferor.[632] The statute in question expressly prevents orders for payments against those who subsequently received the assets from the original transferee, provided they took the assets in good faith, for value and without notice of the circumstances of the original transfer.[633]

---

626. Insolvency Act 1986, s. 424(2).
627. Insolvency Act 1986, s. 423(2). There is an illustrative statutory list of possible orders (Insolvency Act 1986, s. 425) but this does not limit the courts discretion.
628. *In re Paramount Airways Limited* [1993] Ch 223.
629. *Arbuthnot Leasing International Ltd v. Havelet Leasing Ltd (No 2)* [1990] BCC 636.
630. *Dora v. Simper* [2000] 2 BCLC 561.
631. *Chohan v. Saggar* [1994] BCC 134.
632. *Arbuthnot Leasing International Ltd v. Havelet Leasing Ltd (No 2)* [1990] BCC 636.
633. Insolvency Act 1986, s. 425(2)(b).

Chapter 5. The Termination of the Contract

§1. Performance and Breach

332. Contract liability in English law is strict. An action for damages accrues immediately on breach of any kind. The defendant's failure to perform need not be the result of any fault on his part. Indeed, it is 'axiomatic that, in relation to claims the for breach of contract, it is, in general, immaterial why the defendant failed to fulfil his obligations, and certainly no defence to plead that he had done his best'.[634]

333. Although a breach automatically yields a right to sue for damages, no breach automatically terminates the contract. Even repudiation of the contract – where the defendant makes clear that he is unable or unwilling to continue performance of his obligations – will not automatically terminate the contractual relationship.[635] Such breaches only give the claimant a choice whether to affirm the contract or accept the repudiatory breach and terminate.

334. Failure to perform his contractual obligations through no fault of his own can, on one narrow exception to the strict liability on which English contract law is founded, be excused. This is where the contract has become frustrated. In such cases, the contract is terminated automatically on the occurrence of the frustrating event.

§2. Impossibility, Frustration and Hardship

335. English law is extremely slow to allow impossibility of performance to exempt a defendant from liability. Contract liability is strict and the law's point of departure is that the reasons for which the promisee has not performed his undertakings as agreed is immaterial to liability.[636] Breach entails liability regardless of the reasons for breach, or the conduct of the defendant. Indeed, for much of its history English law was unyielding in its attitude to contractual liability, reasoning that the risks of contractual performance becoming impossible simply lay where they fell, unless the contract expressly provided that the obligations were conditional on their continued possibility. If a defendant wished to be excused from his obligations to perform in the event of certain circumstances, he had to ensure this was made an express provision of the contract.[637]

336. As the law of contract came to recognise that the parties' agreement could contain terms other than those the parties had expressly stated at the time of formation, the law began to acknowledge that even contractual undertakings expressed plainly and without qualification could nonetheless be *impliedly* conditional, such that the

634. *Raineri v. Miles* [1981] AC 1050, 1086, per Lord Edmund-Davies.

635. *Geys v. Société Genérale (London Branch)* [2012] UKSC 63, [2013] 1 AC 523.

636. *Raineri v. Miles* [1981] AC 1050, 1086, per Lord Edmund-Davies.

637. *Paradine v. Jane* (1647) Aleyn 26, 82 ER 897.

defendant was not bound if certain events occurred, or failed to occur.[638] In appropriate contexts, the court would identify in the agreement a condition precedent to the enforceability of particular duties: 'a condition is implied that the impossibility of performance...shall excuse the performance'.[639] This was not a dilution of the rule that parties were strictly bound to the obligations that they had undertaken, but a recognition that sometimes those obligations should be taken to have been inherently *conditional* on certain facts, despite the absence of any reference to this condition in the express language of the agreement.

337. This sensitivity to the parties' implied terms ultimately mutated into the claim that contracts would be terminated by the occurrence of certain events, not due to any implied condition in the parties' contract, but simply because of a freestanding rule of law. As a matter of positive law, parties' contracts are now held to be frustrated 'from without'; this is no longer attributed to the parties' own agreement.[640]

338. The doctrine of frustration operates to terminate a contract immediately, when 'without default of either party, a contractual obligation has become incapable of being performed because the circumstances...would render performance a thing radically different from that which was undertaken by the contract'.[641]

339. Some older cases excused defendants from liability where some change in circumstances frustrated the defendant's purpose in entering the contract, even though it was still possible for him to perform his actual contractual *obligations* exactly as agreed.[642] However, the law now insists that it is the actual legal obligations in question that must be rendered impossible by some intervening event. Nonetheless, it is hard to define with precision when a court will conclude that some intervening event has made performance as originally contemplated 'impossible', as opposed to merely more difficult or expensive.

340. The law maintains that mere increased onerousness of performance – 'hardship or inconvenience or material loss' to the defendant – does not qualify as the 'radical difference' necessary for frustration.[643] This is disingenuous. Very little is truly *impossible* if sufficient time and resources are invested, although it may be absurdly wasteful and inefficient to devote huge sums to complete an obligation that has become

638. *Taylor v. Caldwell* (1863) 3 B & S 826, 839, 122 ER 309, 314, per Blackburn J.

639. *Taylor v. Caldwell* (1863) 3 B & S 826, 833, 122 ER 309, 312.

640. Some claim support for an extrinsic doctrine of law in cases such as *Taylor v. Caldwell* (1863) 3 B & S 826, 122 ER 309, but the stated *ratio* of that case was clearly that the parties had themselves impliedly made the obligations subject to conditions precedent.

641. *Davis Contractors v. Fareham Urban District Council* [1956] AC 696, per Lord Radcliffe. In *Pioneer Shipping Ltd v. BTP Tioxide Ltd (The Nema)* [1982] AC 724, Lord Roskill stated that the *Davis Contractors* test was the definitive test for frustration, such that courts should feel no need to look further back into the common law to decide whether intervening events had frustrated a contract.

642. In *Krell v. Henry* [1903] 2 KB 740, the Court of Appeal held a contract for the use of a room frustrated because the procession the room had been hired in order to watch was cancelled. No case has ever directly followed this case, in which the court did not even refer to its own decision in *Herne Bay Steam Boat Co v. Hutton* [1903] 2 KB 683. Here, a boat was hired in order to watch a flotilla that in fact was cancelled. The Court of Appeal denied the contract was frustrated; the risk of cancellation was on the hirer of the boat.

643. *Davis Contractors v. Fareham Urban District Council* [1956] AC 696, 729.

significantly more onerous than was contemplated when the parties made their contract. Despite what the cases claim,[644] it seems that in deciding whether a particular event has frustrated a contract, the court is not distinguishing impossibility from mere onerousness, but is instead answering an impressionistic question of fact and degree, namely whether performance has become *sufficiently* onerous to justify dismissing it as 'impossible'.

341. Importantly, frustration can occur only if the contract itself does not expressly or impliedly allocate the risk of the event in question occurring.[645] It is for this reason that courts very seldom find the doctrine of frustration engaged, since commercial contracts almost always provide extensively for the occurrence of unexpected events.

342. Additionally, the impossibility of performance must not be attributable to the actions of the defendant. Obviously this means the defendant cannot allege frustration where his own breach of contract has made it impossible for him to perform his other contractual obligations, but it additionally excludes frustration where he has had any form of choice or election in whether to perform the obligation in question.[646]

343. When engaged, frustration operates absolutely. Courts have no power to alter the contract to help it survive the frustrating event. Frustration means that the contract is terminated automatically on the occurrence of the frustrating event. Its effect is therefore prospective only, so has no automatic consequences for obligations that have already fallen due, or have already been performed.

344. Frustration is therefore liable to entail significant losses for one party, since there is necessarily no breach of contract on which to base a claim for damages to recoup wasted expenditures. Common law permits restitution for total failure of basis, which means that a claimant can recover the value of services she has provided under the contract if it becomes frustrated before the defendant's own obligations fell due. However, the failure of basis must be total, so this action is excluded if the defendant had performed any of his own obligations under the contract before frustration.[647] Statute provides for the restitution of benefits conferred more widely than the common law rule,[648] but the proper construction of this poorly-drafted legislation is contentious, and there are few cases concerning its effects. In practice, every commercial contract excludes its application by expressly providing for the consequences of impossibility of performance.[649]

644. In *National Carriers Ltd v. Panalpina (Northern) Ltd* [1981] AC 675, Lord Simon stated that the frustration will occur where some supervening occurrence – for which the contract makes no provision – has so significantly changed the nature of the obligation in question, and not just its onerousness, that holding the parties to the contract would be unjust.

645. *Davis Contractors v. Fareham Urban District Council* [1956] AC 696, per Lord Radcliffe.

646. *J Lauritzen AS v. Wijsmuller BV (The Super Servant II)* [1990] 1 Lloyd's Rep 1.

647. *See* for example *Fibrosa Spolka Akcyjna v. Fairbairn Lawson Combe Barbour Ltd* [1943] AC 32.

648. Law Reform (Frustrated Contracts) Act 1943.

649. Although referred to generically as 'force majeure' clauses, such clauses in English contracts do not refer generically to force majeure, which has no recognised meaning in English law: *see* for example, *Thomas Borthwick (Glasgow) Ltd v. Favre Fairclough Ltd* [1968] 1 Lloyd's Rep 16, 28, per Donaldson J. Instead, they tend to list specific qualifying events and their respective effects on the obligations in the contract.

I. Accounting for Discharge for Impossibility

345. The doctrine of frustration is excluded if the contract expressly or impliedly allocates the risk of the event alleged to grand frustration. This demonstrates that the final determinant of the effect of intervening events is the parties' own agreement. With that in mind, it is hard to accept that there is either room or need for a freestanding doctrine of frustration. Rather, the parties' agreement can always be looked to in order to provide – expressly or impliedly – the result of a particular event occurring.

346. In the leading case on frustration, Lord Radcliffe was sceptical of this argument, on the basis that the parties almost certainly did not subjectively contemplate the occurrence of unlikely events. Taken to its logical conclusion, this objection is an assault on the very notion of implied terms. The law is nonetheless content to hold terms to have been implied in fact into the parties' agreement even in the absence of evidence that the parties themselves subjectively considered including the term in question. In this respect Lord Radclifffe's stance has put the law of frustration out of sync with the law's general approach to the implication of contract terms, which employs a hypothetical test,[650] not an historical investigation into what the actual parties considered at the time of contracting.

347. The circle can perhaps be squared by returning to the logic of older cases, which reasoned that parties are taken to have agreed not just their express terms but also 'the general rules of law applicable to such a contract'.[651] Where 'from the nature of the contract, it appears that the parties must from the beginning have known that it could not be fulfilled' unless a certain situation prevailed when performance was due, 'the contract is not to be construed as a positive [i.e., unconditional] contract, but as subject to an implied condition that the parties shall be excused in case, before breach, performance becomes impossible...without default of the contractor'.[652]

§3. Discharge by Agreement

348. As a variation of the parties' contractual obligations, discharge – other than under a mechanism within the contract itself – must be supported by consideration from both parties. Where both parties have outstanding executory obligations, each provides consideration by acquiescing to the discharge of the other party's obligations.

349. In principle, attempts to discharge by agreement where only one party has any outstanding obligations will have to demonstrate that the party whose obligations are discharged provided extrinsic consideration. However, the dilution of the consideration requirement in contract variation to include 'practical benefits' means that in most cases the discharge of one party's obligations only will be effective if freely agreed.[653]

---

650. *Shirlaw v. Southern Foundries (1926) Ltd* [1939] 2 KB 206.
651. *Taylor v. Caldwell* (1863) 3 B & S 826, 833, 122 ER 309, 312.
652. *Taylor v. Caldwell* (1863) 3 B & S 826, 833, 122 ER 309, 312.
653. *Williams v. Roffey Bros & Nicholls (Contractors) Ltd* [1991] 1 QB 1; *MWB Business Exchange Centres Ltd v. Rock Advertising Ltd* [2016] EWCA Civ 553.

Chapter 6. Remedies

§1. General Provisions

350. The law distinguishes between remedies available at common law and remedies available in equity only. The principal common law remedy for breach of contract is an award of damages. A right to damages arises automatically on breach of contract. Equitable remedies are less often awarded, and are discretionary, although their availability is subject to rules established by the precedent of the courts of equity.

§2. Specific Performance and Injunctions

351. When ordering specific performance, a court instructs that the defendant actually perform his contractual obligations precisely as required by the terms of the contract. An injunction, in contrast, orders the defendant to do or refrain from some action, which may not necessarily have been required by the terms of the contract itself. For instance, the defendant may be ordered to remedy a particular breach of contract in some way, or to refrain from breach. Breach of an injunction puts the defendant in contempt of court, for which there is criminal liability.

352. When the claimant seeks specific performance or an injunction, the court can award damages in lieu or in addition.[654] In principle the measure for such damages is assessed as for a direct claim for damages at common law.[655]

353. While damages are always available following a breach of contract, specific performance is available only in limited circumstances. The key situation in which the court will award specific performance is a contract for the sale of a specific thing for which there is no prospect of replacement in the wider market.[656] Specific performance is never available in contracts for personal services,[657] especially contracts of employment.[658]

354. As an equitable remedy, specific performance is also barred by the general rules of equity, such as the rule that a claimant seeking the intervention of equity must come to the court 'with clean hands'; in other words the claimant must have acted fairly and reasonably in relation to the contract she seeks to have specifically enforced.[659]

654. Senior Courts Act 1981, s. 50.
655. *Johnson v. Agnew* [1980] AC 367, 400.
656. This especially means the sale of real property, but specific performance has been awarded in special circumstances in the sale of general goods, for instance where unusual market conditions make finding replacement performance unusually onerous: for example, *Sky Petroleum Ltd v. VIP Petroleum Ltd* [1974] 1 WLR 576.
657. *De Francesco v. Barnum* (1890) 45 Ch D 438.
658. Statute now also precludes an order to make an employee carry out the contracted labour: Trade Union and Labour Relations (Consolidation) Act 1992, s. 236.
659. *See* for example *Coatsworth v. Johnson* (1886) 54 LT 520.

The court will not order specific performance of a contractual obligation not supported by consideration; a gratuitous promise made by deed is therefore binding at common law but will not be specifically enforced in equity.

355. More fundamentally, the courts are unlikely to award specific performance if damages would provide adequate compensation for the claimant. The courts have wavered in the precise threshold required before a claim for specific performance will succeed, and at one point required only that specific performance be the more 'appropriate' remedy to 'meet the justice of the case'.[660] In recent years specific performance has once again become a narrow and exceptional remedy.

356. In *Co-operative Insurance Society v. Argyll Stores*, the House of Lords reasserted the primacy of damages as the standard remedy for breach of contract. In denying the claimant specific performance, The House of Lords focused on the hardship this remedy would cause to the defendant, which they concluded was disproportionate to the actual losses the claimant would suffer due to the breach, and also to the difficulty of checking whether the defendant was complying with the detailed and complex contractual obligations the claimant sought to have specifically enforced. Lord Hoffmann emphasised that the purpose of contract remedies is not to enforce the defendant's promise *per se*, but to protect the claimant's expectation interest, which will usually be achievable by an award of damages.

357. English contract law therefore generally permits defaulting promisors to divest themselves of an obligation to perform their contractual undertakings by compensating the innocent party, on the basis that to hold a defaulting promisor to his promise entails 'a waste of resources' and 'yokes the parties together in a continuing hostile relationship'.[661]

358. The court will not grant an injunction where this would be tantamount to an order for specific performance, if the contract in question is one the court would decline specifically to enforce if the claimant had sought specific performance directly.[662]

§3. Termination

359. The effect of termination is a prospective only. That is to say, it affects only obligations that were executory at the time of termination. Termination discharges executory primary obligations,[663] but does not affect obligations already fallen due under the contract, or clauses interpreted as intended to survive termination.[664] This generally entails terms affecting the parties' secondary obligations, like liquidated damages clauses, exclusion clauses and arbitration clauses. Services performed, property transferred, and monies paid pursuant to obligations triggered before termination are

660. *Beswick v. Beswick* [1968] AC 58, 102, per Lord Upjohn.

661. *Co-operative Insurance Society Ltd v. Argyll Stores (Holdings) Ltd* [1998] AC 1, [15]-[16], per Lord Hoffmann.

662. *Warner Bros Pictures Inc v. Nelson* [1937] 1 KB 209.

663. *Photo Production Ltd v. Securicor Ltd* [1980] AC 827, 849, per Lord Diplock.

664. Frustratingly, this is sometimes referred to as 'rescission', but because it is prospective only in its effects, it is legally distinct from rescission for misrepresentation, etc.

unchallengeable. Termination is absolute and irrevocable in that English law does not admit any doctrine of suspension of contract.

360. Termination will occur when the contract is frustrated. It can also occur in circumstances that fall short of frustration, by virtue of either (i) an express termination clause in the contract, or (ii) the common law rules of termination for breach. In either case, termination does not require judicial approval. Although a court will often be called upon to decide the lawfulness of a purported termination, in principle termination is an act of the party suffering a breach of contract, not a remedy provided by the court.

361. Termination can be particularly advantageous to the victim of a breach where it has become possible to secure alternative performance elsewhere at a lower price than that agreed under the contract that has been breached. Nonetheless, judges and scholars have divergent views as to the desirability of easy termination. This has affected the courts' interpretation of express contractual termination clauses, and the development of termination at common law for breach of contract.

I. Termination under the Express Terms of the Contract

362. In principle, the parties have total freedom to designate the circumstances under which a contract may be terminated. Commercial contracts frequently contain clauses permitting termination in specified circumstances, and stipulating the effect of such termination on other obligations under the contract. This allows for more nuanced outcomes than permitted by termination at common law, which automatically discharges the contract prospectively, yet leaves executed obligations intact. However, the presence of a termination clause does not affect the right to terminate at common law.

363. The general law of contract interpretation requires courts to apply termination clauses as written, without attempting to manipulate them in order to protect parties in breach. This is particularly the case in cases between commercial parties' optical bargaining power, where termination clauses fall to be interpreted strictly in pursuit of certainty.[665] However, courts have occasionally applied strained and even counter-textual interpretations of express termination clauses, to prevent parties in breach losing the benefit of the continuing contractual relationship.

364. In *Rice v. Great Yarmouth Borough Council*, the contract explicitly granted the right to terminate following 'breach of any...obligations'.[666] This term, though perhaps onerous and commercially unwise, was unambiguous, but nonetheless Hale LJ in the Court of Appeal rejected the 'draconian consequences' of applying this term

665. For example, *Union Eagle Ltd v. Golden Achievement Ltd* [1997] AC 514, 519, per Lord Hoffmann. The express language of a broad termination clause will exclude any implied duty of good faith the court may have found to be part of the contract: *Yam Seng Pte Ltd v. International Trade Corp Ltd* [2013] EWHC 111, [2013] 1 Lloyd's Rep 526, [149].

666. *Rice v. Great Yarmouth Borough Council* (2001) 3 LGLR 4.

literally.[667] Cases like *Rice* impliedly assume a judicial power to review the reasonableness of termination clauses in particular, a power that has not been granted by statute, and is expressly denied by leading authoritative decisions at the highest level.

II. Termination for Breach at Common Law

365. All breaches of contract give the victim a right to damages. In addition, in some circumstances a breach also creates a right to terminate the contract, notwithstanding the absence of any express termination clause in the contract itself. An innocent party can both terminate the contract and sue for damages consequent on the breach that produced the right to terminate. In that case the damages will compensate the innocent party for the results of the contract's termination.[668]

366. A right to terminate will arise following a repudiatory breach of contract, including breach of a 'condition' of the contract. Importantly, such a breach does not automatically terminate the contract.[669] It only gives the victim a choice; she can either reject the repudiation and simply sue for damages for breach, or she can accept the repudiation and terminate the contract.

367. The innocent party can terminate as soon as the breach in question occurs, and is under no obligation to give the party in breach an opportunity to correct his late or defective performance. The decision whether or not to terminate is irrevocable, and the innocent party cannot avoid making this decision. If the innocent party prevaricates, she may be held impliedly to have affirmed the contract,[670] provided she knew or should reasonably have known of her right to terminate. Once the right to terminate is lost, any future attempt to terminate will itself constitute a wrongful repudiation of the contract.[671]

368. The orthodox position is that the innocent party has unencumbered freedom to accept or reject repudiation. However, some cases have suggested this freedom may be subject to limits, for instance where the innocent party has 'no legitimate interest'

667. *Rice v. Great Yarmouth Borough Council* (2001) 3 LGLR 4, [27]. Instead Arden LJ she treated 'any breach' as meaning only any *repudiatory* breach. In *Dominion Corporate Trustees Ltd v. Debenhams Properties Ltd* [2010] EWHC 1193, Kitchin J applied the decision in *Rice*, holding that a similar provision whose literal wording allowed termination for any breach 'however minor the provision and however insignificant the failure' (at [29]) could not bear this meaning, which 'flouts business common sense' (at [32]).

668. *Photo Production Ltd v. Securicor Ltd* [1980] AC 827, 849, per Lord Diplock.

669. Recently reiterated by the Supreme Court in *Geys v. Société Genérale (London Branch)* [2012] UKSC 63, [2013] 1 AC 523.

670. *Peyman v. Lanjani* [1985] Ch 457.

671. This may not be the case if the purported termination was done in the good faith belief that a right to terminate still existed: *Woodar Investment Development Ltd v. Wimpey Construction UK Ltd* [1980] 1 WLR 277, 283. This is, however, inconsistent with the wider principle that what matters is the objective legal presence of a right to terminate. That is reflected in the rule that termination is valid and effective even if the innocent party was mistaken as to the reason she had a right to terminate, provided she in fact had the right to terminate for other – unknown – reasons: *Maredelanto Compania Naviera SA v. Bergbau-Handel GmbH* [1971] 1 QB 164.

in keeping the defendant bound to a contractual relationship and therefore subject to increasing liabilities as more obligations fall due under the unterminated contract.[672]

369. Whether a breach of contract occasions a right to terminate depends first on the nature of the term that has been breached, and sometimes also on the gravity of the consequences. Traditionally, the law distinguished exhaustively between terms that were 'conditions' and terms that were 'warranties'.[673] Any breach of a condition, no matter how trivial the consequences, entailed an automatic right to terminate in addition to the action for damages. Conversely, no breach of a warranty, no matter how grave the results, created a right to terminate.

370. This traditional picture has been complicated by the introduction of a third category of term, breach of which will sometimes but not always produce a right to terminate. In *Hong Kong Fir*, Diplock LJ considered it artificial to divide exhaustively into conditions and warranties, positing the existence of a third variety of contract term, a category that has come to be known as innominate, or intermediate terms. Breach of such a term will permit termination only if 'fundamental', meaning that the breach is so severe as to deprive the innocent party of 'substantially the whole benefit which it was the intention of the parties that he should obtain from the contract'.[674] In addition to repudiatory breaches,[675] this will include non-repudiatory breaches where the consequences are particularly severe.

371. Sometimes an innocent party's right to terminate for breach of a condition is limited by statute.[676] Also, judges have sometimes been prepared to do significant violence to the language of the contract to avoid a right to terminate for minor breaches. In *Schuler v. Wickman Machine Tool Sales,*[677] the parties' contract designated as a 'condition' a term requiring the promisor to make an enormous number of visits to interested commercial parties. Lord Reid felt that the result of construing the term as a condition – that any breach permitted termination by the promisee – was 'so unreasonable that it must make me search for some other possible meaning'. The term would be regarded as a condition 'only if that is the only possible interpretation'.[678] Lord Reid considered the term an intermediate term, since it was at least possible that the parties had used the word 'condition' in another sense.[679] It emerges that contractual

672. *White & Carter (Councils) Ltd v. McGregor* [1962] AC 413, 431, per Lord Reid. The other members of the House of Lords did not indicate this potential exception, which in any case was *obiter*.

673. English contract law uses the words condition and warranty in many different senses. Their meanings in this instance should not be confused with meanings these terms carry in other contexts within contract law discourse.

674. *Photo Production Ltd v. Securicor Ltd* [1980] AC 827, 849, per Lord Diplock.

675. Including 'anticipatory' repudiation: *Hochster v. De La Tour* (1852) 2 El & Bl 678, 690, 118 ER 922, 926.

676. For example, the Sale of Goods Act 1979, s. 15A.

677. *Schuler AG v. Wickman Machine Tool Sales Ltd* [1974] AC 235.

678. *Schuler AG v. Wickman Machine Tool Sales Ltd* [1974] AC 235, 251.

679. Namely its English common parlance meaning, as a general synonym of 'term' (in the sense of 'Terms and Conditions Apply'). Lord Wilberforce in dissent emphasised that the law must not impose a requirement of reasonableness for a term to be validly designated a condition. Commercial parties such as the litigants did not intend 'easygoing tolerance' but rather 'insistent punctuality and efficiency' (at 263).

designation of a term as a condition is probably inadequate to ensure with certainty that an English court will approve termination for any breach of it.[680]

§4. Exceptio Non Adimpleti Contractus

372. Generally, to sue for breach of the defendant's contractual obligation, the claimant must have performed her own obligations, or be willing and able to perform them, to the extent required by the contract itself as the condition precedent for the enforcement of the defendant's obligation in question. Many contractual obligations are 'entire', in that the defendant's obligations fall due only on full completion of the claimant's relevant obligations. In other words, full completion is a condition precedent for the right to enforce the other party's undertakings.

373. In *Sumpter v. Hedges*, the claimant partially performed his contractual undertaking to build two houses, then abandoned the project and claimed for payment representing the work he had completed to date. The Court of Appeal declared that the contractor's obligations were entire, and therefore that he was unable to sue for pro rata payment on the basis of his partial completion.[681] However, in some instances the court will permit such claims. In *Hoenig v. Isaacs*, where a contractor had performed his obligations defectively and therefore in breach of contract, the court permitted a claim for the contract price, less the amount for which the contractor would be liable in damages for breach.[682] This was on the basis that the obligations had been substantially performed.

374. However, this is not a retreat from the entire obligation rule, but only a recognition that not all contracts are comprised of a single 'entire' obligation; many contracts are in fact *divisible* into multiple legally discrete obligations, and therefore accommodate a claim for a proportion of the overall contract price where a proportion of the overall contract has been performed. This depends on the construction of contract.[683] Many obligations are expressly stated not to be entire, for instance where contracts provide for payment in instalments on incremental completion of the overall

680. Even expressly providing for termination in case of *any breach* might not be adequate in light of interventionist decisions such as *Rice v. Great Yarmouth Borough Council* (2001) 3 LGLR 4.

681. *Sumpter v. Hedges* [1898] 1 QB 673, per Smith LJ. Collins LJ noted that the claimant could recover a pro rata sum if the defendant had freely accepted the part performance.

682. *Hoenig v. Isaacs* [1952] 2 All ER 176.

683. This is shown by close attention to the old cases. For instance, in *Cutter v. Powell* (1795) 6 Term Rep 320, 101 ER 573, a widow failed in her action to recover a proportion of the money that her husband's employer had agreed to pay him for his services as a ship's carpenter on a lengthy sea voyage. The court did not suggest that his dying before the voyage was completed constituted a breach of contract, but only that he had thereby failed to satisfy the condition precedent necessary to trigger the employer's obligation to pay. This decision is erroneously assumed to have established a rule of law – since abolished – that employment contracts are entire obligations. In fact, the decision turned entirely on the interpretation of the nature of the deal the parties had struck. The court considered this not an ordinary employment contract but – in light of the fact that the remuneration was four times more than the market rate – that it was in the nature of an all-or-nothing exchange of a fixed sum for a fixed performance.

contract services. If an obligation is interpreted not to be entire,[684] then the claimant can recover provided she has substantially performed the obligation in question. Whether substantial performance has been rendered will depend on the facts.[685]

§5. Faulty Behaviour of the Debtor

375. See general material on breach, at paragraphs [332]–[334].

§6. Limitation of Actions

376. The limitation period for contracts made other than by deed is six years from the date of breach, whether or not the breach was discoverable when it occurred,[686] except for breaches resulting in personal injury or death.[687] However, if the claimant's action is based on the defendant's fraud, or if the defendant has concealed from the claimant any information relevant to the claim,[688] or if the action is for relief from the consequences of a mistake, the limitation period runs only from the time the claimant discovered or could reasonably have discovered these facts.[689] The limitation period for obligations made by deed is twelve years.[690]

377. Courts have been critical of the rule that the limitation period begins even before the claimant was aware of the breach in question. This has led them to adapt other legal rules in order to prevent the intuitive injustice of a claimant losing a cause of action she could not possibly have known about. This is one reason for the recognition of concurrent liability in tort.

684. Courts tend to lean against finding obligations entire, due to concern that entire obligations invite unjust enrichment of the defendant, who obtains a benefit at no cost. The Law Commission has recommended replacing the *Sumpter v. Hedges* rule with a restitutionary approach: Law Commission Report No 121.
685. *Bolton v. Mahadeva* [1972] 2 All ER 1322. Here, a boiler had been installed so defectively that it emitted noxious fumes. Sachs LJ denied that the installer had given any substantial performance since the installation was not just substandard, but useless.
686. Limitation Act 1980, s. 14. Cf the rule in tort, where the six-year limitation period runs from the time harm was suffered. The Law Commission has recommended reform of the contract rule to match the tort rule: Law Commission Report No 270.
687. Where breach of contract results in an injury, the limitation period is three years from the breach of contract or the date on which the injured person became aware of the identity of the wrongdoer, that the injury sustained was significant and at least partially attributable to the breach (Limitation Act 1980, ss. 11(4) and 14(1)), unless the claimant dies before the expiration of that period, in which case the action may be brought up to three years from the date of death (or, if later, when deceased's personal representative becomes aware of the death: s. 11(5)).
688. Concealment includes the deliberate commission of a breach of duty in circumstances where it is unlikely to be discovered for a long time: Limitation Act 1980, s. 32(2).
689. Limitation Act 1980, s. 32(1).
690. Limitation Act 1980, s. 8.

378. Where a debt would otherwise become time-barred, the limitation period begins again if the debtor acknowledges the debt in writing. The limitation period is six years from the date of the last written acknowledgment.

§7. Damages and Exemption Clauses

379. The purpose of contract damages is to put the claimant, as far as money can achieve, in the position she would have occupied had the contract been performed according to its terms.[691] Their stated goal is therefore to protect the claimant's expectation interest. In some instances it may also be possible to sue for and recover someone else's loss, such as where a parent sues for their child's non-pecuniary loss resulting from the substandard provision of a contracted holiday,[692] or where a commissioner of building work sues for losses in fact suffered by the eventual occupier of the property.[693]

380. The expectation measure can be estimated in two ways, which often, but not always, arrive at roughly equivalent figures. The court may award the diminution in value, calculated by calculating the value of the performance and subtracting the value of the result actually provided by the defendant (which may be nothing). The court may alternatively award the cost of cure, which is the amount required to bring the results into conformity with those required by the contract, for instance by contracting elsewhere.

381. In principle the claimant is free to choose between these estimates, and the courts have been willing to award cost-of-cure damages even when the diminution in value is negligible.[694] However, the claimant will not be able to recover the cost of cure if this sum is 'wholly disproportionate' to the diminution in value.[695] In *Ruxley Electronics v. Forsyth*, the House of Lords asked whether it was *reasonable* to seek to cure the defect in question, holding on the facts that this was not reasonable and therefore that the claimant was limited to recovering the diminution in value (which was minimal). However, it is hard to extract a *test* of reasonableness from their Lordships' speeches.

382. In many respects the award of damages – even at the cost of cure measure – is unable fully to compensate for actual performance. Not all types of loss are readily recoverable. Moreover, the claimant is required to mitigate her losses, and cannot recover losses that are judged too remote. In *Hadley v. Baxendale*, it was established that the claimant can recover only losses (a) that are natural consequences of the breach,

691. *Robinson v. Harman* (1848) 1 Ex Rep 850, 154 ER 363. Contract damages are therefore compensatory, and there are no punitive damages in contract actions: *Addis v. Gramophone Co Ltd* [1909] AC 488.

692. *Jackson v. Horizon Holidays Ltd* [1975] 1 WLR 1468.

693. At least where the builder in breach also knows that the property will eventually be occupied by someone other than the client: *Linden Gardens Trust Ltd v. Lanesta Sludge Disposals Ltd* [1994] 1 AC 85; *Darlington Borough Council v. Wiltshier Northern Ltd* [1995] 1 WLR 68; *Alfred McAlpine Construction Ltd v. Panatown Ltd* [2001] 1 AC 518.

694. *Radford v. De Froberville* [1977] 1 WLR 1262.

695. *Ruxley Electronics and Construction Ltd v. Forsyth* [1994] 3 All ER 801, per Lord Mustill.

or (b) that ought reasonably to have been contemplated by the defendant as being likely to occur on breach, at the time of contract formation.[696] Only the *type* of loss, not the exact nature or extent, need be foreseeable.[697]

383. In *The Achilleas*,[698] Lord Hoffmann understood the two limbs of *Hadley v. Baxendale* as merely illustrative of a general principle, namely that the only losses recoverable are those that were reasonably foreseeable based on the knowledge of the reasonable person in the position of the defendant at the time of contracting. The crucial test was therefore one of presumed intention: for what losses did the claimant reasonably understand the defendant to be assuming responsibility? On the facts, Lord Hoffmann held that the defendant was not liable for certain losses even though they were entirely foreseeable consequences of breach, since the parties had contracted on the basis of industry standards, which excluded liability for such losses.

384. *The Achilleas* has not displaced the *Hadley v. Baxendale* rule as the general formula for remoteness, but the traditional approach is now understood as representing the parties' expectations and the defendant's assumed liabilities. In principle the claimant can only recover losses 'from which the party in breach may reasonably be taken to have assumed a responsibility to protect the victim'.[699] It is possible for the parties' understanding of the defendant's liability to differ from the outcome suggested by the traditional remoteness rule. Applying this refined understanding of the remoteness rule, the defendant may not be liable for losses that were nonetheless of a foreseeable type, or may be liable for losses that were not foreseeable. In the absence of an express term dictating what types of loss the promisor is liable to compensate on breach, the law will look to the parties' implied agreement as a whole for an answer. While it will usually be concluded that the promisor impliedly undertakes responsibility for losses that were foreseeable at the time of contracting, this will not be the case where the commercial context suggests the opposite conclusion.[700] *The Achilleas* has therefore had a lasting impact in that an assumption of responsibility analysis now has an acknowledged role in the remoteness test. However, it seems generally confined to unusual cases, and courts typically refer principally to the *Hadley v. Baxendale* rule in deciding questions of remoteness.

385. The claimant cannot recover losses that might have resulted from the breach in question if the claimant in fact managed to avert these losses. Indeed, the law actively requires the claimant to take all reasonable steps to avoid the losses the breach of contract might otherwise cause, and thereby to mitigate her losses. A claimant will therefore be unable to claim from the defendant losses that she could reasonably have

696. *Hadley v. Baxendale* (1854) 9 Ex Ch 341, 156 ER 145.

697. *Parsons (Livestock) Ltd v. Uttley Ingham & Co Ltd* [1978] QB 791.

698. *Transfield Shipping Inc v. Mercator Shipping Inc (The Achilleas)* [2008] UKHL 48, [2008] 3 WLR 345. It is actually unclear on what basis the case was decided. Lord Rodger and Baroness Hale applied the conventional remoteness test, although reached on the facts the odd conclusion that it was not foreseeable that ship owners might have future contracts with which a delayed return of the vessel would interfere.

699. *Supershield Ltd v. Siemens Building Technologies Fe Ltd* [2010] EWCA Civ 7, [2010] 1 Lloyd's Rep 349, per Toulson LJ.

700. *See* for example *John Grimes Partnership Ltd v. Gubbins* [2013] EWCA Civ 37.

avoided.[701] In resisting a claim for certain losses, the defendant must prove that the claimant failed to take reasonable steps to avoid incurring them.

386. Instead of seeking the expectation measure of damages, the claimant can in principle claim for the expenditure incurred in reliance on the expectation of performance. This will be an attractive course of action where it is particularly hard to quantify the value of the expectation. The reliance measure includes the costs the claimant has incurred in performing her own contractual obligations, and even costs incurred prior to contract formation, provided the defendant should reasonably have contemplated his breach leading to the waste of such expenditures.[702] However, the claimant cannot claim more in reliance damages than the value of the performance.[703] This prevents escape from bad bargain; the law will not allow breach to be more profitable than performance.[704]

387. Traditionally the law refused to permit recovery of non-pecuniary losses in an action for breach of contract. It remains the law that claimants cannot generally recover for the hurt feelings, frustration or disappointment resulting from a breach of contract.[705] This has been described as a rule of legal policy rather than logic, since distress and displeasure are foreseeable consequences of breach in the same was as pecuniary losses.[706]

388. Nonetheless the law is now more accommodating of claims for non-pecuniary losses in some circumstances, although it has struggled to identify a principled test for when such losses will be recoverable.

389. In *Watts v. Morrow*, Bingham LJ identified two broad exceptions to the law's general refusal to compensate claimants for non-pecuniary losses resulting from breach of contract. Claimants could recover where the 'very object of the contract' was the provision of pleasure, relaxation, peace of mind or freedom from molestation, and the breach meant that this was not achieved, or in fact that the opposite result emerged. More generally, claimants could recover for physical inconvenience and discomfort caused by breach of contract, and mental suffering directly connected to that physical discomfort (and not resulting merely from the fact of breach).[707] However,

701. *British Westinghouse Electric and Manufacturing Co Ltd v. Underground Electric Railways Company of London Ltd* [1912] AC 673.
702. *Anglia Television Ltd v. Reed* [1972] 1 QB 60, per Lord Denning MR.
703. *CCC Films (London) Ltd v. Impact Quadrant Films Ltd* [1985] 1 QB 16.
704. This principle might extent to stopping the claimant suing for reliance damages where, as a result of the breach, she has been able to make more profit than she could have made if the contract had been performed: *Omak Maritime Ltd v. Mamola Challenger Shipping Co Ltd* [2010] EWHC 2026 (Comm), [2010] WLR (D) 230, per Teare J.
705. *Addis v. Gramophone Co Ltd* [1909] AC 488.
706. *Watts v. Morrow* [1991] 1 WLR 1421, per Bingham LJ. However this will surely depend on the context. Even if distress were generally recoverable in principle, it would often be excluded by the remoteness test, since it is hardly foreseeable for seasoned commercial actors to suffer emotional distress on breach of contract. The complexity regarding liability for non-pecuniary losses can perhaps be resolved by reference to the reasoning in *Transfield Shipping Inc v. Mercator Shipping Inc (The Achilleas)* [2008] UKHL 48, [2008] 3 WLR 345. The defendant will be liable for a specific type of loss if, properly interpreted, the contract reveals him implicitly to have undertaken the liability to compensate this in the event of breach.
707. *Watts v. Morrow* [1991] 1 WLR 1421.

in *Farley v. Skinner*, the House of Lords doubted the cogency of Bingham LJ's firm distinction between physical and non-physical inconvenience, preferring to distinguish between (i) distress caused by an unwelcome sensory experience and (ii) pure internal disappointment at the breach.[708]

390. In addition, a further method of recovering non-pecuniary losses has gathered support in recent years. In an influential scholarly article, Harris, Ogus and Phillips advanced the notion of the 'consumer surplus', namely the value the claimant attaches to performance above and beyond its empirical monetary value. Provided it was foreseeable to the defendant at the time of contracting that the claimant attached to performance this additional – necessarily non-pecuniary – value, the claimant should be able to recover the consumer surplus.[709]

391. This notion gained some support in *Ruxley Electronics and Construction Ltd v. Forsyth*[710] and also in *Farley v. Skinner*. Even though there is no diminution in value as a result of the breach, the claimant is held to have suffered a loss of some kind and must be compensated for this if her expectation interest is to be fully protected.[711] It has moreover been linked to the notion of the sanctity of contractual undertakings: 'the principle of *pacta sunt servanda* would be eroded if the law did not take account of the fact that the consumer often demands specifications which, although not of economic value, have value to him'.[712] In other words, it has been felt improper that the defendant should escape liability for breaches simply because they entail no monetary disadvantage to the claimant.

392. In *Farley v. Skinner*, Lord Scott noted that the *Watts* test and the consumer surplus might both be relevant on the same facts, but that they functioned as mutually exclusive approaches to the valuation of the claimant's expectation interest. Moreover, claims for sensory inconvenience (and indeed distress, to the extent that this is recoverable) protect the claimant's reliance interest, in that in suing for these losses the claimant is seeking compensation for losses she would not have suffered but for contracting. The consumer surplus – and certain claims under the *Watts* criteria – protects the claimant's expectation interest, in that they seek to award the monetary

708. *Farley v. Skinner* [2001] 4 All ER 801, per Lord Scott. However, although physicality is certainly a difficult distinction, so is a requirement that inconvenience be 'sensory'. Indeed, one cannot *sense* anything that is not *physical*. It is unclear whether the majority supported Lord Scott's rephrasing.

709. D Harris, A Ogus and J Phillips, 'Contract remedies and the consumer surplus' (1979) 95 LQR 581.

710. '[T]he law must cater for those occasions where the value of the promise to the promisee exceeds the financial enhancement of his position which full performance will secure...[Although] it represents a personal, subjective and non-monetary gain...the law should recognise it and compensate the promisee if the misperformance takes it away.': *Ruxley Electronics and Construction Ltd v. Forsyth* [1994] 3 All ER 801, per Lord Mustill.

711. Although Lord Mustill and Lord Bridge enthusiastically endorsed the consumer surplus, Lord Lloyd explained the recoverability of non-pecuniary losses in this case in terms of the *Watts v. Morrow* [1991] 1 WLR 1421 criteria.

712. *Farley v. Skinner* [2001] 4 All ER 801, per Lord Steyn, discussing Lord Mustill's judgment in *Ruxley Electronics and Construction Ltd v. Forsyth* [1994] 3 All ER 801.

equivalent of the benefit the claimant was supposed to receive under the contract. Sums awarded under either test will be modest.[713]

§8. Restitution

393. *See* paragraphs [32]–[34] and [432]–[435].

713. *Farley v. Skinner* [2001] 4 All ER 801, per Lord Steyn.

Part II. Specific Contracts

394. English contract law ascribes little importance to *ex ante* classifications of contracts into distinct categories. There is no role for the kind of categorisation of specific contracts familiar to civil law thinking. The law does not provide general frameworks or blueprints for contracts of particular types. The law asserts that each contract is independently created by the parties' own design out of a single, undifferentiated body of contract law doctrine. While the law also implies additional terms into contracts in some contexts, most are excludable by sufficiently express language, particularly those implied-in by the common law rather than statute,[714] and are understood as specific intrusions into a bespoke contract, rather than a general blueprint which the parties tailor to their own needs.

395. In sophisticated commercial contracts, the drafters focus on the extensive delineation of the parties' rights and obligations, with the goal of leaving as few gaps as possible and little room for courts to conclude the contract contains terms other than those expressly contained in the contractual document. Sometimes a contract will nonetheless be deemed to contain express terms that the parties did not specifically negotiate, for instance where these terms are sufficiently widespread norms within the relevant industry. Nonetheless this too is attributed to the parties' (objectively deduced) intentions, since in the absence of evidence to the contrary, the reasonable person in the parties' position would understand themselves to be contracting in accordance with the established norms of the industry in which they operate.

396. Importantly, these industry standards are not legal rules but simply market conventions, and are therefore distinct from 'specific contracts' in the civil law sense. The discussion below refers only to legal doctrinal rules applicable only to certain contracts, and only where knowledge of these rules is genuinely helpful for understanding English contract law as a body of doctrine. In many cases there is nothing of particular relevance to be said in addition to the discussions of English contract law above.

714. *Liverpool City Council v. Irwin* [1977] AC 239, 257, per Lord Cross.

Chapter 1. Agency

397. Where an agent concludes a contract on behalf of his principal, the contract is made not with the agent himself but with the principal.[715] It follows that, generally, the agent is not liable on the contract,[716] nor able to enforce it.[717] A relationship recognised by the law as agency can arise in several ways. It usually predates (or at least coincides with) a particular transaction, but in some circumstances agency can be recognised retroactively, through ratification of a transaction that was not in fact authorised by the principal at the time the agent made it.

398. In some circumstances, agency sometimes arises by operation of law. The law deems one party to have acted as the agent for another, notwithstanding the consent or non-consent of this principal. This may occur due to statute or based on the common law doctrine of agency of necessity.[718] Generally, however, agency emerges out of express or implied agreement,[719] and relies on the presence of an intention to act specifically on behalf of the principal in question. A relationship of agency does not have to rise under a contract; indeed, it can arise even where the terms of the parties' contract expressly denies such a relationship,[720] provided the substance of the parties' relationship is sufficient to establish agency in law. Likewise, even expressly declaring oneself to be acting as an agent is not conclusive if in fact the actor intended to contract for his own benefit.[721]

399. It is a question of fact whether the putative agent really intended to act on behalf of his principal, although this is decided objectively. An agent with authority to conclude an agreement may nonetheless be held to have contracted in his personal capacity and therefore be personally liable, depending on the construction of the contract with the third party.

---

715. The other party can raise against the principal any defences he would have had against the agent if he had been the true party.
716. *Robins v. Bridge* (1837) 3 M& W 114.
717. *Lucas v. Beale* (1851) 10 CB 739.
718. Examples include a shipmaster's authority to sell part of the ship's cargo, to borrow money against the credit of the ship owner, and to enter salvage agreements as the agent of the cargo's owner. These powers are, however, subject to limits: *China Pacific SA v. Food Corp of India (The Winson)* [1982] AC 939: *See* the material on 'quasi-contracts' below.
719. Authority can be established by reference to 'the conduct of the parties and the circumstances': *Hely-Hutchinson v. Brayhead Ltd* [1968] 1 QB 549, 583. This is a significantly less exacting threshold than the test for implication of terms into a contract.
720. *Ormrod v. Crosville Motor Services Ltd* [1953] 1 WLR 1120; *Garnac Grain Co Inc v. Faure & Fairclough Ltd* [1968] AC 1130, 1137.
721. *Kennedy v. De Trafford* [1897] AC 180, 188. This is particularly relevant given the tendency of commercial intermediaries to describe themselves as 'agents', when in fact their business structure is to contract entirely in their own capacity, buying and reselling. They thereby act as commercial conduits and facilitators, but not as legal agents.

400. There is no particular formula for the conclusive demonstration that one is contracting solely as an agent and therefore not assuming any personal liability,[722] but it is generally sufficient to declare oneself contracting 'on behalf of' (or '*per procurationem*') the principal. Generally, if the agent is held to be personally liable, he will also be able to enforce the contract, if this is not inconsistent with its true construction.[723] It is also possible in principle for the agent to be able to enforce the contract despite not being personally liable under it.

401. No formality is required for the valid creation of a relationship of agency and the vesting of authority in the agent, even when formality is required for the formation of the contract the agent is authorised to conclude on behalf of the principal.[724]

402. The scope of the agent's authority is defined by the agreement, in the first instance by its express language. The principal is liable provided the agent genuinely and reasonably[725] interpreted the principal's language as conferring the necessary authority, even if the principal did not intend to bestow authority of the requisite extent.[726]

403. A principal is liable on the contract with the third party whether or not the agent disclosed her existence at the time of contracting.[727] If the agent was acting within his authority as agent but nonetheless failed to disclose that he was contracting as an agent, then the principal can insist on her own status as the relevant party as long as there is nothing expressly contradicting this in the contract,[728] and unless the agent knew or ought reasonably to have known that the third party consented to contract specifically and uniquely with the agent personally. Generally a third party seeking to avoid liability to the principal has the burden of showing that the identity of the agent was so indispensable to the decision to contract that he would not have contracted with anyone but the agent.[729]

722. The law distinguishes between *representative* references to agency, which will validly prevent any personal liability, and merely descriptive references, such as statements of the putative agent's general profession. These will generally not be sufficient to prevent personal liability: *Burrell v. Jones* (1819) 3 B & Ald 47; *Parker v. Winlow* (1857) 7 E& B 942.

723. *Repetto v. Millar's Karri & Jarrah Forests Ltd* [1901] 2 KB 306, 310.

724. *Heard v. Pilley* (1869) LR 4 Ch 548.

725. If the words would have struck the reasonable person in the putative agent's position as unclear as to the extent of the authority, it will in many cases be unreasonable to proceed with a transaction without first checking directly with the principal, and thus the putative agent will not be able to invoke her own interpretation of the extent of her authority in order to avoid personal liability: *European Asian Bank v. Punjab & Sind Bank (No 2)* [1983] 1 WLR 642, 656.

726. *Weigall v. Runciman* (1916) 85 LJKB 1187.

727. *Boyter v. Thomson* [1995] 2 AC 629, 632.

728. *Humble v. Hunter* (1842) 12 QB 316.

729. *Siu Yin Kwan v. Eastern Ins Co Ltd* [1994] 2 AC 199, 210. The law is imperfectly clear on whether an action by the undisclosed principal would be defeated not because the other party was uniquely interested in contracting with this particular agent, but because he was uniquely interested in not contracting with this particular principal (or someone sharing one of the principal's characteristics). To the extent that this enquiry can be reduced to orthodox offer and acceptance analysis, the answer should be the same in either case.

404. In consensual agency, the agent's authority is always terminable by the principal, even when the original agency agreement purports to be irrevocable.[730] Authority will end at the time specified in the agency agreement, or after reasonable notice, in the absence of specification of term.[731] Revocation of authority is effective even if in breach of contract, in which case it will nonetheless give the wrongfully dismissed agent an independent action for breach.[732] Authority also ends following (i) incapacity of the principal,[733] even though unknown to the agent,[734] (ii) the death of either party, whether or not known to the other[735] and (iii) the bankruptcy of principal,[736] or sometimes of the agent.[737]

405. English law distinguishes between the actual authority and the *apparent* authority of a putative agent. A principal can be liable on a contract even though in fact the agent acted outside his authority in entering it, on the basis of the agent's having apparent authority to enter the contract on her behalf. [738] Apparent authority arises where the principal[739] represents either expressly or impliedly[740] to a third party[741] that she has appointed an agent to contract on her behalf.[742]

406. The principal's representation must in fact have induced the third party to believe he was contracting with an agent authorised by the principal to conclude the

730. *Bailey v. Angove's PTY Ltd* [2016] UKSC 47.
731. *Martin-Baker Aircraft Co Ltd v. Canadian Flight Equipment Ltd* [1955] 2 QB 556.
732. The normal remedy will be damages (*Denmark Productions Ltd v. Boscobel Productions Ltd* [1969] 1 QB 699), and/or a declaration of the wrongfulness of dismissal (*Taylor v. NUS* [1967] 1 WLR 532). There may also be available an injunction to prevent the principal breaching of contractual duties not to appoint another agent: *Decro-Wall International SA v. Practitioners in Marketing Ltd* [1971] 1 WLR 361.
733. Principals have no more capacity through their agent than they would have if contracting directly.
734. *Yonge v. Toynbee* [1910] 1 KB 215, although this rule was criticised (obiter) in *Blankley v. Central Manchester & Manchester University Children's Hospitals NHS Trust* [2015] EWCA Civ 18.
735. *Campanari v. Woodburn* (1854) 15 CB 400; *Pool v. Pool* (1889) 58 LJP 67. However, principal may be liable on a contract on the basis of the agent's apparent authority even though in fact the actual authority was destroyed, for instance by the principal's loss of capacity: *Drew v. Nunn* (1879) 4 QBD 661.
736. *Elliott v. Turquand* (1881) 7 App Cas 79.
737. If it makes agent unable to perform duties: *McCall v. Australian Meat Co Ltd* (1870) 19 WR 188.
738. *Summers v. Solomon* (1857) 7 E & B 879.
739. Not the agent (*Attorney General for Ceylon v. Silva* [1953] AC 461; *In re Selectmove Ltd* [1995] 1 WLR 474, 478) and not some other person (*Rhodian River Shipping Co SA and Rhodian Sailor Shipping Co SA v. Halla Maritime Corp (The Rhodian River and Rhodian Sailor)* [1984] 1 Lloyd's Rep 373).
740. The third party must genuinely and reasonably have concluded that the principal had invested the agent in question with the relevant authority.
741. A representation made 'to the world' in general is inadequate: *Dickinson v. Valpy* (1829) 10 B & C 128, 140.
742. The representation must be specifically as to the putative agent's status *as agent*.

transaction on her behalf.[743] It appears to be no defence that the reasonable person in the third party's position would not have believed such a representation.[744]

407. In partial deviation from the above common law rules on consensual agency, the relationship of 'commercial agency' is now regulated by secondary legislation.[745] These regulations apply between a principal and a commercial agent, defined as 'a self-employed intermediary who has continuing authority to negotiate the sale or purchase of goods on behalf of and in the name of the principal'. They contain provisions regulating various issues such as the earning of commission,[746]and the notice periods required successfully to terminate actual authority.[747]

408. Even in the absence of agency on the basis of either actual or apparent authority, then provided the agent purported to be transacting on the principal's behalf,[748] in some circumstances the principal can retrospectively ratify that unauthorised transaction. Such ratification is effective only if the principal in fact had a free choice whether or not to ratify.

409. Ratification can be by express communication, or can be inferred from the principal's conduct, provided she knows of the unauthorised transaction,[749] where her conduct unequivocally shows that she has affirmed it, notwithstanding an express denial of having ratified.[750] Total inaction or passive acquiescence alone are generally inadequate,[751] but may demonstrate implied ratification in certain circumstances, such as where the principal knows that the agent believed he was authorised to enter the transaction in question, and the principal fails to correct this error.[752]

410. Ratification must be done within a reasonable period after the time that the principal ought to have become aware of the transaction,[753] and certainly before the time specified for performance of the contract.[754] Ratification will also be barred when to permit it would unfairly prejudice the interests of the third party.

---

743. A representation will therefore not render the principal liable on the contract either if the third party was unaware of it, or realised its falsity prior to contracting.
744. *Gaydamak v. Leviev* [2012] EWHC 1740 (Ch), [249]. This corresponds with the general rule on contractual misrepresentation in *Redgrave v. Hurd* (1881) 20 Ch D 1. Cf *Jacobs v. Morris* [1902] 1 Ch 816; *Overbrooke Estates Ltd v. Glencombe Properties Ltd* [1974] 1 WLR 1335.
745. Commercial Agents (Council Directive) Regulations 1993 (SI 1993/3053) (Implementing EC Council Directive 86/653), as amended by Commercial Agents (Council Directive) (Amendment) Regulations 1993 (SI 1993/3173) and 1998 (SI 1998/2868).
746. Commercial Agents (Council Directive) Regulations 1993 (SI 1993/3053), regs 10(1)–(4).
747. Commercial Agents (Council Directive) Regulations 1993 (SI 1993/3053), regulation 15.
748. *Wilson v. Tumman* (1843) 6 Man & G 236. It is therefore impossible for an undisclosed principal retrospectively to ratify: *Keighley, Maxsted & Co v. Durrant* [1901] AC 240 (cf. a disclosed but *unspecified* principal: *Hagedorn v. Oliverson* (1814) 2 M & S 485).
749. *Lewis v. Read* (1845) 13 M & W 834.
750. *Cornwall v. Henson* (1750) 1 Ves Sen 509.
751. *Moon v. Towers* (1840) 8 CB (NS) 611.
752. *Suncorp Ins & Finance v. Milano Assicurazioni SpA* [1993] 2 Lloyd's Rep 225, 241.
753. *In re Portuguese Consolidated Copper Mines* (1890) 45 Ch D 16.
754. *Metropolitan Asylums Board v. Kingham* (1890) 6 TLR 217.

Chapter 2. Bailment

411. Bailment describes the transfer of physical possession of personal property for some specific purpose without any change in legal title. Bailment requires the bailee voluntarily to take possession,[755] which is differentiated from a mere licence to use the property by a degree of control and exclusivity of access. Bailment gives rise to a cause of action independent of contract, so is established even where the property is bailed gratuitously (without consideration from the bailee). The bailee has an obligation to take reasonable care of the property and return it in the condition required by the express or implied terms on which possession has been transferred. Statute now permits sale of uncollected bailed property in some instances,[756] preventing liability in the tort of conversion.

755. Someone who receives possession involuntarily will not become a bailee, but will still be liable in the tort of conversion.

756. Torts (Interference with Goods) Act 1977, ss. 12 and 13.

Chapter 3. Gaming and Wagering

412. At common law, arrangements of wager were enforceable as contractual undertakings.[757] However, in the Victorian period, increasing public concern about the immorality of gambling lead to statutory intervention, with the Gaming Act 1845 rendering all bets and wagers unenforceable.[758]

413. Today, the law favours the regulation of gambling rather than its suppression. Statute therefore provides that a contract is not unenforceable simply because it 'relates to gambling',[759] which is defined as gaming, betting, or participating in a lottery.[760] Nonetheless, the statutory language leaves open the possibility that a specific gambling contract could be unenforceable for some other reason, such as under the illegality rule.[761] Indeed, a gambling contract may offend the illegality rule for failure to conform to the rules laid down elsewhere in the statutory regulatory framework.

757. *Gilbert v. Sykes* (1812) 16 East 150.
758. Gaming Act 1845, s. 18.
759. Gambling Act 2005, s. 335(1).
760. Gambling Act 2005, s. 3. The meaning of 'betting' is furthermore declared to exclude regulated activities within the meaning of the Financial Services and Markets Act 2000, s. 22: Gambling Act 2005, s. 10.
761. Gambling Act 2005, s. 335(2).

Chapter 4. Sale of Goods

414. In contracts for the sale of goods, common law and statute supply many terms in addition to those agreed specifically by the parties. A contract for the sale of goods contains an implied undertaking by the seller that she has title to the goods, that they are free from undisclosed encumbrances, and that the buyer will enjoy quiet possession of them following the contract.[762] Contracts for the sale of goods by description or sample also contain an implied undertaking that the goods will in fact correspond with the description or sample.[763] Where goods are sold in course of business, the contract also contains an implied term that the goods will be of satisfactory quality and reasonably fit for any planned purpose that the buyer makes known to the seller either expressly or impliedly.[764]

415. Only some of these implied terms can be excluded by express provision. In the case of consumer contracts, the terms cannot be excluded or restricted by the trader against the consumer.[765] For non-consumer contracts, attempts to exclude these implied terms are subject to the test of reasonableness contained in the Unfair Contract Terms Act 1977.[766]

762. For non-consumer contracts, Sale of Goods Act 1979, s. 12. For consumer contracts, Consumer Rights Act 2015, s. 17.
763. For non-consumer contracts, Sale of Goods Act 1979, ss. 13 and 15. For consumer contracts, Consumer Rights Act 2015, ss. 11 and 13.
764. For non-consumer contracts, Sale of Goods Act 1979, s. 14. For consumer contracts, Consumer Rights Act 2015, ss.9–10.
765. Consumer Rights Act 2015, s. 31.
766. Unfair Contract Terms Act 1977, s. 6.

Chapter 5. Building Contracts, Hire of Work & Skills

416. Where the supplier of a service is acting in course of business, statute imposes an implied term that the service will be carried out with reasonable care and skill.[767] Where this term has been implied into a consumer contract, they cannot be excluded or restricted by the trader against the consumer.[768] For non-consumer contracts, it is possible to exclude or vary these duties by express agreement or by reference to trade custom or course of dealing between the parties,[769] subject to the statutory test of reasonableness.[770]

767. For non-consumer contracts, Supply of Goods and Services Act 1982, s. 13. For consumer contracts, Consumer Rights Act 2015, s. 49.
768. Consumer Rights Act 2015, s. 57.
769. Supply of Goods and Services Act 1982, ss. 11 and 16.
770. Unfair Contract Terms Act 1977, s. 6.

Chapter 6. Lease, Commercial and Agricultural Leases

417. There is much statutory reduction of contractual freedom in this area. Subject to express exclusion, the law implies into lease contracts a term obliging the landlord to guarantee the tenant quiet possession of the property,[771] and an undertaking that properties let furnished will be fit for habitation as soon as the tenancy begins.[772] Statutory rent control has declined with the ascendance of free market ideology, but there remain statutory limitations on landlords' rights to terminate the tenancy for breach of the tenant's obligations.

418. Where the contract is between a tenant and the landlord who owns many premises within the same building, the contract is deemed to contain an implied term that the landlord undertakes to maintain common areas,[773] unless there are express terms to the contrary. Landlords also have implied statutory duties to repair the premises, and in a tenancy of a dwelling house for a turn less than seven years these implied terms cannot be excluded.[774]

771. *Markham v. Paget* [1908] 1 Ch 697.
772. *Collins v. Hopkins* [1923] 2 KB 617.
773. *Liverpool City Council v. Irwin* [1977] AC 239.
774. Landlord and Tenant Act 1985, s. 12.

Chapter 7. Compromise Settlement

419. See paragraphs [348]–[349].

Chapter 8. Suretyship

420. See paragraphs [126] and [129].

Chapter 9. Pledge

421. In a pledge agreement, the pledgor (borrower) transfers possession of an asset to the pledgee (lender) as security for a debt. The lender has the right to dispose of the asset in the event that the borrower defaults on the loan. The lender thus enforces her security interest by exercising her power of sale to recoup the value of the loan advanced.

422. A pledge removes the pledged assets from the pool of assets available to the borrower's liquidators, and other creditors with fixed or floating charges over the borrower's assets.

423. Essential to the creation of a pledge is a manifested intention to create this kind of security interest, and the transfer of possession of the assets. The possession transferred to the lender can be constructive rather than actual, and often involves delivering the keys to property in which the pledged goods are stored. Once the pledge is made, the lender only loses her security interest in the asset if she voluntarily surrenders legal possession,[775] which does not necessarily result from merely giving temporary detention of the goods to another.

775. *Bassano v. Toft* [2014] EWHC 377 (QB).

Chapter 10. Loans

424. Loans are subject to statutory control, particularly for the purposes of protecting consumers. For instance, the court can intervene where a contract is unfair to the debtor due to its terms or the way the creditor has acted, including the way the creditor has enforced her own rights under the contract. The court can order the creditor to repay some of the money paid, reduce the sums payable by the debtor, or alter the terms of the contract.[776]

776. Consumer Credit Act 1974, ss. 140A-C.

Chapter 11. Contracts with the Government and Other Public Administrations

425. See paragraphs [15]–[17].

Chapter 12. Contract of Partnership

426. Statute defines partnership as 'the relationship which subsists between persons carrying on a business in common with a view of profit'.[777] Although often concluded in a written contract, a partnership can validly be created by oral agreement, or even without any express statements, simply by being inferred from the respective parties' conduct. There is no requirement that the parties understand the notion of legal partnership or intend specifically to bring one into existence; parties are deemed to be legal partners if they conduct themselves in accordance with the law's understanding of partnership.

427. A partnership has no separate legal personality, and therefore cannot be used to achieve limited liability.[778] Rather, each partner is jointly and severally liable for the debts of the partnership arising during her time as a partner.

428. The Partnership Act 1890 provides that each partner is entitled to participate in the management of the concern, to have an equal share in its profits, to an indemnity in respect of liabilities undertaken in the course of business, and not to be excluded from the partnership by the other partners. Nonetheless, partnerships can expressly exclude or modify the default provisions of the Act, and indeed this is the norm for partnerships created by written contracts.

777. Partnership Act 1890, s. 1.

778. An exception is provided by the Limited Liability Partnerships Act 2000, which allows liability to be limited with respect to the debts incurred in general business, but does not allow the limiting of individual partners' liability for negligence.

Chapter 13. Quasi-contracts

§1. Negotiorum Gestio

429. In some circumstances, someone who acts to preserve another's property without the owner's prior authorisation – i.e., where there exists no consensual agency – can claim against the owner.[779] To succeed, the intervener must have acted in good faith, believing that her actions were in the owner's interests and commercially necessary.[780] Moreover, it must have been impossible to check with the owner to determine his wishes in advance of the intervention.[781]

430. It does not seem that a cause of action arises simply for improving the condition of another's property without prior authorisation. However, if sued in the tort of conversion for interference with property, the law will offset the intervener's liability to take account of the improvements made to the property in question.[782]

431. English law does not recognise the above claims as a species of quasi-contract *per se*. Instead it regards the intervener as having been the agent of the property owner. However, the intervener's right to compensation from the owner does not necessarily entail that the intervener would have had authority to commit the owner to contract with a third party in service of the property in question; the doctrine of 'agency of necessity' can, but need not, [783] entail agency in this ordinary legal sense. Nonetheless there is an important link with true agency in that the intervener's claim against the owner will fail if the intervener acted in the genuine but mistaken belief that the property saved was her own, on the basis that she cannot therefore have been acting on behalf of another, but in her own interests.

§2. Enrichment Without Cause

432. There can be a claim in the absence of a contract to prevent unjust enrichment where the claimant conferred a benefit on the defendant at the defendant's request in a context in which the conferral of this benefit was not expected to be gratuitous. If

779. This does not amount to a proprietary claim on the property saved, only to a personal right against the owner: *Binstead v. Buck* (1776) 2 Wm Bl 1117; *Nicholson v. Chapman* (1793) 2 H Bl 254.
780. Merely alleviating an inconvenience will generally not qualify: *Sachs v. Miklos* [1948] 1 KB 23.
781. Or if that person, once contacted, nonetheless fails to give instructions: *China Pacific SA v. Food Corp of India (The Winson)* [1982] AC 939, 962.
782. *Peruvian Guano Co v. Dreyfus Bros* [1892] AC 166, 176; in the context of goods, *see* Torts (Interference with Goods) Act 1977, ss. 6(1) and 3(7). At least at common law, this is rationalised not as compensating the intervener, but at more accurately reflecting the value of the property of which the claimant has been deprived: *Munro v. Wilmott* [1949] 1 KB 295.
783. *China Pacific SA v. Food Corp of India (The Winson)* [1982] AC 939.

this is established, the defendant must pay a *quantum meruit* (the value of the benefits conferred) as restitution of the benefits conferred by the claimant's actions.

433. This is important for pre-contractual expenditures, where the claimant confers a benefit on the defendant as premature performance of obligations the final contract is intended to impose, but this action has not been specifically *requested* by the defendant in a sense that will support a finding of actual contract formation with an implied term to pay a reasonable sum.[784] If such a benefit has been provided in the pre-contractual stage, the court can look to the negotiations for help valuing the benefit, because this shows the values the parties ascribed to its conferral.[785]

434. It is less certain whether actions of the claimant can found a claim independent of any benefit that they confer on the defendant. In some cases such actions have been allowed,[786] although the juristic basis is unclear. It is not a situation of unjust enrichment because the quantum awarded does not equate to the value of the benefit conferred. Indeed, the cases that have allowed a cause of action on this basis have tended to value recovery by the costs incurred by the claimant, rather than the value of the benefits received by the defendant.[787] Clearly therefore, this action curiously protects reliance, even in the absence of an express or implied contract.

§3. Money Paid but Not Due

435. Generally a payer can recover money that was paid pursuant to a void contract,[788] no matter the cause of the contract's voidness.[789] This right exists despite the fact that both parties may have performed their putative contractual obligations.[790] In this way, recoverability of money under this principle is distinct from recovery for total failure of the basis of a valid contract. However, the recoverability of the money ultimately depends on the reason for which the contract is void. For example, if the contract is void for illegality, there may be cases in which the court would conclude it is contrary to public policy even to permit the recovery of the money. However, a contract's illegality will be less likely to defeat the recovery of money paid than to defeat an action to enforce the contract itself.[791]

---

784. Both of those two situations must be distinguished from the third possibility, namely that the conferral of the benefit is just one party's attempt to put herself in the best position to win the eventual contract. This comes under the normal non-recoverability of pre-contractual expenditures: *Regalian Properties Plc v. London Docklands Development Corp* [1995] 1 WLR 212; *William Lacey (Hounslow) Ltd v. Davis* [1957] 1 WLR 932.
785. *Way v. Latilla* [1937] 3 All ER 759, 764, per Lord Atkin; *Benedetti v. Sawiris* [2013] UKSC 50, [2014] AC 938, [168].
786. *William Lacey (Hounslow) Ltd v. Davis* [1957] 1 WLR 932, 939.
787. *Brewer Street Investments Ltd v. Barclay Woollen Co Ltd* [1954] 1 QB 428.
788. *In re London City Commercial Reinsurance Office* [1922] 2 Ch 67
789. This is true even if the payment was made in the mistaken belief that the contract was legally valid: *Kleinwort Benson Ltd v. Lincoln City Council* [1999] 2 AC 349.
790. *Kleinwort Benson Ltd v. Lincoln City Council* [1999] 2 AC 349.
791. *Patel v. Mirza* [2016] UKSC 42.

Selected Bibliography

P Atiyah, 'Consideration: A Restatement' in *Essays on Contract* (Oxford University Press, 1986)

R Brownsword, 'Good Faith in Contracts Revisited' (1996) 49 Current Legal Problems 111

R Brownsword, *Contract Law: Themes for the Twenty-First Century*, 2nd edn (Oxford University Press, 2006)

A Burrows, 'Reforming privity of contract: Law Commission Report No. 242' (1996) Lloyd's Maritime and Commercial Law Quarterly 467

J Carter, A Phang and J Poole, 'Reactions to *Williams v Roffey*' (1995) 8 JCL 248

E Cooke, 'Working Together? Contract, estoppel and the business relationship' [2002] 1 Journal of Obligations and Remedies 5

C Fried, *Contract as Promise: A Theory of Contractual Obligation* (Oxford University Press, 1981)

D Harris, A Ogus and J Phillips, 'Contract remedies and the consumer surplus' (1979) 95 LQR 581

W Howarth, 'The Meaning of Objectivity in Contract' (1984) 100 LQR 265

W Howarth, 'A note on the objective of objectivity in contract' (1987) 103 LQR 527

J Langbein, 'The Contractarian Basis of the Law of Trusts' (1995) 105 Yale Law Journal 625

J Langbein, 'Why the rule in *Saunders v Vautier* is wrong' in P Turner (ed), *Equity and Administration* (Cambridge University Press, 2016)

P Luther, 'Campbell, Espinasse and the sailors: text and context in the common law' (1999) 19 Legal Studies 526

P Matthews, 'Why the rule in *Saunders v. Vautier* is wrong: A commentary' in P Turner (ed), *Equity and Administration* (Cambridge University Press, 2016)

J McCaughran, 'Implied terms: the journey of the man on the Clapham omnibus' (2011) 70 CLJ 607

P Millet, 'Equity's Place in the Law of Commerce' (1998) 114 LQR 214

J O'Sullivan, 'In defence of *Foakes v. Beer*' (1996) 55 CLJ 225

V Palmer, *The Paths to Privity: the History of Third Party Beneficiaries in English Law* (Austin & Winfield, 1992)

S Perry, 'Judicial Obligation, Precedent and the Common Law' (1987) 7 Oxford Journal of Legal Studies 215

C Slade, 'The Myth of Mistake in the English law of Contract' (1954) 70 LQR 885

J Stapleton, 'Duty of care and economic loss: a wider agenda' (1991) 107 LQR 249

R Stevens, 'The Contracts (Rights of Third Parties) Act 1999' (2004) 120 LQR 292

J Vorster, 'A Comment on the Meaning of Objectivity in Contract' (1987) 104 LQR 274

Table of Cases

Actionstrength Ltd v. International Glass Engineering [2003] UKHL 17, [2003] 2 AC 581

Adam Opel GmbH v. Mitras Automotive (UK) Ltd [2007] EWHC 3205 (QB), [2008] Bus LR D55

Adams v. Lindsell (1818) 1 B & Ald 681, 106 ER 250

Addis v. Gramophone Co Ltd [1909] AC 488

Adler v. Dickson [1955] 1 QB 155

AIB Group (UK) Plc v. Mark Redler & Co [2014] UKSC 58, [2015] AC 1503

Ajayi v. RT Briscoe (Nigeria) Ltd [1964] 1 WLR 1326

Alfred McAlpine Construction Ltd v. Panatown Ltd [2001] 1 AC 518

Allcard v. Skinner (1887) 36 Ch D 145

Allied Marine Transport Ltd v. Vale do Rio Doce Novagacao SA (The Leonidas D) [1985] 1 WLR 925

Amalgamated Investment and Property Co Ltd v. Texas Commerce International Bank Ltd [1982] QB 84

Andrews v. Australia and New Zealand Banking Group Ltd [2012] HCA 12

Anglia Television Ltd v. Reed [1972] 1 QB 60

Antios Compania Naviera SA v. Salen Referierna AB [1985] AC 191

Arbuthnot Leasing International Ltd v. Havelet Leasing Ltd (No 2) [1990] BCC 636

Arnold v. Britton [2015] UKSC 36, [2015] AC 1619

Associated Japanese Bank (International) Ltd v. Credit du Nord SA [1989] 1 WLR 255

Astley v. Reynolds (1731) 2 Str 915

Atlas Express Ltd v. Kafco (Importers and Distributors Ltd) [1989] 1 QB 833

Attorney General for Ceylon v. Silva [1953] AC 461

Attorney General of Belize v. Belize Telecom Ltd [2009] 1 WLR 1988

Attorney General v. Blake [2001] 1 AC 268

Bailey v. Angove's PTY Ltd [2016] UKSC 47

Baird Textiles Holdings Ltd v. Marks and Spencer Plc [2001] EWCA Civ 274, [2002] 1 All ER (Comm) 737

Balfour v. Balfour [1919] 2 KB 571

Ballet v. Mingay [1943] KB 281

Bank of Credit and Commerce International v. Aboody [1990] 1 QB 923

Bank of Credit and Commerce International v. Ali [2002] 1 AC 251

Banque Financière de la Cité SA v. Westgate Insurance Co Ltd [1991] 2 AC 249

Barclays Bank v. O'Brien [1994] 1 AC 180

Barton v. Armstrong [1976] AC 104

Bassano v. Toft [2014] EWHC 377 (QB)

Benedetti v. Sawiris [2013] UKSC 50, [2014] AC 938

Beswick v. Beswick [1968] AC 58

Binstead v. Buck (1776) 2 Wm Bl 1117

Bisset v. Wilkinson [1927] AC 177

Blackpool and Fylde Aero Club Ltd v. Blackpool Borough Council [1990] 1 WLR 1195

Blankley v. Central Manchester & Manchester University Children's Hospitals NHS Trust [2015] EWCA Civ 18

Blomley v. Ryan [1956] HCA 81, (1956) 99 CLR 362

Bolton v. Mahadeva [1972] 2 All ER 1322

Borrelli v. Ting [2010] UKPC 21

Boulton v. Jones (1857) 2 H & N 564

Boustany v. Piggott [1995] 69 P&CR 298

Boyter v. Thomson [1995] 2 AC 629

BP Refinery v. Shire of Hastings (1977) 52 ALJR 20

Bradbury v. Morgan (1862) 1 H & C 249, 158 ER 877

Bremer Handelgesellschaft mbH v. Vanden Avenne-Izegem PVBA [1978] 2 Lloyd's Rep 109

Brennan v. Bolt Burden [2004] EWCA Civ 1017, [2005] QB 303

Brewer Street Investments Ltd v. Barclay Woollen Co Ltd [1954] 1 QB 428

Brikom Investments Ltd v. Carr [1979] QB 467

Brinkibon v. Stahag Stahl [1983] 2 AC 34

British Car Auctions v. Wright [1972] 1 WLR 1519

British Concrete Co v. Schleff [1921] 2 Ch 563

British Crane Hire Corp Ltd v. Ipswich Plant Hire Ltd [1975] QB 303

British Steel Corp v. Cleveland Bridge and Engineering Co Ltd [1984] 1 All ER 504

Table of Cases

British Westinghouse Electric and Manufacturing Co Ltd v. Underground Electric Railways Company of London Ltd [1912] AC 673

Brown v. Gould [1972] Ch 53

Bull v. Pitney Bowes Ltd [1966] 2 All ER 384

Burrell v. Jones (1819) 3 B & Ald 47

Butler Machine Tool Company v. Ex-Cell-O Corporation (England) [1979] 1 WLR 401

Byrne v. Van Tienhoven & Co (1880) 5 CPD 344

C Czarnikow Ltd v. Koufos (The Heron II) [1969] 1 AC 350

C.A. Norgren Co and others v. Technomarketing and others (1983) (unreported)

Callisher v. Bischoffshein (1870) LR 5 QB 449

Campanari v. Woodburn (1854) 15 CB 400

Caparo Industries Plc v. Dickman [1990] 2 AC 605

Car and Universal Finance v. Caldwell [1965] 1 QB 525

Carewatch Care Services Ltd v. Focus Caring Services Ltd [2014] EWHC 2313

Carlill v. Carbolic Smoke Ball Co [1893] 1 QB 256

Carter v. Boehm (1766) 3 Burr 1905, 97 ER 1162

Cassel & Co Ltd v. Broome [1972] AC 1027

Cavendish Square Holding BV v. Talal El Makdessi and *ParkingEye Ltd v. Beavis* [2015] UKSC 67, [2015] 3 WLR 1373

CCC Films (London) Ltd v. Impact Quadrant Films Ltd [1985] 1 QB 16

Central London Property Trust Ltd v. High Trees House Ltd [1947] KB 130

Centrovincial Estates Plc v. Merchant Investors Assurance Co [1983] Com LR 158

Channel Tunnel Group Ltd v. Balfour Beatty Construction Ltd [1993] AC 334

Chapelton v. Barry Urban District Council [1940] 1 KB 532

Chappel & Co Ltd v. Nestle Co Ltd [1960] AC 87

Chapple v. Cooper (1844) 13 M & W 252, 153 ER 105

Charlock v. Liverpool Corporation [1968] 1 WLR 1498

Chartbrook Ltd v. Persimmon Homes Ltd [2009] UKHL 38, [2009] 1 AC 1101

Cheese v. Thomas [1994] 1 WLR 129

China Pacific SA v. Food Corp of India (The Winson) [1982] AC 939

Chohan v. Saggar [1994] BCC 134

CIBC Mortgages Plc v. Pitt [1994] 1 AC 200

Clea Shipping Corporation v. Bulk Oil International Ltd (The Alaskan Trader) [1983] 1 Lloyd's Rep 315

Clements v. London & North Western Railway [1894] 2 QB 482

Clydebank Engineering and Shipbuilding Co Ltd v. Yzquierdo y Castaneda [1905] AC 6

Co-operative Insurance Society Ltd v. Argyll Stores (Holdings) Ltd [1998] AC 1

Coatsworth v. Johnson (1886) 54 LT 520

Cobbe v. Yeoman's Row Management Ltd [2008] UKHL 55, [2008] 1 WLR 1752

Collier v. P and M J Wright (Holdings) Ltd [2007] EWCA Civ 1329, [2008] 1 WLR 643

Collins v. Godefroy (1831) B & Ad 950

Collins v. Hopkins [1923] 2 KB 617

Combe v. Combe [1951] 2 KB 215

Commercial Plastics Ltd v. Vincent [1964] 3 WLR 820

Commission for the New Towns v. Cooper (Great Britain) Ltd [1995] Ch 259

Commonwealth v. Verwayen [1990] HCA 39

Compagnie de Commerce et Commission SARL v. Parkinson Stove Co Ltd [1953] 1 Lloyd's Rep 532

Conlon v. Simms [2006] EWCA Civ 1749, [2008] 1 WLR 484

Cook v. Wright (1861) 1 B & S 559, 121 ER 822

Cornwall v. Henson (1750) 1 Ves Sen 509

Couchman v. Hill [1947] KB 554

Courtney & Fairbairn Ltd v. Tolani Bros (Hotels) Ltd [1975] 1 WLR 297

Coward v. Motor Insurers' Bureau [1963] 1 QB 259

Cowern v. Nield [1912] 2 KB 419

Credit Lyonnais Bank Nederland v. Burch [1977] 1 All ER 144

Cresswell v. Potter [1978] 1 WLR 255

CTN Cash and Carry Ltd v. Gallaher Ltd [1994] 4 All ER 714

Currie v. Misa (1875) 10 Exch 153

Curtis v. Chemical Cleaning [1951] 1 KB 805

Cutter v. Powell (1795) 6 Term Rep 320, 101 ER 573

Czarnikow v. Roth Schmidt & Co [1922] 2 KB 478

D & C Builders v. Rees [1966] 2 WLR 28

Darlington Borough Council v. Wiltshier Northern Ltd [1995] 1 WLR 68

Daulia Ltd v. Four Millbank Nominees Ltd [1978] Ch 231

Davis Contractors v. Fareham Urban District Council [1956] AC 696

Table of Cases

Dawson v. Great Northern & City Railway [1905] 1 KB 260

De Francesco v. Barnum (1890) 45 Ch D 438

Decro-Wall International SA v. Practitioners in Marketing Ltd [1971] 1 WLR 361

Denmark Productions Ltd v. Boscobel Productions Ltd [1969] 1 QB 699

Dicke Bentley Productions Ltd v. Harold Smith (Motors) Ltd [1965] 1 WLR 623

Dickinson v. Dodds [1876] 2 Ch D 463

Dickinson v. Valpy (1829) 10 B & C 128

Dimmock v. Hallet (1866) 2 Ch App 21

Dimskal Shipping Co SA v. International Transport Workers Federation [1992] 2 AC 152

Doleman & Sons v. Osset Corporation [1912] 3 KB 257

Dolphin Maritime & Aviation Services Ltd v. Sveriges Angfartygs Assurans Forening [2009] EWHC 716 (Comm), [2009] 2 Lloyd's Rep 123

Domb and another v. Isoz [1980] Ch 548

Dominion Corporate Trustees Ltd v. Debenhams Properties Ltd [2010] EWHC 1193

Don King Productions Inc v. Warren [2000] Ch 291

Dora v. Simper [2000] 2 BCLC 561

Drew v. Nunn (1879) 4 QBD 661

DSND Subsea Ltd v. Petroleum Geo Services ASA [2000] BLR 530

Dunhill v. Burgin (Nos 1 and 2) [2014] UKSC 18, [2014] 1 WLR 933

Dunlop Pneumatic Tyre Co Ltd v. New Garage & Motor Co Ltd [1915] AC 79

Dunlop Pneumatic Tyre Co Ltd v. Selfridge & Co Ltd [1915] AC 847

Durham Bros v. Robertson [1898] 1 QBD 765

Durham Fancy Goods Ltd v. Michael Jackson (Fancy Goods) Ltd [1968] 2 QB 839

Dutton v. Poole (1678) 2 Lev 210

Earl of Aylesford v. Morris (1873) 8 Ch App 484

Eastwood v. Kenyon (1840) 11 Ad & E 438, 113 ER 482

Edgington v. Fitzmaurice (1885) 29 Ch D 459

Edwards v. Skyways [1964] 1 QB 349

Elliott v. Turquand (1881) 7 App Cas 79

Else (1982) Ltd v. Parkland Holdings Ltd [1994] 1 BCLC 130

Entores Ltd v. Miles Far East Corporation [1955] 2 QB 327

Erlanger v. New Sambrero Phosphate Co (1878) 3 App Cas 1218

Errington v. Errington Woods [1952] 1 KB 290

Esso Petroleum Co Ltd v. Mardon [1976] QB 801

Euro-Diam v. Bathurst Ltd [1988] 2 WLR 517

European Asian Bank v. Punjab & Sind Bank (No 2) [1983] 1 WLR 642

Ex parte Agra Bank (1868) LR 3 Ch App 555

Exxonmobil Sales and Supply Corporation v. Texaco Ltd [2003] EWHC 1964 (Comm), [2003] 2 Lloyd's Rep 686

Farley v. Skinner [2001] 4 All ER 801

Fawcett v. Smethurst (1914) 84 LJKB 473

Federal Commerce and Navigation Co Ltd v. Tradax Export SA (The Maratha Envoy) [1978] AC 1

Felthouse v. Bindley (1862) 11 CB NS 869, 142 ER 1037

Fibrosa Spolka Akcyjna v. Fairbairn Lawson Combe Barbour Ltd [1943] AC 32

Financings Ltd v. Stimson [1962] 3 All ER 386

First National Securities Ltd v. Jones [1978] Ch 109

Fisher v. Bell [1961] 1 WLR 394

Foakes v. Beer (1884) 9 App Cas 605

Foley v. Classique Coaches Ltd [1934] 2 KB 1

Forster v. Baker [1910] 2 KB 636

Fry v. Lane (1888) 40 Ch D 312

Garnac Grain Co Inc v. Faure & Fairclough Ltd [1968] AC 1130

Gaydamak v. Leviev [2012] EWHC 1740 (Ch)

Georgi Velichkov Barbudev v. Eurocom Cable Management Bulgaria Eood [2012] EWCA Civ 548

Geys v. Société Genérale (London Branch) [2012] UKSC 63, [2013] 1 AC 523

Gibson v. Manchester City Council [1978] 1 WLR 520; [1979] 1 WLR 294

Gil v. Baygreen Properties Ltd [2004] EWHC 1732 (Ch), [2005] BPIR 95

Gilbert v. Sykes (1812) 16 East 150

Glasbrook Bros v. Glamorgan County Council [1925] AC 270

Goddard's Case (1584) 2 Co Rep 4b, 76 ER 396

Goodchild v. Bradbury [2006] EWCA Civ 1868, [2006] All ER (D) 247

Gore v. Gibson (1845) 13 M & W 621, 153 ER 260

Government of Zanzibar v. British Aerospace (Lancaster House) Ltd [2000] 1 WLR 2333

Granatino v. Radmacher [2010] UKSC 42, [2010] 3 WLR 1367

Table of Cases

Great Atlantic Insurance Co v. Home Insurance Co (The New York Star) [1981] 1 WLR 138

Great Peace Shipping Ltd v. Tsavliris (International) Ltd [2002] EWCA Civ 1407, [2003] QB 679

Groom v. Crocker [1939] 1 KB 194

Hadley v. Baxendale (1854) 9 Ex Ch 341, 156 ER 145

Hagedorn v. Oliverson (1814) 2 M & S 485

Halki Shipping Corporation v. Sopex Oils Ltd [1998] 1 WLR 726

Halpern v. Halpern [2007] EWCA Civ 291, [2008] QB 195

Hamilton v. Watson (1845) 12 Cl & Fin 109, 8 ER 1339

Harding v. Harding (1886) 17 QBD 442

Hardwick Game Farm v. Suffolk Agricultural and Poultry Producers' Association [1966] 1 WLR 287

Harris v. Great Western Railway Co (1876) 1 QBD 515

Harris v. Sheffield United Football Club Ltd [1988] QB 77

Hart v. O'Connor [1985] AC 1000

Hartley v. Ponsonby (1857) 26 LJ QB 322, 119 ER 1471

Hartog v. Colin & Shields [1939] 3 All ER 566

Harvela Investments Ltd v. Royal Trust Co of Canada (CI) Ltd [1986] AC 207

Harvey v. Facey [1893] AC 552

Heard v. Pilley (1869) LR 4 Ch 548

Hedley Byrne & Co Ltd v. Heller & Partners Ltd [1964] AC 465

Heilbut, Symons & Co v. Buckleton [1913] AC 30

Helstan Securities Ltd v. Hertfordshire County Council [1978] 3 All ER 262

Hely-Hutchinson v. Brayhead Ltd [1968] 1 QB 549

Henderson v. Merrett Syndicates Ltd [1995] 2 AC 145

Henthorn v. Fraser [1892] 2 Ch 27

Herbert v. Doyle [2010] EWCA Civ 1095, [2011] 1 EGLR 119

Hercules Piling Ltd v. Tilbury Construction Ltd (1992) 61 Build LR 107

Herne Bay Steam Boat Co v. Hutton [1903] 2 KB 683

HIH Casualty and General Insurance Ltd v. Chase Manhattan Bank [2001] EWCA Civ 1250, [2001] 2 Lloyd's Rep 483; [2003] UKHL 6, [2003] 2 Lloyd's Rep 61

Hochster v. De La Tour (1852) 2 El & Bl 678, 118 ER 922

Hoenig v. Isaacs [1952] 2 All ER 176

Hollier v. Rambler Motors (AMC) [1972] 2 WLR 401

Holman v. Johnson (1775) 1 Cowp 341, 98 ER 1120

Holwell Securities v. Hughes [1974] 1 WLR 155

Home Insurance Co v. Administrata Asigurarilor [1983] 2 Lloyd's Rep 674

Hounga v. Allen [2014] UKSC 47, [2014] 1 WLR 2889

Household Fire Insurance v. Grant (1878–79) LR 4 Ex D 216

Howard Marine and Dredging Co Ltd v. A Ogden & Sons [1978] QB 574

Hughes v. Metropolitan Railway (1876–77) LR 2 App Cas 439

Humble v. Hunter (1842) 12 QB 316

Huyton SA v. Peter Cremer GmbH & Co [1999] 1 Lloyd's Rep 620

Huyton SA v. Peter Cremer GmbH and Co [1999] 1 Lloyd's Rep 620

Hyde v. Wrench (1840) 3 Beav 334, 49 ER 132

Imperial Loan Co v. Stone [1892] 1 QB 599

In re Brocklehurst [1978] Ch 14

In re Craig [1971] Ch 95

In re London City Commercial Reinsurance Office [1922] 2 Ch 67

In re Marini Ltd [2004] BCC 172

In re Paramount Airways Limited [1993] Ch 223

In re Portuguese Consolidated Copper Mines (1890) 45 Ch D 16

In re Schebsman [1944] Ch 83

In re Selectmove Ltd [1995] 1 WLR 474

In re Sinclair's Life Policy [1938] 3 All ER 124

Ingram v. Little [1961] 1 QB 31

Inland Revenue Commission v. Hashimi [2002] EWCA Civ 981, [2002] BCC 943

Inntrepreneur Pub Co (GL) v. East Crown Ltd [2000] 2 Lloyd's Rep 611

Interfoto Picture Library Ltd v. Stiletto Visual Programmes Ltd [1989] QB 433

Investors Compensation Scheme v. West Bromwich Building Society [1998] 1 WLR 896

Italmare Shipping Co v. Ocean Tanker Co Inc (The Rio Sun) [1981] 2 Lloyd's Rep 489

J Lauritzen AS v. Wijsmuller BV (The Super Servant II) [1990] 1 Lloyd's Rep 1

Jackson v. Horizon Holidays Ltd [1975] 1 WLR 1468

Jacobs v. Morris [1902] 1 Ch 816

Jacoby v. Whitmore (1883) 49 LT 335

Table of Cases

JEB Fasteners Ltd v. Marks, Bloom & Co [1983] 3 All ER 289

Jetivia SA v. Bilta (UK) Ltd [2015] UKSC 23

John Grimes Partnership Ltd v. Gubbins [2013] EWCA Civ 37

Johnson v. Agnew [1980] AC 367

Jones v. Padavatton [1969] 1 WLR 328

Jones v. Sherwood Computer Services [1992] 1 WLR 227

Jones v. Vernon Pools Ltd [1938] 2 All ER 626

Jorden v. Money (1854) 5 HL Cas 185, 10 ER 868

Kay v. Lambeth London Borough Council [2006] UKHL 10, [2006] 2 AC 465

Keighley, Maxsted & Co v. Durrant [1901] AC 240

Kennedy v. De Trafford [1897] AC 180

Kleinwort Benson Ltd v. Lincoln City Council [1999] 2 AC 349

Kleinwort Benson Ltd v Malaysia Mining Corp Berhad [1989] 1 WLR 379

Kolmar Group AG v. Traxpo Enterprises Pty Ltd [2010] EWHC 113 (Comm), [2010] 2 Lloyd's Rep 653

Krell v. Henry [1903] 2 KB 740

Kyle Bay Ltd (T/A Astons Nightclub) v. Underwriters [2006] EWHC 607 (Comm), [2006] Lloyd's Rep IR 718

L'Estrange v. Graucob [1934] 2 KB 394

Lampleigh v. Braithwait (1615) Hobart 105, 80 ER 255

Lancashire Loans Ltd v. Black (1934) 1 KB 380

Leaf v. International Galleries [1950] 2 KB 86

Les Laboratoires Servier v. Apotex Inc [2012] EWCA Civ 593, [2013] RPC 21; [2014] UKSC 55, [2014] 3 WLR 1257

Lewis v. Averay [1971] 3 WLR 603

Lewis v. Read (1845) 13 M & W 834

Linden Gardens Trust Ltd v. Lenesta Sludge Disposals Ltd [1994] 1 AC 85

Little v Courage (1994) 70 P & CR 469

Liverpool City Council v. Irwin [1977] AC 239

Lloyds Bank Ltd v. Marcan [1973] 1 WLR 1387

Lloyds Bank v. Bundy [1975] QB 326

Lucas v. Beale (1851) 10 CB 739

Lumley v. Gye (1852) 2 El & Bl 216, 118 ER 749

Luxor (Eastbourne) Ltd v. Cooper [1941] AC 108

Mahoney v. Purnell [1996] 3 All ER 61

Manai Investment Co Ltd v. Eagle Star Life Assurance Co Ltd [1997] AC 749

Maredelanto Compania Naviera SA v. Bergbau-Handel GmbH [1971] 1 QB 164

Markham v. Paget [1908] 1 Ch 697

Marks and Spencer Plc v. BNP Paribas Securities Services Trust Company (Jersey) Ltd [2015] UKSC 72

Martin-Baker Aircraft Co Ltd v. Canadian Flight Equipment Ltd [1955] 2 QB 556

Martyn v. Hind (1776) Cowp 437

Matthews v. Baxter (1873) LR 8 Exch 132

May & Butcher v. R [1934] 2 KB 17

McCall v. Australian Meat Co Ltd (1870) 19 WR 188

McCutcheon v. David MacBrayne Ltd [1964] 1 WLR 165

McRae v. Commonwealth Disposals Commission [1951] HCA 79

Megaro v. Di Popolo Hotels Ltd [2007] EWCA Civ 309, [2007] All ER (D) 210

Mercantile Union Guarantee Corporation v. Ball [1937] 2 KB 498

Merritt v. Merritt [1970] 1 WLR 1211

Metropolitan Asylums Board v. Kingham (1890) 6 TLR 217

Midland Bank Trust Co Ltd v. Hett, Stubbs & Kemp [1979] Ch 348

Miliangos v. George Frank (Textiles) Ltd [1976] AC 443

Moon v. Franklin [1996] BPIR 196

Moon v. Towers (1840) 8 CB (NS) 611

Moore Stephens v. Stone & Rolls Ltd (in liquidation) [2008] EWCA Civ 644; [2009] UKHL 39, [2009] 1 AC 1391

Munro v. Wilmott [1949] 1 KB 295

Murray v. Leisureplay Plc [2005] EWCA Civ 963, [2005] IRLR 946

MWB Business Exchange Centres Ltd v. Rock Advertising Ltd [2016] EWCA Civ 553

Nash v. Inman [1908] 2 KB 1

National Carriers Ltd v. Panalpina (Northern) Ltd [1981] AC 675

National Westminster Bank Plc v. Morgan [1985] AC 686

Nicholson v. Chapman (1793) 2 H Bl 254

Nisshin Shipping Co Ltd v. Cleaves & Co Ltd [2003] EWHC 2602, [2004] 1 Lloyd's Rep 38

Nordenfelt v. Maxim Nordenfelt Guns and Ammunition Co Ltd [1894] AC 535

Nottingham Patent Brick & Tile Co v. Butler (1889) 16 QBD 778

Table of Cases

NZ Shipping Co Ltd v. A M Satterthwaite & Co Ltd (The Eurymedon) [1975] AC 154

O'Sullivan v. Management Agency and Music Ltd [1985] QB 428

OBG Ltd v. Allan [2007] UKHL 21, [2008] 1 AC 1

Occidental Worldwide Investment Corp v. Skibs A/S Avanti (The Siboen and the Sibotre) [1976] 1 Lloyd's Rep 293

Office of Fair Trading v. Abbey National Plc [2009] UKSC 6, [2010] 1 AC 696

Olley v. Marlborough Court Ltd [1949] 1 KB 532

Omak Maritime Ltd v. Mamola Challenger Shipping Co Ltd [2010] EWHC 2026 (Comm), [2010] WLR (D) 230

Ormrod v. Crosville Motor Services Ltd [1953] 1 WLR 1120

Oscar Cess Ltd v. Williams [1957] 1 WLR 370

Overbrooke Estates Ltd v. Glencombe Properties Ltd [1974] 1 WLR 1335

Overseas Tankship (UK) Ltd v. Morts Dock and Engineering Co Ltd (The Wagon Mound) (No 1) [1961] AC 388

Paal Wilson & Co A/S v. Partenreederei Hannah Blumenthal (The Hannah Blumenthal) [1983] 1 AC 854

Pankhania v. London Borough of Hackney [2002] EWHC 2441

Pao On v. Lau Yiu Long [1980] AC 614

Paradine v. Jane (1647) Aleyn 26, 82 ER 897

Parker v. South Eastern Railway (1877) 2 CPD 416

Parker v. Winlow (1857) 7 E& B 942

Parsons (Livestock) Ltd v. Uttley Ingham & Co Ltd [1978] QB 791

Partridge v. Crittenden [1968] 2 All ER 421

Patel v. Mirza [2014] EWCA Civ 1047, [2015] 1 Ch 271; [2016] UKSC 42

Payne v. Cave (1789) 3 TR 148

Peachy v. Duke of Somerset (1720) 1 Strange 447

Pearce v. Brooks (1866) LR 1 Exch 213

Peek v. Gurney (1873) LR 6 HL 377

Peekay Intermark Ltd v. Australia and New Zealand Banking Group Ltd [2006] EWCA Civ 386; [2006] 2 Lloyd's Rep 511

Persimmon Homes Ltd v. Ove Arup & Partners Ltd [2017] EWCA Civ 373

Peruvian Guano Co v. Dreyfus Bros [1892] AC 166

Peters v. Fleming (1840) 6 M & W 42, 151 ER 314

Petromec Inc v. Petroleo Brasiliero SA [2005] EWCA Civ 891, [2006] 1 Lloyd's Rep 121

Peyman v. Lanjani [1985] Ch 457

Pharmaceutical Society of Great Britain v. Boots Cash Chemists (Southern) Ltd [1953] 1 QB 401

Phillips Products Ltd v. Hyland [1987] 1 WLR 659

Phillips v. Brooks [1919] 2 KB 243

Photo Production Ltd v. Securicor Ltd [1980] AC 827

Pillans & Rose v. Van Mierop & Hopkins (1765) 3 Burr 1663

Pinnel's Case (1602) 5 Co Rep 117a, 77 ER 237

Pioneer Shipping Ltd v. BTP Tioxide Ltd (The Nema) [1982] AC 724

Pool v. Pool (1889) 58 LJP 67

Portman Building Society v. Dusangh [2000] 2 All ER (Comm) 221

Powell v. Lee (1908) 99 LT 284

Price v. Easton (1833) 4 B & Ad 433

Prudential Assurance Co Ltd v. David Monroe Ayres & Christopher Grew [2007] EWHC 775 (Ch), [2007] All ER (D) 43

R Leslie Ltd v. Sheill [1914] 3 KB 607

R v. Attorney General for England and Wales [2003] UKPC 22, [2003] All ER (D) 246

Radford v. De Froberville [1977] 1 WLR 1262

Raiffeisen Zentralbank Osterreich AG v. Five Star General Trading LLC (The Mount I) [2001] EWCA Civ 68, [2001] 1 Lloyd's Rep 597

Raineri v. Miles [1981] AC 1050

Rainy Sky SA v. Kookmin Bank [2011] UKSC 50, [2011] 1 WLR 2900

Ramsgate Victoria Hotel Ltd v. Montefiore (1866) LR 1 Ex 109

Rann v. Hughes (1778) 7 Term Rep 350

Re London and Northern Bank, ex parte *Jones* [1900] 1 Ch 220

Record v. Bell [1991] 1 WLR 853

Redgrave v. Hurd (1881) 20 Ch D 1

Regalian Properties Plc v. London Docklands Development Corp [1995] 1 WLR 212

Repetto v. Millar's Karri & Jarrah Forests Ltd [1901] 2 KB 306

Republic of India v. Indian Steamship Co Ltd (No 2) [1998] AC 878

Rhodian River Shipping Co SA and Rhodian Sailor Shipping Co SA v. Halla Maritime Corp (The Rhodian River and Rhodian Sailor) [1984] 1 Lloyd's Rep 373

Rice v. Great Yarmouth Borough Council (2001) 3 LGLR 4

Robins v. Bridge (1837) 3 M& W 114

Robinson v. Harman (1848) 1 Ex Rep 850, 154 ER 363

Robophone Facilities Ltd v. Blank [1966] 1 WLR 1468

Rookes v. Barnard [1964] AC 1129

Routledge v. Grant (1828) 4 Bing 653

Royal Bank of Scotland Plc v. Etridge [1998] 4 All ER 705

Royal Bank of Scotland Plc v. Etridge (No 2) [2002] 2 AC 773

Royscott Spa Leasing v. Lovett [1995] BCC 502

Royscott Trust Ltd v. Rogerson [1991] 2 QB 297

RTS Flexible Systems Ltd v. Molkerei Alois Miller GmbH [2010] UKSC 14, [2010] 1 WLR 753

Ruxley Electronics and Construction Ltd v. Forsyth [1994] 3 All ER 801

Ryder v. Wombwell (1868) LR 4 Ex 32

S Pearson & Son Ltd v. Dublin Corporation [1907] AC 351

Sachs v. Miklos [1948] 1 KB 23

Salt v. Stratstone Specialist Ltd [2015] EWCA Civ 745

Saunders v. Anglia Building Society (Gallie v Lee) [1970] AC 1004

Saunders v. Edwards [1987] 1 WLR 1116

Scally v. Southern Health & Social Services Board [1992] 1 AC 294

Schuler AG v. Wickman Machine Tool Sales Ltd [1974] AC 235

Scotson v. Pegg (1861) 6 H & N 295, 158 ER 121

Scott v. Avery (1855) 5 HLC 811

Scriven v. Hindley [1913] 3 KB 564

Scruttons Ltd v. Midland Silicones Ltd [1962] AC 446

Shadwell v. Shadwell (1860) 9 CB (NS) 159

Shah v. Shah [2001] EWCA Civ 527, [2002] QB 35

Shanklin Pier v. Detel [1951] 2 KB 854

Shirlaw v. Southern Foundries (1926) Ltd [1939] 2 KB 206

Shogun Finance v. Hudson [2003] UKHL 62, [2004] 1 AC 919

Simpkins v. Pays [1955] 1 WLR 975

Sirius International v. FAI Insurance Ltd [2004] UKHL 54

Siu Yin Kwan v. Eastern Ins Co Ltd [1994] 2 AC 199

Skansa Rashleigh Weatherfoil Ltd v. Somerfield Stores Ltd [2006] EWCA Civ 1732, [2007] CILL 2449

Sky Petroleum Ltd v. VIP Petroleum Ltd [1974] 1 WLR 576

Sloman v. Walter (1784) 1 Bro Ch 418

Smith New Court Securities Ltd v. Scrimgeour Vickers [1996] 3 WLR 1051

Smith v. Hughes (1871) LR 6 QB 597

Smith v. Land & House Property Corporation (1884) LR 28 Ch D 7

Soleimany v. Soleimany [1999] QB 785

Solle v. Butcher [1950] 1 KB 671

Spellman v. Spellman [1961] 1 WLR 921

Spencer v. Harding (1870) LR 5 CP 561

Springwell Navigation Corp v. JP Morgan Chase Bank [2010] EWCA Civ 1221, [2010] 2 CLC 705

Spurling v. Bradshaw [1956] 1 WLR 461

Stevenson, Jaques & Co v. McLean (1880) 5 QBD 346

Stewart Gill Ltd v. Horatio Myer & Co Ltd [1992] QB 600

Stilk v. Myrick (1809) 2 Camp 317, 170 ER 1168, 6 Esp 129, 170 ER 851

Summers v. Solomon (1857) 7 E & B 879

Sumpter v. Hedges [1898] 1 QB 673

Suncorp Ins & Finance v. Milano Assicurazioni SpA [1993] 2 Lloyd's Rep 225

Supershield Ltd v. Siemens Building Technologies Fe Ltd [2010] EWCA Civ 7, [2010] 1 Lloyd's Rep 349

Tai Hing Cotton Mill Ltd v. Liu Chong Hing Bank Ltd [1986] AC 80

Tancredo v. Delagoa Bay (1889) 23 QBD 239

Tang v. Grant Thornton International Ltd [2012] EWHC 3198 (Ch), [2014] 2 CLC 663

Taylor v. Caldwell (1863) 3 B & S 826, 122 ER 309

Taylor v. Motability Finance Ltd [2004] EWHC 2619 (Comm)

Taylor v. NUS [1967] 1 WLR 532

Tekdata Interconnections Ltd v. Amphenol Ltd [2009] EWCA Civ 1209, [2010] 1 Lloyd's Rep 357

Tenax Steamship Co v. Owners of the Motor Vessel Brimnes (The Brimnes) [1975] QB 929

Thanakharn Kasikhorn Thai Chamkat (Mahachon) v. Akai Holdings Ltd [2010] HKCFA 64

The Moorcock (1889) LR 14 PD 64

Thomas Borthwick (Glasgow) Ltd v. Favre Fairclough Ltd [1968] 1 Lloyd's Rep 16

Thomas v. Thomas (1842) 2 QB 851, 114 ER 330

Table of Cases

Thomas Witter Ltd v. TBP Industries Ltd [1996] 2 All ER 573

Thompson v. London, Midland and Scotland Railway Co [1930] 1 KB 41

Thornton v. Shoe Lane Parking [1971] 2 QB 163

Tilden Rent-a-Car Co v. Clendenning (1978) 83 DLR (3d) 400

Timothy v. Simpson (1834) 6 C & P 499, 172 ER 1337

Tinn v. Hoffman & Co (1873) 29 LT 271

Tinsley v. Milligan [1994] 1 AC 340

Tito v. Waddell (No 2) [1977] Ch 106

Tool Metal Manufacturing Co Ltd v. Tungsten Electric Co Ltd [1955] 2 All ER

Torrington v. Magee [1902] 2 KB 427

Transfield Shipping Inc v. Mercator Shipping Inc (The Achilleas) [2008] UKHL 48, [2008] 3 WLR 345

Tweddle v. Atkinson (1861) 1 B & S 393, 121 ER 762

UCB Bank Plc v. Hepherd Winstanley and Pugh [1999] Lloyd's Rep PN 963

Union Eagle Ltd v. Golden Achievement Ltd [1997] AC 514

Universe Tankships Inc of Monrovia v. International Transport Workers Federation (The Universe Sentinel) [1983] AC 366

Vandepitte v. Preferred Accident Insurance Corporation of New York [1933] AC 70

Vesta v. Butcher [1988] 2 All ER 43

Wade v. Simeon (1846) 2 CB 548, 135 ER 1061

Wales v. Wadham [1977] 1 WLR 199

Walford v. Miles [1992] 2 AC 128

Walker v. Bradford Old Bank (1884) 12 QBD 511

Waltons Stores (Interstate) Ltd v. Maher [1988] HCA 7

Ward v. Byham [1956] 1 WLR 496

Warner Bros Pictures Inc v. Nelson [1937] 1 KB 209

Watford Electronics Ltd v. Sanderson CFL Ltd [2001] EWCA Civ 317, [2001] 1 All ER (Comm) 696

Watts v. Morrow [1991] 1 WLR 1421

Way v. Latilla [1937] 3 All ER 759

Weigall v. Runciman (1916) 85 LJKB 1187

Wellesley Partners LLP v. Withers LLP [2014] EWHC 556 (Ch), [2014] PNLR 22; [2015] EWCA Civ 1146

White & Carter (Councils) Ltd v. McGregor [1962] AC 413

White v. Jones [1995] 2 AC 207

William Lacey (Hounslow) Ltd v. Davis [1957] 1 WLR 932

William Sindall Plc v. Cambridgeshire County Council [1994] 1 WLR 1016

Williams v. Bayley (1866) LR 1 HL 200

Williams v. Roffey Bros & Nicholls (Contractors) Ltd [1991] 1 QB 1

Wilson v. Tumman (1843) 6 Man & G 236

With v. O'Flanagan [1936] Ch 575

Woodar Investment Development Ltd v. Wimpey Construction UK Ltd [1980] 1 WLR 277

Woodhouse AC Israel Cocoa Ltd SA v. Nigerian Produce Marketing Co Ltd [1972] AC 741

Wright v. Carter [1903] 1 Ch 27

Yam Seng Pte Ltd v. International Trade Corp Ltd [2013] EWHC 111, [2013] 1 Lloyd's Rep 526

Yates Building Co Ltd v. Pulleyn & Son (York) Ltd (1975) 237 EG 183

Yaxley v. Gotts [2000] Ch 162

Yonge v. Toynbee [1910] 1 KB 215

Zamet v. Hyman [1961] 1 WLR 1442

Table of Legislation

Arbitration Act 1996

Commercial Agents (Council Directive) Regulations 1993 (SI 1993/3053)

Commercial Agents (Council Directive) (Amendment) Regulations 1993 (SI 1993/3173) and 1998 (SI 1998/2868)

Companies Act 2006

Consumer Contracts (Information, Cancellation and Additional Charges) Regulations 2013 (SI 2013/3134)

Consumer Credit Act 1974

Consumer Insurance (Disclosure and Representations) Act 2012

Consumer Protection from Unfair Trading Regulations 2008 (SI 2008/1277), amended by SI 2014/870

Consumer Rights Act 2015

Contracts (Rights of Third Parties) Act 1999

Family Law Reform Act 1969

Financial Services and Markets Act 2000

Fraudulent Conveyances Act 1571

Gambling Act 2005

Gaming Act 1845

Insolvency Act 1986

Insurance Act 2015

Interpretation Act 1978

Judicature Act 1873

Landlord and Tenant Act 1985

Law of Property (Miscellaneous Provisions) Act 1989

Law of Property Act 1925

Law Reform (Enforcement of Contracts) Act 1954

Law Reform (Frustrated Contracts) Act 1943

Limitation Act 1980

Limited Liability Partnerships Act 2000

Marine Insurance Act 1906
Minors' Contracts Act 1987
Misrepresentation Act 1967
Occupiers' Liability Act 1957
Partnership Act 1890
Sale of Goods Act 1979
Senior Courts Act 1981
Statute of Frauds 1677
Supply of Goods (Implied Terms) Act 1973
Supply of Goods and Services Act 1982
Supreme Court of Judicature Act 1873
Torts (Interference with Goods) Act 1977
Tribunals, Courts and Enforcement Act 2007
Unfair Arbitration Agreements (Specified Amounts) Order 1999 (SI 1999/2167)
Unfair Contract Terms Act 1977

Index

The numbers here refer to paragraph numbers

Acceptance 68–77
communication 68–77
by post 69–71
silence 75
unilateral contract 72–73
unqualified 58
Actio Pauliana 327–331
Administrative contracts (*see* Public contracts)
Administrative law (*see* Public law)
Agency 397
actual authority 399–402
apparent authority 405–407
in collateral contracts 325–326
commercial 407
by operation of law 398
ratification 397, 408–410
termination 404
undisclosed principals 403
Arbitration 276–283
Assessment of damages 379–392
Assignment 316–323
in equity 322
formalities 321
at law 318
novation 316
of obligations 316
of rights 316–317
Auctions 57

Bailment 411
Bargain theory of contract (*see* Consideration)
Benefit of third party, contract for (*see* Privity)
Breach, strict liability for 332–334
Business contracts (*see* Commercial contracts)

Cancellation (*see* Rescission and termination)
Capacity 152–160
Case law (*see* Precedent)
Children (*see* Capacity)
Coercion (*see* Duress)
Common law (*see also* Sources of law) 5–7, 9–12, 21–25
Collateral contracts 133, 296, 324–326
Commercial contracts 18–19
Communication of acceptance 68–77
Compensation (*see* Damages)
Conditional contract 162, 336, 372
Conditions 366–371
intermediate terms, distinguished from 370–371
warranties, distinguished from 369
Consent (*see* Intention to create legal relations)
Consideration
adequacy 90
benefit and detriment 89–90
gratuitous undertakings 88, 99–100
as motive 101
past consideration 101–102
promissory estoppel 113–123
value 90, 92
Constitution 8
Consumer protection 186, 261, 265–267
Contract 20
Contractual intention (*see* Intention to create legal relations)

Damages

assessment of 379–392
causation 385
liquidated damages 268
nature of remedy 379
punitive damages 379
remoteness 382–384
Death
effect on agency 404
effect on offers 60
effect on rights 316
Debt, limitation of 378
Deceit, tort of 143–145, 181
Deeds 100
Devolution, effect on contract law 1
Discharge of obligations
by agreement 348–349
impossibility, supervening 337–344
repudiation, acceptance of 366–368
rescission 239
termination 359–361
Drunkenness 158–159
Duress 187–198
Duty to disclose information 139–142

Economic duress 191–196
End of contract (*see* Discharge of obligations)
Entire obligations 372–374
Equity 23, 25
Estoppel
by convention 113
promissory 114–123
by representation 113
Evidence
burden of proof 136–137
parol evidence rule 130–133
standard of proof 136
Exclusion clauses
rules of interpretation 184
special notice 184
validity 185–186, 261–264
Exemption clauses (*see* Exclusion clauses)
Expectation interest (*see* Damages)

Fair dealing (*see* Good faith)
Fault (*see* Strict liability)
Force majeure clauses (*see also* Frustration) 341, 344
Formal contracts (*see* Deeds and formalities)
Formalities 124–129
company seal 124
real property 125
non-compliance, effect of 127–129
notarisation 134
signature 125
writing 125–126
Formation of contract (*see also* Offer and acceptance) 49–53
Fraud (*see* Deceit)
Frustration (*see also* Impossibility) 335–347

Gifts 99
Good faith 41, 140, 194, 237, 242, 266
Government contracts (*see* Public contracts)
Gratuitous contracts (*see also* Gifts, Consideration) 99–100, 354
Gross disparity (*see* Unequal bargaining power)
Guarantee 126, 129, 140

Hardship 335, 340

Illegality (*see* Public policy)
Immorality (*see* Public policy)
Implied terms 253–260
in fact 254–256
at law 259–260
juristic basis 257–258
Impossibility 214–223, 335–347
Injunctions 351–352, 358
Insolvency 327–331
Insurance 140
Innominate terms (*see* Intermediate terms)
Intention to create legal relations 84–87
Intermediate terms
conditions, distinguished from 371
warranties, distinguished from 370
Interpretation 261–264, 284–293
Invitation to tender (*see* Invitation to treat)
Invitation to treat 54–57

Judgments (*see* Precedent)

Index

Judiciary 11–14
Jurists, writings of 48

Lease 417–418
Legislation 8–10, 47
Licit cause 210
Limitation 376–378
Limited Liability Partnership 427
Liquidated damages (*see also* Penalty clauses) 268–269
Loan 424

Mental illness (*see* Unsound mind)
Minors (*see* Capacity)
Misrepresentation 143–147, 172–186
  definition 145–146, 172–177
  exclusion of liability 183–186
  fact and opinion 173–174
  remedies 147, 178–182
Mistake 161–171
  common 215–224
  of identity 166–171
  juristic basis 162, 220–223
  payment under (*see* Money paid but not due)
  unilateral 161–171
Mitigation 385
Modification (*see* Variation)
Money paid but not due 435

Natural obligations 101–102
Negotiation (*see* Pre-contractual liability)
Negotiorum gestio 429–431
Non est factum 163, 251
Non-performance (*see* Breach)
Non-performance as bar to enforcement (*see* Entire obligations)
Notarisation 134
Notary 135
Novation 316

Objectivity 78–85
Offer 54–67
  counter-offer 58
  invitation to treat, distinguished from 54–56
  unilateral contracts, in the case of 72
  termination 59–60
  withdrawal 61–67
Offer and acceptance 49–77

Parol evidence rule 130–133
Partnership 426–428
Past consideration 101–102
Payment for work done (*see Quantum meruit*)
Payment under mistake 435
Penalty clauses (*see also* Liquidated damages) 268–275
Performance (*see* Breach, strict liability for)
Pledge 421–423
Postal rule (*see also* Communication of acceptance) 69–71
Precedent 12, 45–46
Pre-contractual liability 138–151
Presumptions (*see* Burden of proof)
Principal and agent (*see* Agency)
Privity 294–315
  collateral contracts 324–326
  consideration 302
  contract for the benefit of a third party 304
  subcontracts 324
  tort, actions in 296
Promisor disabling himself 338
Promissory estoppel 113–123
Proposal (*see* Offer)
Public contracts 16–17
Public law 17
Public policy
  illegal contracts 225–233
  immoral contracts 225, 233
  restraint of trade 234–235
  wagers 412–413
Punitive damages 379

Quantum meruit 432–433
Quasi-contract 32–34, 432–435
  payment for non-gratuitous act 432–434
  supplying to persons without capacity 159

Ratification
accepting part performance 373
unauthorised acts of agents 397, 408–410
Ratio decidendi (*see* Precedent)
Reciprocity (*see* Consideration)
Release by promisee (*see* Discharge of obligations)
Reliance interest 386
Remedies for breach
account 40, 205
damages 379–392
injunctions 351–352, 358
specific performance 351
termination 239, 359–360, 362–371
Repudiation 333, 366–368
Rescission 172–179, 182, 187, 205, 207, 237, 239–242
bars to 241–242
damages in lieu 178–179
effect 237, 239
Restitution (*see also* Quasi-contract) 32–34, 432–435
Restraint of trade 234–235
Revocation (*see* Withdrawal)

Sale of goods 414–415
Seal, contracts under (*see* Formalities)
Silence
as acceptance 75
as misrepresentation 139, 142
Sources of law 44
juristic writings 48
legislation 8–10, 47
precedent 9, 11, 45–46
Specific performance 351
bars to 353–354
damages in lieu 352
discretion 355–357
nature of remedy 351
Standard form contracts 261
Stare decisis (*see* Precedent)
Stranger to contract (*see* Privity)
Strict liability 332
Style of drafting 42–43
Subcontracts 324
'Subject to contract' (*see* Offer and acceptance and intention to create legal relations)
Surety (*see* Guarantee)

Termination
effect 239, 359
power to terminate 360, 362–371
Third party rights (*see* Privity)
Tort, contract and 28–31
Transfer of contractual rights (*see* Assignment)
Trusts
and contract 37–40
of promises 297–298

Uncertainty 211–213
Unconscionability 207–209
Undue influence 187–190
Unenforceable contracts (*see* Public policy and uncertainty)
Unequal bargaining power 206–209
Unilateral contracts 62–64, 67, 72–73
Unjust enrichment (*see also* Quasi-contracts) 432–434
Unsound mind 158–159

Vagueness (*see* Uncertainty)
Variation of contracts 103–112
Vitiating factors (*see* Duress, Undue influence and unconscionability)
Voidability (*see also* Rescission) 236–237
Voidness 236, 238

Wagers 412–413
Warranties
conditions, distinguished from 369
intermediate terms, distinguished from 370–371
unincorporated representations, distinguished from 245–246
Withdrawal of offer 61–67
Written contracts (*see* Formalities)

www.ingramcontent.com/pod-product-compliance
Ingram Content Group UK Ltd.
Pitfield, Milton Keynes, MK11 3LW, UK
UKHW020144290926
15471UKWH00004B/691